# Fine Food from Country Australia

# Fine Food from Country Australia

*Recipes from Australia's best country restaurants and guesthouses*

### Edited by Pam Brewster

### Photography by Oliver Strewe

**RANDOM HOUSE**
AUSTRALIA

# Fine Food from Country Australia

## Acknowledgments

The publishers would like to thank Tourism Victoria and the Tasmanian Tourist Authority for their valuable assistance in those states. Restaurant reviewers, restauranteurs, chefs and foodies from around the nation pitched in with valuable advice on the places we might have missed but particular thanks goes to Rita Erlich, John Rozentals, Jackie Passmore, Stephano Manfredi, Howard Bromley and Nicole Lehmann. And thanks goes also to the friends in far away places who helped with their personal dining experiences.

Most of all, though, our thanks go to the chefs and owners of Australia's country restaurants who are leading this quiet revolution.

First published in 1996 by

Random House Australia Pty Ltd
20 Alfred Street, Milsons Point, NSW 2061

Sydney, New York, Toronto
London, Auckland, Johannesburg
and agencies throughout the world

Created and produced by
Modern Times Pty Ltd
PO Box 908, Bondi Junction
New South Wales 2022
Australia

Copyright © in this collection Modern Times Pty Ltd 1996
Copyright © in the individual recipes remains with the individual contributing restaurants
Copyright © of the photographs in this collection
Modern Times Pty Ltd

All rights reserved. No part of this publication may be reproduced, stored in a retrieval system, or transmitted in any form or by any means, electronic, mechanical, photocopying, recording or otherwise, without the prior written permission of the copyright holder.

National Library of Australia
Cataloguing-in-Publication Data

Fine food from country Australia: recipes from Australia's best country restaurants and guest houses.

Includes index.
ISBN 0 09 183335 3.

1. Cookery. 2. Cookery, Australian. I. Brewster, Pam, 1952- .
641.5994

Designed by Modern Times Pty Ltd
Produced by Mandarin Offset

# INTRODUCTION

IN RESEARCHING this book it was exciting to find what I had always felt must be true: that out in the country, the Australian bush, there are wonderful chefs and restaurants equal to any of their city or suburban counterparts. The fact that they are only occasionally reviewed or talked about is purely a problem of distance and locality. Food reviewers write mostly about city restaurants for their city readers; even though *they know* there are marvellous country eateries out there waiting to be discovered.

It's a matter of finding them – tucked away as part of a little country hotel or guest house, often off the beaten track. But when you do the rewards are great.

What a change this is from even a decade and a half ago. Travelling with my family on holidays when I was young, my one consistent memory is the awful food. Invariably it was badly cooked. Guest house food was like boarding school food; the country town restaurant was actually a greasy cafe. And the food was seldom fresh. If you had fish on the south coast of New South Wales, it came frozen from Sydney; if you had vegetables with your roast mutton in north east Victoria, they came wilted from Melbourne. Hardly ever could you enjoy fresh local produce cooked simply and healthily. Now, travelling through Australia is like travelling through France or Italy: fine food is everywhere.

Local produce truly is the theme of this book because without it these wonderful establishments could not create the marvellous food they do. They rely on their local game farmer, tropical fruit grower, local fishermen and oyster growers, orchardists and vineyards. They also rely on the seasons. Unlike their city counterparts who can buy anything from anywhere at any time of year. Visit a country restaurant's kitchen and you will understand just how hard it is to get good produce if it has to travel a long way. So, by necessity, this is where you can see the seasons at their best.

The chefs and owners of these little pockets of gastronomy deserve high praise. They are the heroes. Often, they have to work in isolation while maintaining high standards. They ferret out the produce from within their locality and invent wonderful menus. Many of them do it hard though, with only their local communities and a small amount tourism to support them. But we were struck by their professionalism and high standards, by their innovative menus and their commitment, right across the country, to fine food.

A number of restaurants have not been included in this book and I hope they will forgive me. Some would have been except for timing; some were thinking of selling or were so busy that another thing to do, like putting together recipes for this book, was simply beyond their resources. Others were just opening and are established now, but not then.

In *Fine Food From Country Australia* you will find mouth-watering recipes like a salad of rabbit fillets from a cottage restaurant or char-grilled salmon from a seaside guest house, lemon curd tart that would melt any heart and confit of duck that makes it sound so, so easy. All the recipes are told simply and with just the right amount of detail.

Pam Brewster

# Fine Food from Country Australia

# CONTENTS

## SUMMER

CHARDONNAY LODGE • *page* 12
Coonawarra, South Australia

THE WILD OLIVE • *page* 16
Barossa Valley, South Australia

COTSWOLD HOUSE
RESTAURANT • *page* 20
Dandenongs, Victoria

TALGAI HOMESTEAD • *page* 24
Darling Downs, Queensland

MIETTA'S QUEENSCLIFF HOTEL • *page* 28
Bellarine Peninsula, Victoria

ANABEL'S OF SCOTTSDALE • *page* 30
Northeastern Tasmania

HOWQUA DALE GOURMET
RETREAT • *page* 34
Northeastern Victoria

CARRINGTON HOUSE • *page* 40
Newcastle, New South Wales

RED OCHRE GRILL • *page* 42
Cairns, Queensland

THE MOUNT INN • *page* 45
Blue Mountains, New South Wales

FLUTES OF BROOKLAND
VALLEY • *page* 48
Margaret River Region, Western Australia

THE COTTAGE RESTAURANT • *page* 52
Hunter Valley, New South Wales

BAWLEY POINT GUEST HOUSE • *page* 56
South Coast, New South Wales

THE PARLOUR AND PANTRY • *page* 57
Northeastern Victoria

LOUISA'S RESTAURANT • *page* 61
Bunbury, Western Australia

ARCOONA • *page* 64
Deloraine, Northern Tasmania

NEWTOWN HOUSE
RESTAURANT • *page* 66
Margaret River Region, Western Australia

LUCINDA • *page* 69
North Coast, Tasmania

SUNNYBRAE COUNTRY
RESTAURANT • *page* 71
Southern Coast, Victoria

FRANKLIN MANOR • *page* 74
West Coast, Tasmania

PEREGIAN PARK HOMESTEAD
RESTAURANT • *page* 77
Sunshine Coast, Queensland

MOUNT LOFTY HOUSE, MERCURE
GRAND HOTEL • *page* 82
Adelaide Hills, South Australia

SEVEN SPIRIT BAY • *page* 86
Cobourg Peninsula, Northern Territory

PROSPECT HOUSE • *page* 88
Richmond, Southeast Tasmania

## AUTUMN

SAN SOLERO BAY • *page* 92
Cox Peninsula, Northern Territory

DARLEYS RESTAURANT,
LILIANFELS • *page* 93
Blue Mountains, New South Wales

# Fine Food from Country Australia

THORN PARK COUNTRY
HOUSE • *page* 97
Clare Valley, South Australia

THE WILD OLIVE • *page* 100
Barossa Valley, South Australia

ADAMS OF NORTH RIDING • *page* 102
St Andrews, Victoria

ARTHURS RESTAURANT • *page* 106
Mornington Peninsula, Victoria

LAKE HOUSE • *page* 109
Central Victoria

LOUISA'S RESTAURANT • *page* 113
Bunbury, Western Australia

HOWQUA DALE GOURMET
RETREAT • *page* 117
Northeastern Victoria

THE MOUNT INN • *page* 122
Blue Mountains, New South Wales

THE URAIDLA
ARISTOLOGIST • *page* 125
Adelaide Hills, South Australia

THE COTTAGE RESTAURANT • *page* 128
Hunter Valley, New South Wales

LUCINDA • *page* 132
North Coast, Tasmania

LEEUWIN ESTATE • *page* 134
Margaret River, Western Australia

ELLIMATTA GUEST HOUSE AND
RESTAURANT • *page* 138
Central Victoria

ANABEL'S OF SCOTTSDALE • *page* 142
Northeastern Tasmania

SILK'S BRASSERIE • *page* 146
Blue Mountains, New South Wales

PROSPECT HOUSE • *page* 149
Richmond, Southeast Coast, Tasmania

PEREGIAN PARK HOMESTEAD
RESTAURANT • *page* 152
Sunshine Coast, Queensland

VUE GRAND HOTEL • *page* 158
Bellarine Peninsula, Victoria

PADTHAWAY ESTATE • *page* 160
Padthaway, South Australia

TALGAI HOMESTEAD • *page* 162
Darling Downs, Queensland

## WINTER

TAYLOR'S COUNTRY
HOUSE • *page* 168
Byron Bay, New South Wales

COTSWOLD HOUSE
RESTAURANT • *page* 172
Dandenongs, Victoria

TYNWALD • *page* 176
New Norfolk, Southern Tasmania

ADAMS OF NORTH RIDING
RESTAURANT • *page* 180
St Andrews, Victoria

ROBERTS AT PEPPER TREE • *page* 182
Hunter Valley, New South Wales

NEWTOWN HOUSE
RESTAURANT • *page* 186
Margaret River Region, Western Australia

SILK'S BRASSERIE • *page* 190
Blue Mountains, New South Wales

SKILLOGALEE • *page* 193
Clare Valley, South Australia

SAN SOLERO BAY • *page* 194
Cox Peninsula, Northern Teritory

LAKE HOUSE • *page* 198
Central Victoria

PICNICS AT FAIRHILL • *page* 204
Sunshine Coast, Queensland

ARCOONA • *page* 208
Deloraine, Northern Tasmania

WARRENMANG VINEYARD
RESORT • *page* 212
Pyrenees, Central Victoria

# CONTENTS

DARLEYS RESTAURANT, LILIANFELS • *page 216*
Blue Mountains, New South Wales

BAWLEY POINT GUEST HOUSE • *page 220*
South Coast, New South Wales

LAMONT'S WINERY AND RESTAURANT • *page 221*
Swan Valley, Western Australia

ELLIMATTA GUEST HOUSE AND RESTAURANT • *page 224*
Central Victoria

THE VALLEY COUNTRY HOME • *page 228*
Tilba Tilba, Southern Coast, New South Wales

VUE GRAND HOTEL • *page 232*
Bellarine Peninsula, Victoria

THORN PARK COUNTRY HOUSE • *page 233*
Clare Valley, South Australia

FLUTES OF BROOKLAND VALLEY • *page 238*
Margaret River Region, Western Australia

SUNNYBRAE COUNTRY RESTAURANT • *page 244*
Southern Coast, Victoria

DEAR FRIENDS GARDEN RESTAURANT • *page 246*
Swan Valley, Western Australia

## SPRING

THE URAIDLA ARISTOLOGIST • *page 252*
Adelaide Hills, South Australia

CHARDONNAY LODGE • *page 254*
Coonawarra, South Australia

FRANKLIN MANOR • *page 258*
West Coast, Tasmania

ARTHURS RESTAURANT • *page 261*
Mornington Peninsula, Victoria

MIETTA'S QUEENSCLIFF HOTEL • *page 264*
Bellarine Peninsula, Victoria

TAYLOR'S COUNTRY HOUSE • *page 268*
Byron Bay, New South Wales

THE PARLOUR AND PANTRY • *page 270*
Northeastern Victoria

THE VALLEY COUNTRY HOME • *page 273*
Tilba Tilba, Southern Coast, New South Wales

WARRENMANG VINEYARD RESORT • *page 276*
Pyrenees, Central Victoria

WILLOWVALE MILL • *page 278*
Southern Highlands, New South Wales

LEEUWIN ESTATE • *page 281*
Margaret River, Western Australia

SKILLOGALEE • *page 286*
Clare Valley, South Australia

RED OCHRE GRILL • *page 290*
Cairns, Queensland

LAMONT'S WINERY AND RESTAURANT • *page 294*
Swan Valley, Western Australia

TYNWALD • *page 297*
New Norfolk, Southern Tasmania

DEAR FRIENDS GARDEN RESTAURANT • *page 300*
Swan Valley, Western Australia

MOUNT LOFTY HOUSE, MERCURE GRAND HOTEL • *page 304*
Adelaide Hills, South Australia

PICNICS AT FAIRHILL • *page 308*
Sunshine Coast, Queensland

SEVEN SPIRIT BAY • *page 309*
Cobourg Peninsula, Northern Territory

CARRINGTON HOUSE • *page 312*
Newcastle, New South Wales

RESTAURANTS AND GUEST HOUSES • *page 315*

INDEX • *page 317*

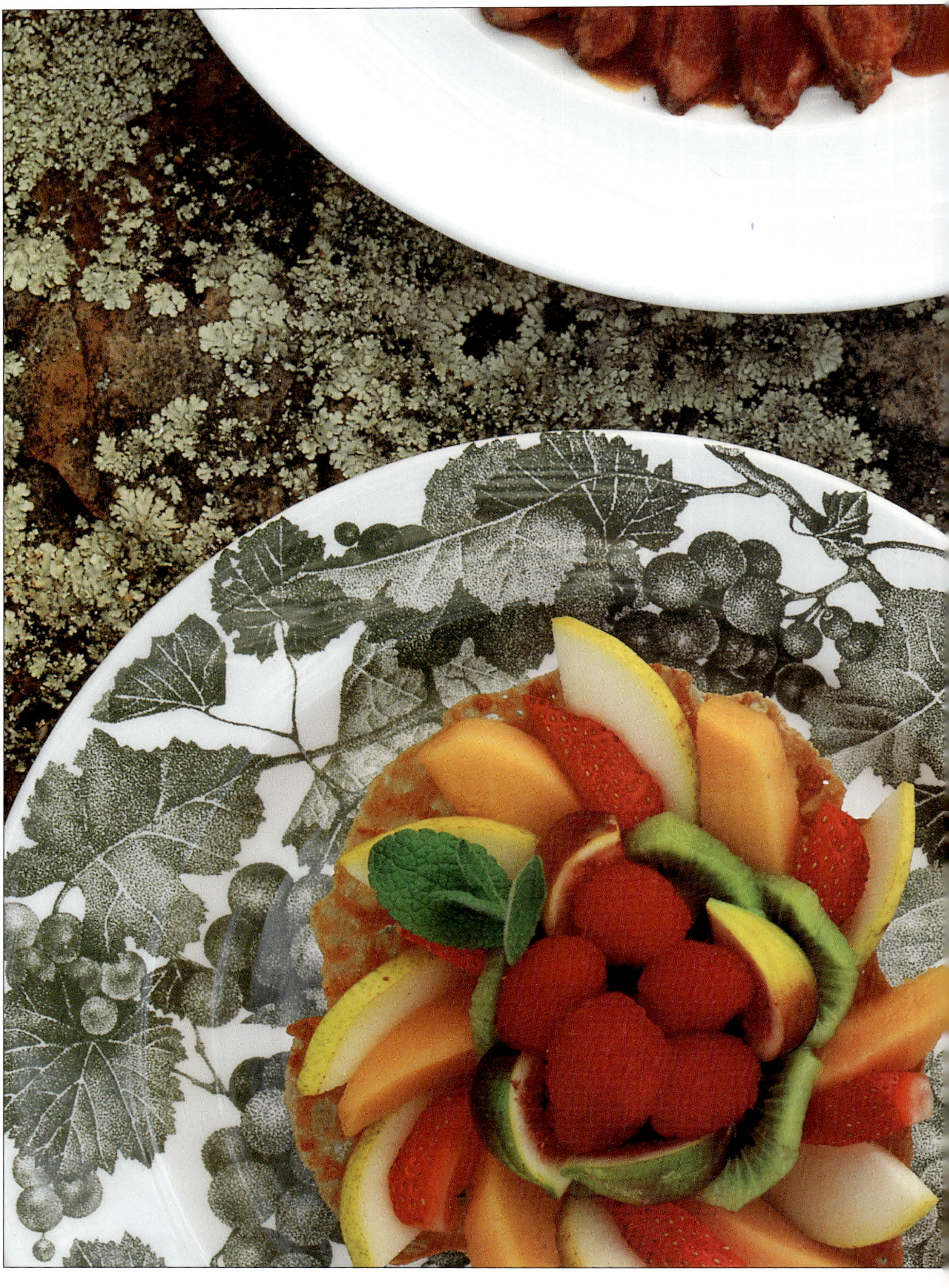

# SUMMER

## CHARDONNAY LODGE
Coonawarra, South Australia

•

*Penola yabbies and dhal salad with a tomato and coriander salsa*

•

*Roast breast of duck with brandied figs and braised caraway cabbage*

•

*Savarin of berries with a champagne sabayon*

# PENOLA YABBIES AND DHAL SALAD WITH A TOMATO AND CORIANDER SALSA

### CHARDONNAY LODGE

*6 yabbies per portion*
*5 litres water*
*200 ml white vinegar*
*200 ml white wine*
*1 carrot*
*1 onion, peeled*
*white of 1 leek*
*2 bay leaves*
*12 black peppercorns, crushed*
*Dhal Salad*
*Tomato and Coriander Salsa*
*mixed salad leaves*

Place all the ingredients, except the yabbies, into a large saucepan, place on a high heat until the water boils. Place the yabbies into the water and bring back to the boil. Cook for 1 minute then remove the yabbies from the water and place into iced water, leave for 5 minutes and drain. Peel the yabbies and remove the vein. Store in a refrigerator.

To serve, mix together the yabbies and some of the Dhal Salad and place in the centre of the plate, arrange mixed salad leaves around the yabbies. Spoon some of the salsa around.

## DHAL SALAD

*15 ml olive oil*
*75 grams onions, chopped*
*250 grams red lentils, soaked overnight*
*15 ml raspberry vinegar*
*1 orange, grated zest and juice*
*5 grams fresh ginger, finely chopped*
*500 ml chicken stock*
*2.5 grams dijon mustard*
*salt and pepper*
*⅓ bunch coriander, leaves only*

Heat the oil in a medium saucepan over a medium heat, add the onion and cook until soft, add the drained lentils, raspberry vinegar, orange zest and juice. Reduce the liquid then add the ginger and chicken stock, reduce the heat and simmer until the liquid has evaporated. Skim from time to time. Remove from the heat, stir in the mustard, add salt and pepper to taste and allow to cool. Add the coriander.

## TOMATO AND CORIANDER SALSA

*300 grams tomato, peeled, seeded and diced*
*3 grams lime leaves, chopped*
*2 grams lemon grass, finely chopped*
*2 grams shallots, peeled and sliced*
*1 gram diced red chilli*
*⅓ bunch coriander leaves*
*1 lime juice and zest*
*8 ml Thai fish sauce*
*8 ml olive oil*
*8 ml red wine vinegar*

Combine all the ingredients.

# ROAST BREAST OF DUCK WITH BRANDIED FIGS AND BRAISED CARAWAY CABBAGE

### CHARDONNAY LODGE

*500 ml sauterne wine*  
*2 litres duck stock*  
*1 duck breast per portion*  
*brandied figs*  
*salt and pepper*  
*oil*  
*Braised Caraway Cabbage*

Place the wine in a saucepan over a medium heat and reduce by two thirds. Add the duck stock and reduce to the desired consistency, strain and put aside.

Heat the oil in a medium sauté pan over a high heat, season the duck with the salt and pepper and place in the sauté pan skin side up. Turn the breast onto the skin side and place in a medium hot oven for approximately 8 minutes or until the duck is cooked. Remove from the oven and allow to rest for ten minutes.

To serve, place the heated brandied figs in the centre of the plate along with the cabbage ball, slice the duck into thin pieces and arrange around the figs. Pour the sauce around the duck breast.

## BRAISED CARAWAY CABBAGE

*1 small cabbage*  
*75 grams butter*  
*salt and pepper*

Remove the outer leaves from the cabbage and blanch in boiling water until tender, refresh and set aside. Shred the remaining cabbage. Melt the butter in a medium pan and add the shredded cabbage and caraway seeds, cover and place in a medium oven, cook until tender. Add salt and pepper to taste.

Line a 125 ml ladle with the blanched cabbage and fill with the braised cabbage. Remove from the ladle and place into a clean tea towel, twist the towel to remove excess moisture. Place cabbage ball aside and keep warm.

# SAVARIN OF BERRIES WITH A CHAMPAGNE SABAYON

### CHARDONNAY LODGE

*30 ml warm milk*
*8 grams fresh yeast*
*115 grams plain flour*
*125 grams castor sugar*
*1 ½ eggs*
*pinch salt*
*50 grams melted butter*
*225 ml water*
*25 ml cassis liqueur*
*500 grams mixed berries*
*200 grams castor sugar, extra*
*300 ml water*
*Champagne Sabayon*
*500 grams mixed whole berries, to serve*
*mint*

Mix the warm milk with the yeast and 20 grams of the flour to start the fermentation. When the process has started and the mixture is foaming add the rest of the flour, 8 grams of the sugar, eggs and the salt, mix to a dough. Make an indentation in the top of the dough and pour the melted butter into it. Cover the dough with a cloth and leave it to prove in a warm place until it has doubled in volume.

Knead the dough until the butter has been absorbed, use the dough to half fill greased and floured savarin moulds, leave in a warm place until the dough has doubled in volume. Bake in an oven at 220°C for 15 minutes. Turn out onto a rack and allow to cool.

Heat the remaining sugar, water and cassis in a medium saucepan until the sugar has dissolved. Using a slotted spoon dip each savarin into the syrup until they are thoroughly soaked, leave on a wire rack to drain.

Put the berries, extra sugar and water into a medium saucepan and bring to a boil over a medium heat, simmering gently for about 5 minutes. Place the mixture into a food processor, process and strain. Return the liquid to the pan and bring to the boil, reduce the liquid by about a third until it reaches the consistency of a light glaze. Glaze the savarins with the syrup.

To serve, place some of the sabayon in the centre of the plate, place a savarin on top of the sabayon. Fill the centre of the savarin with mixed berries combined with a little of the berry glaze. Garnish the plate with 5 piles of mixed berries and top each pile with a mint leaf.

ARCOONA, TASMANIA
*Raspberries in Cointreau with Arcoona's lavender ice-cream, Page 65*

*S*UMMER

## THE WILD OLIVE
### Barossa Valley, South Australia

*Vine-ripe tomatoes filled with goat's cheese and blue swimmer crab with a basil-scented jus*

•

*Honey-glazed duck breast with wontons of braised leg meat, cumin carrots and jasmine sauce*

•

*Almond and orange basket of fresh fruit and chantilly cream*

## CHAMPAGNE SABAYON

*3 egg yolks*
*50 grams castor sugar*
*120 ml champagne*
*100 ml double cream, whipped to soft peaks*

Place the egg yolks, sugar and champagne into a large stainless steel bowl and whisk over a hot water bath, continue whisking over the heat for approximately 5 minutes until mixture is frothy and creamy. Remove from heat and continue to whisk until mixture is cool, fold in the double cream.

## VINE-RIPE TOMATOES FILLED WITH GOAT'S CHEESE AND BLUE SWIMMER CRAB WITH A BASIL-SCENTED JUS

### THE WILD OLIVE

*30 vine-ripe, squashball-sized tomatoes*
*500 grams fresh goat's cheese*
*300 ml thickened cream*
*2 carrots, finely diced*
*3 zucchini, seeded and finely diced*
*600 grams blue swimmer crab meat*
*salt and pepper, to taste*
*700 ml chicken stock*
*200 grams butter, chopped*
*1 bunch basil, chopped*

Cut a cross on the base of the tomatoes and blanch in boiling salted water for 10 seconds. Refresh in cold water and peel off the skin. Remove the tops of the tomatoes and scoop out the pulp. Discard the pulp.

Place the goat's cheese in a stainless steel bowl and soften over a pot of simmering water or a bain marie. Add the cream and remove from the heat. Blanch the carrots and zucchini, then strain and combine thoroughly with the cheese mixture, crab meat and salt and pepper.

Fill the tomatoes with spoonfuls of the mixture and place in a buttered baking dish. Pour in the chicken stock and replace the tops of the tomatoes. Cook at 200°C for 8 to 10 minutes. The tomatoes will soften slightly and the mixture inside will be hot. Remove the tomatoes from the liquid and keep warm.

Transfer the remaining mixture to a saucepan and heat over medium heat. Blend in the butter, then add the basil. Place 3 tomatoes on each serving plate and spoon the sauce over. Serves 10.

# HONEY-GLAZED DUCK BREAST WITH WONTONS OF BRAISED LEG MEAT, CUMIN CARROTS AND JASMINE SAUCE

## THE WILD OLIVE

*5 x No. 18 or 20 ducks*
*honey*
*1 tablespoon vegetable oil or lard*
*6 carrots, roughly diced*
*1 bunch celery, roughly diced*
*2 leeks, roughly chopped*
*6 onions, roughly chopped*
*1 head of garlic, halved*
*1 kilogram ripe tomatoes, chopped or 2 tablespoons tomato paste*
*1 litre red wine*
*8–10 cardamom pods*
*8–10 star anise*
*8–10 juniper berries*
*parsley stalks*
*few sprigs of thyme*
*salt and pepper, to taste*
*2 teaspoons jasmine tea*
*wonton wrappers*
*Cumin Carrots*

REMOVE the legs and breasts from the duck carcasses and clean off any excess fat and sinew. Score the skin in a crisscross fashion, then place the breasts on a tray and smear with slightly warmed honey. Set aside. Chop the carcasses into pieces and roast in a 250°C oven until brown.

Heat the oil in a saucepan. Add three-quarters of the vegetables and the garlic and cook until well browned. Add the tomatoes and cook for a further 5 minutes. Add the roasted bones, red wine, herbs and spices and enough water to just cover. Bring to the boil and skim. Reduce the heat to low and simmer for 4–5 hours, skimming the surface when necessary. Strain through a fine strainer into another saucepan, and cook over medium heat until reduced by one-quarter. This is the stock.

Place the remaining vegetables in the bottom of a roasting tray. Place the duck legs, skin side down, in a hot pan and brown (no oil is required as the skin has enough fat). Arrange on top of the chopped vegetables in the tray, then pour in enough of the stock to cover the vegetables but not submerge the duck. Season with salt and pepper, cover and bake at 160°C for about 2 hours. The meat should come away from the bones easily.

Sear the duck breast skin side down in an oven-proof dish over high heat (again, no oil is required). Season with salt and pepper. When the skin starts to colour and crisp, transfer to a 190°C oven for about 5 minutes, longer if you like your meat well done. Remove from the oven and rest. Slice.

Strain the remaining stock into a saucepan and cook over a medium heat until reduced to a sauce consistency. Remove from the heat and add the jasmine tea. Cover and infuse for 10 minutes before straining again.

When the duck legs are cool enough to handle, remove the

bones and skin. Shred the meat by hand, mould into small balls and enclose between two wonton wrappers. Eggwash the edges of the wrappers to seal. Just before serving, simmer in salted water for 3–4 minutes, drain and arrange on a serving plate. Serve with the sauce and the Cumin Carrots. Serves 10.

## CUMIN CARROTS

*2 bunches Dutch carrots*
*250 ml orange juice*
*1 tablespoon castor sugar*
*1 tablespoon butter*
*1 teaspoon cumin seeds*
*salt and pepper, to taste*
*water*

Peel and thinly slice the carrots and place in a pot with the remaining ingredients. Barely cover with water and simmer until soft.

## ALMOND AND ORANGE BASKET OF FRESH FRUIT AND CHANTILLY CREAM

### THE WILD OLIVE

*200 grams pure icing sugar*
*50 grams plain flour*
*75 ml fresh orange juice*
*25 grams flaked almonds*
*75 grams almonds, chopped*
*grated zest of one orange*
*75 grams melted butter*
*500 ml cream*
*2 tablespoons castor sugar*
*fresh fruit: raspberries, strawberries, peaches, plums, blueberries*

SIFT THE icing sugar and flour into a bowl. Slowly whisk in the orange juice. Fold in the flaked almonds, chopped almonds and orange zest, then the butter. Stir until combined. Place in the refrigerator until cold.

Spoon dessertspoonfuls of the mixture onto a non-stick tray, spacing them well apart. Bake at 180°C until golden brown. Remove from the oven and let cool for 2–3 minutes. While still warm, lift off the tray with a spatula and sit over a cup or dome shape until cool and hard.

Whip the cream and castor sugar together until stiff peaks form. Place a spoonful of the cream mixture in the bottom of each basket and arrange the fruit on top. Serves 10.

---

THE WILD OLIVE.
SOUTH AUSTRALIA
*Vine-ripe tomatoes filled with goat's cheese and blue swimmer crab with a basil-scented jus, page 16*
*Honey-glazed duck breast with wontons of braised leg meat, cumin carrots and jasmine sauce, page 17*
*Almond and orange basket of fresh fruit and chantilly cream*

## Summer

## COTSWOLD HOUSE RESTAURANT
### Dandenongs, Victoria

•

*Spicy tuna tartare in crispy somen noodles*

•

*Barbequed boneless quail stuffed with wild cherry farce, served with a garlic tuille and a sweet potato swirl*

•

*Strawberry and mascarpone trifle*

# SPICY TUNA TARTARE IN CRISPY SOMEN NOODLES

### COTSWOLD HOUSE RESTAURANT

*1 packet of somen noodles*
*1 tablespoon sesame oil*
*salt and pepper*
*300 grams yellow fin tuna*
*1 tablespoon sambal olek*
*2 teaspoons of dark sesame oil*
*1 tablespoon worcestershire sauce*
*10 large spinach leaves*
*2 teaspoons wasabi powder*
*4 tablespoons ketjap manis*
*250 ml yoghurt*
*1 cucumber, sliced and seeded*

Cook the somen noodles to al dente and refresh in cold water. Drain and add sesame oil and salt and pepper to taste.

Cut the tuna finely and put it into a bowl with the sambal olek, dark sesame oil, worcestershire sauce.

Wilt the spinach leaves in boiling water.

Spread out a sheet of plastic wrap, 10 x 10 cm, and place the wilted spinach in a 5 cm square. Using a small ice-cream scoop, shape the tuna tartare into a ball and place in the centre of the spinach. Take the plastic wrap by each corner and twist to make a firm ball.

Using plastic wrap again, spread out another 10 x 10 cm square and place a small amount of the somen noodles in the centre. Place a similar sized piece of plastic wrap on top and roll with a rolling pin until they are flat and about 2 mm thick. Remove the top layer of plastic wrap, unwrap the tuna ball and place on top of the noodles. Lift the corners of the bottom layer of plastic wrap together and twist until a ball is formed. Leave to set in the refrigerator for 3 to 4 hours.

Combine the ketjap manis and wasabi powder.

Combine the yoghurt and cucumber in a food processor until it has a sauce consistency.

Heat enough oil in a pot to fry the somen ball. Fry the ball in the hot oil for 30 seconds. Remove from the oil and cut in half.

Serve with withered mescalin leaves, cucumber and yoghurt sauce and soy and wasabi sauce. Mix some wasabi powder and water into a paste and serve on a side dish.

# BARBECUED BONELESS QUAIL STUFFED WITH WILD CHERRY FARCE, SERVED WITH A GARLIC TUILLE AND SWEET POTATO SWIRL

### COTSWOLD HOUSE RESTAURANT

*1 boned quail per person*
*lemon juice*
*virgin olive oil*
*fresh or dried tarragon*
*salt and pepper to taste*

*Wild Cherry Farce*
*Quail Jus*
*Garlic Tuilles*
*Sweet Potato Purée*
*White Potato Purée*

Marinate the quails in a mixture of lemon juice, virgin olive oil, fresh or dried tarragon, salt and pepper to taste for 2 to 3 hours. Remove from the marinade and fill the quails with Wild Cherry Farce. Cook on a barbecue for 15 to 20 minutes, basting with the Quail Jus and turn the quail to cook both sides.

Make two paper piping bags and fill each bag with one of the potato purées. Evenly place the two paper piping bags side by side inside a large piping bag and reheat in the microwave.

Pipe swirls of the potato purées into the garlic tuille baskets. When the quail is cooked, slice the quail and serve with the tuille baskets.

## WILD CHERRY FARCE

*1 chicken breast*
*1 teaspoon basil, chopped*
*1 pinch sage, chopped*
*100 ml cream*
*1 egg*
*200 grams sour cherries*
*salt and pepper*

Combine the chicken breast and herbs in a food processor and purée to a fine paste. Add the cream and egg and mix until it has a whipped cream consistency. Place the mixture in a bowl, fold in the cherries and add salt and pepper to taste.

## QUAIL JUS

*200 grams quail bones, chopped roughly*
*40 grams carrots, chopped finely*
*40 grams onions, chopped finely*
*40 grams celery, chopped finely*
*1 litre cold water*
*150 ml Herman's barbecue sauce*

Roast all of the ingredients in the oven until the vegetables and quail bones are dark brown. Place in a pot with the water and bring to the boil. Simmer for 1 to 2 hours or until the liquid has reduced by half. Skim well.

Strain and discard the vegetables and bones. Reduce the liquid to approximately 250 ml. Add the barbecue sauce.

## GARLIC TUILLES

3 eggs
4 egg whites
¾ cup simple syrup (½ cup sugar and ½ cup water, boiled together)
¼ cup meat or vegetable stock
2 cloves garlic, puréed
2 ¼ cups plain flour, sifted
2 ½ teaspoons rosemary, finely chopped
225 grams butter, melted
salt and white pepper

Whisk together the eggs and egg whites, simple syrup, stock and garlic purée. Work the flour and rosemary into the mixture and stir in the butter. Add salt and pepper. Spread thinly on a non-stick oven tray forming circles of about 15 cm diameter.

Bake at 190°C until just set. Remove from the tray while still hot and drape over upturned cups. Place the cups in the oven and leave until the tuilles are crisp and brown.

Remove from the oven and leave the tuilles to cool on the cups. Store in an airtight container for up to 7 days.

## SWEET POTATO PURÉE & WHITE POTATO PURÉE

sweet potato
potatoes
salt and pepper
Boursin garlic and fine herbs cheese
cream

Separately peel and dice the sweet potato and potatoes, and separately boil until cooked. Mash and season well. Mix each mixture with some of the cheese and a little cream to bring it to piping consistency.

## STRAWBERRY AND MASCARPONE TRIFLE
### COTSWOLD HOUSE RESTAURANT

4 eggs
½ cup sugar
⅛ teaspoon vanilla essence
½ cup plain flour
¼ cup self raising flour
pinch of salt
1 tablespoon sugar, extra
¼ cup hot water
½ teaspoon of kirsch
Strawberries
Mascarpone Cream

Whisk the eggs, sugar and vanilla essence together until very thick. Sift the flours together with the salt and gently fold into the mixture.

Pour into a greased and lined 20 x 20 cm square tin. Bake until golden brown at 160°C, for approximately 20 minutes. Turn out on a rack to cool then cut into 3 x 3 cm squares, 1 cm thick.

To make a syrup, dissolve the extra sugar in the hot water and add the kirsch.

---

COTSWOLD HOUSE RESTAURANT, VICTORIA
*Spicy tuna tartare in crispy somen noodles, page 20*

*S*UMMER

23

### TALGAI HOMESTEAD
#### Darling Downs, Queensland

• 

*Olive and Parmesan bread*

•

*Timbale of Thai noodles with chicken encased in smoked salmon with chilli beurre blanc*

•

*Fillet of Darling Downs beef with peppered raspberry onion marmalade*

•

*Terrine of tropical fruit ice-cream with raspberry coulis and double cream*

---

In a deep casserole or glass bowl, spread a thin coating of mascarpone cream. Place a single layer of sponge cake squares on this base and sprinkle with the kirsch syrup. Spread a layer of strawberries on top of the cake. Cover with the mascarpone cream and repeat. Finish with mascarpone cream on top and a few slices of fresh strawberries to garnish.

### STRAWBERRIES

*2 punnets of strawberries, hulled and coarsely sliced*
*2 tablespoons of icing sugar*
*several drops of lemon juice*
*2 tablespoons of kirsch*

Soak the strawberries in liquid for approximately 30 minutes.

### MASCARPONE CREAM

*2 eggs*
*3 tablespoons sugar*
*1 cup mascarpone cream cheese*
*1 cup whipped cream*

Beat the eggs and the sugar, add the mascarpone and mix well. Fold in the whipped cream.

## OLIVE AND PARMESAN BREAD
#### TALGAI HOMESTEAD

*3 cups self-raising flour*
*¼ cup olive oil*
*½ teaspoon salt*
*2 tablespoons gluten flour*
*30 grams fresh yeast*
*½ cup kalamata olives*
*½ cup finely grated parmesan cheese*
*1 to 1½ cups lukewarm water (approximately)*
*1 egg, lightly beaten*

COMBINE the flour, olive oil, salt, gluten flour and yeast in a mixer bowl. Mix on a low speed until combined, then add the roughly chopped olive, half the cheese and all the water. Mix well and adjust the water content until bread dough has a uniform consistency. Let the dough rise until it has doubled in size, knock down and lightly knead the dough. Divide into 8 equal portions and shape into rolls. Brush with lightly beaten egg and sprinkle with remaining cheese. Allow to double in size again and bake for 20 minutes in an oven preheated to 220°C. Double serving for four.

# TIMBALE OF THAI NOODLES WITH CHICKEN ENCASED IN SMOKED SALMON WITH CHILLI BEURRE BLANC

### TALGAI HOMESTEAD

*2 chicken breasts, skin removed*
*1 red capsicum, finely chopped*
*1 small piece of fresh ginger, grated*
*6 spring onions, finely chopped*
*2 cloves of garlic, finely chopped*
*2 sprigs coriander, including roots and leaves, finely chopped*
*1 fresh lime leaf, finely chopped*
*440 grams tin coconut cream*
*2 teaspoons soy sauce*
*200 grams angel hair vermicelli*
*300 grams sliced smoked salmon*
*1 bottle champagne*
*150 grams butter*
*2 tablespoons sweet chilli sauce*
*2 tablespoons castor sugar*
*capers, deep fried*
*yellow marigold petals*
*chives, finely chopped*

Finely dice the chicken breast and place in a marinade made of capsicum, ginger, spring onions, garlic, coriander, lime leaf, coconut cream and soy sauce, leave overnight. Remove the chicken from the marinade and brown in a pan with a little olive oil, add marinade and reduce by half.

Bring a large pot of water to the boil, add the vermicelli and cook until al dente. Remove from the pot and run under cold water momentarily (vermicelli should remain warm).

Combine chicken, reduced marinade and vermicelli together. Line the timbale moulds with smoked salmon and spoon the chicken mixture into the moulds, pressing it down well. Refrigerate until set.

To make the beurre blanc, place the champagne in a large pan and reduce by half, add the butter, chilli sauce and castor sugar, replace on the heat until the mixture bubbles.

To serve, remove the timbales from the moulds and place on the plates. Pour hot beurre blanc over them. Garnish with deep fried capers, a sprinkle of yellow marigold petals and finely chopped chives. Serves 4.

## FILLET OF DARLING DOWNS BEEF WITH PEPPERED RASPBERRY ONION MARMALADE

### TALGAI HOMESTEAD

4 beef butt fillet steaks (at least 2½ cm thick, trimmed of all fat and sinew)
2 tablespoons olive oil
salt and pepper
1 kg Spanish onions
4 tablespoons raspberry vinegar
2 tablespoons pink peppercorns
1 cup castor sugar
4 large leeks
1 sweet potato

Brush the beef with olive oil and season, cover and refrigerate. Peel and slice the onions, place in a large saucepan with raspberry vinegar, remaining olive oil, peppercorns, castor sugar and cover with water. The onions should be cooked slowly over a moderate heat until the liquid is reduced by three quarters and the onion is very soft. Cut the leeks and sweet potato into thin straws, deep fry and drain on absorbent paper. Reserve for garnishing.

Heat a griddle pan until just smoking, place the beef on the pan and cook until sealed, turn and continue cooking until medium rare (or to your liking). Place the fillets on plates and spoon over the raspberry onions. Garnish with the mixture of deep fried leeks and sweet potato. Serve with seasonal vegetables. Serves 4.

## TERRINE OF TROPICAL FRUIT ICE-CREAM WITH RASPBERRY COULIS AND DOUBLE CREAM

### TALGAI HOMESTEAD

150 grams cream cheese
½ cup castor sugar
2 eggs
300 grams cream
300 grams milk
1 teaspoon vanilla essence
2 large mangoes, flesh
½ cup of toasted macadamia nuts, chopped
1 small pineapple
1 small rockmelon
½ kg fresh or frozen raspberries
½ cup castor sugar
30 ml vodka
double cream

Mix the cream cheese, sugar and eggs together until smooth, gradually add cream, milk and vanilla essence. Divide the mixture into three equal portions. Place the first portion into a food processor and add the flesh of the mango and purée. Place the mango mixture into an ice-cream churn and follow manufacturer's instructions. Line a loaf tin with plastic film and place macadamia nuts on the bottom of the tin. When the ice-cream mixture is ready

*Mietta's Queenscliff Hotel, Victoria
Steamed whiting fillets with chervil mousseline, oysters and champagne sauce, page 28*

𝒮ummer

27

**MIETTA'S QUEENSCLIFF HOTEL**
Bellarine Peninsula,
Victoria

•

*Steamed whiting fillets with chervil mousseline, oysters and champagne sauce*

•

*Roast medallions of Queenscliff crayfish with balsamic vinaigrette, peppers and char-grilled vegetables*

•

*Apricot soufflé with apricot sorbet and poached stone fruit*

spoon it into the loaf tin and spread out evenly. Freeze and continue this process with the second portion being flavoured by pineapple and the third with rockmelon.

To make a raspberry coulis, place the raspberries into a large pan, add the sugar and bring to the boil, remove immediately and cool. Force the raspberry mixture through a fine sieve and add the vodka. Refrigerate.

Remove the terrine from the freezer five minutes before serving. Cut the terrine into slices 1½ cm thick. Place on plates with a tablespoon of double cream to one side and finished with raspberry coulis. Serves 8.

# STEAMED WHITING FILLETS WITH CHERVIL MOUSSELINE, OYSTERS AND CHAMPAGNE SAUCE

### MIETTA'S QUEENSCLIFF HOTEL

*6 x 100 gram whiting fillets, skinned and boned*
*1 egg*
*400 ml thickened cream*
*3 teaspoons chopped chervil*
*1 cup champagne*
*2 tablespoons vinegar*
*1 cup fish stock*
*salt and pepper, to taste*
*125 grams butter*
*½ cup chervil sprigs*
*24 oysters*

DICE 2 of the fish fillets and place in a food processor. Blend with the egg until it forms a smooth paste. Remove from the processor, place in a bowl and refrigerate for 30 minutes. Carefully fold in 100 ml of the cream and the chervil. Refrigerate.

Place the champagne, vinegar and fish stock in a saucepan and simmer until it reduces by three-quarters. Add the remaining cream and simmer over a moderate heat until the sauce reduces by half.

Roll the 4 remaining fillets from the thick end to the tail, leaving a 3 cm wide cavity in the middle. Secure with toothpicks. Fill the cavity with the blended fish mixture and season to taste with salt and pepper.

Place the stuffed fillets on greased paper on a steamer basket and place over a pot of boiling water. Steam for approximately 10 minutes or until the fish filling is firm.

Meanwhile, place the sauce in a saucepan, bring to the boil then turn off the heat. Whisk in the butter until it is fully incorporated. Just before serving, season to taste with more salt and pepper and add some of the chervil sprigs and the oysters, allowing to warm for 1 minute. Divide the sauce between 4 plates, garnish with the oysters and the remaining chervil sprigs. Place the stuffed whiting in the centre of each plate. Serves 4.

# ROAST MEDALLIONS OF QUEENSCLIFF CRAYFISH WITH BALSAMIC VINAIGRETTE, PEPPERS AND CHAR-GRILLED VEGETABLES

### MIETTA'S QUEENSCLIFF HOTEL

*2 large crayfish*
*2 yellow peppers*
*2 red peppers*
*1 Spanish onion, peeled*
*1 clove garlic*
*150 ml extra virgin olive oil*
*50 ml balsamic vinegar*
*1 cup mixed chopped herbs: chervil, chives, tarragon and parsley*
*salt and pepper*
*4 small zucchini*
*2 medium eggplants*
*500 ml vegetable oil*
*50 grams unsalted butter*
*sea salt flakes, to taste*
*cracked black pepper, to taste*

CUT THE crayfish tails through the shell into 6 medallions and cut the heads in half lengthwise. Remove the gut. Roast the peppers in a little oil until the skin blisters and browns. Remove from the heat. When cool, peel and seed. Finely chop one half of the red pepper and one half of the yellow pepper; slice the remaining peppers into serving size pieces.

Finely chop the onion and garlic and mix with the olive oil, balsamic vinegar, ½ cup of the mixed herbs and the finely chopped peppers. Season to taste with salt and pepper.

Slice the zucchini and eggplant into 1 cm thick slices and marinate with the chopped peppers, ¼ cup of the mixed herbs and the vegetable oil.

Place the crayfish pieces in a frying pan and sear over very hot heat with a little olive oil, turning once. Place on a baking tray and cook at 230°C for 6–8 minutes. When cooked, remove from the oven and toss with the butter and remaining herbs. Meanwhile, char-grill or pan fry the marinated vegetables.

Divide the char-grilled vegetables and the crayfish into 4 and place on serving plates. Spoon the vinaigrette over and sprinkle with the sea salt and cracked pepper. Accompany with a raddichio salad. Serves 4.

# Fine Food from Country Australia

**ANABEL'S OF SCOTTSDALE**
Northeastern Tasmania

•

*Medallions of crayfish with asparagus spears and strawberry mayonnaise*

•

*Grilled Tasmanian salmon with scallops in coral sauce*

•

*A mille feuille of Tasmanian berry fruit*

## APRICOT SOUFFLÉ WITH APRICOT SORBET AND POACHED STONE FRUIT

MIETTA'S QUEENSCLIFF HOTEL

10 apricots
2 peaches
24 cherries
250 ml water
200 grams castor sugar
10 egg whites
4 egg yolks
4 dessertspoons icing sugar

Cut the fruit in half and remove the stones. Place the water and sugar in a saucepan, bring to the boil over high heat and cook until the sugar dissolves. When the sugar has dissolved, put the fruit in and remove from the heat.

Pick out the apricots and purée in a food processor, then pass through a sieve. Churn half of the purée and 150 ml of the sugar syrup in an ice-cream machine. When ready, fold through one lightly beaten egg white and freeze. This is the apricot sorbet.

Strain off the other fruit and slice into nice pieces.

In a bowl, mix the remaining purée with the egg yolks and icing sugar. Gently fold one-third of the remaining egg whites through the purée mixture, then fold in the rest, being careful not to over mix.

Fill 4 ramekins with the soufflé, smooth the tops flat with the back of a knife then gently run the knife around the inside of the ramekin to a depth of 1 cm. Place on the middle shelf of the oven at 180°C and cook for 10–14 minutes. Dust the tops with icing sugar.

Neatly pile the fruit on serving plates and top with the apricot sorbet. Serve with the soufflés. Serves 4.

## MEDALLIONS OF CRAYFISH WITH ASPARAGUS SPEARS AND STRAWBERRY MAYONNAISE

ANABEL'S OF SCOTTSDALE

1.5 to 2 kg large cooked crayfish, chilled
12 spears asparagus
200 grams butter
16 strawberries, washed and hulled
300 ml mayonnaise
1 lettuce, finely sliced into chiffonnade

Holding the head of the crayfish firmly, pull out the tail using a side to side movement. Break the limbs from the carcass and retain. Wash the tail and cut out the soft underside by snipping down both sides with scissors. Ease the tail out of the shell in one piece. Cut into 1 cm medallions, extracting the piece of waste gut, which

**MIETTA'S QUEENSCLIFF HOTEL, VICTORIA**
*Roast medallions of Queenscliff crayfish with balsamic vinaigrette, peppers and char-grilled vegetables*
page 29

*Summer*

31

runs the entire length of the tail, with tweezers. Keep in the refrigerator.

Trim the asparagus to a length of 10 to 12 cm. Place into a pot of quickly boiling water with the butter. Continue to boil until the stems will take the point of a knife easily. Do not overcook, the asparagus should still retain a crispness. Refresh in cold water and keep in the refrigerator.

Crush 12 strawberries evenly with a fork until you have a rough mash. Combine this with the mayonnaise, stirring until it is pink.

On each plate arrange three asparagus spears on top of a pile of chiffonnade. Cover the cut ends of the spears with medallions of crayfish and top with strawberry mayonnaise. Garnish with the crayfish legs and remaining strawberries. Serves 4.

## GRILLED TASMANIAN SALMON WITH SCALLOPS IN CORAL SAUCE

### ANABEL'S OF SCOTTSDALE

*16 Tasmanian scallops*
*50 grams butter, solid*
*50 ml Pipers Brook Riesling*
*⅔ cup King Island cream*
*4 salmon cutlets*
*½ cup flour*
*100 grams butter, melted*
*salt and pepper*
*4 lemon wedges*
*4 cucumber twists*

WASH AND pat dry the scallops and separate the corals. Melt 50 grams butter in a pan until frothing, add the scallops and their corals and gently cook for 1 minute on each side. Remove the scallops from the pan and keep warm leaving the corals in the pan. Raise the heat. Add the wine and season with salt and pepper. Reduce a little, then add the cream and allow to thicken slightly. Purée the sauce and corals in a food processor. Reheat in a clean saucepan, adjusting the thickness with wine or cream.

Dredge the salmon in flour and place on a buttered grilling tray. Season and brush with the melted butter. Grill under a hot grill for approximately 5 minutes until cooked through. Add the scallops for the last minute and finish cooking.

To serve, place the salmon cutlets on plates and top with 4 scallops each. Mask each one with coral sauce. Garnish with lemon wedges and cucumber twists. Serves 4.

# A MILLE FEUILLE OF TASMANIAN BERRY FRUIT

## ANABEL'S OF SCOTTSDALE

*325 grams bakers flour*
*110 grams plain cake flour*
*½ teaspoon salt*
*450 grams butter cut into 2 cm cubes and chilled*
*1¾ cups King Island cream*
*1 egg, beaten*
*1 cup Tasmanian raspberries*
*1 cup Tasmanian blackberries*
*1 cup Tasmanian blueberries*
*1 cup mixed black and red currants*
*¾ cup castor sugar*
*1 dessertspoon lemon juice*
*8 strawberries, to serve*
*400 ml King Island cream*
*icing sugar*

To make a puff pastry, sift the two flours and salt together into a bowl. Cut in the butter and stir in the cream, forming a coarse dough that is neither wet nor dry. Shape the dough into a 15 cm square and on a floured surface roll it out into a 30 cm square. Fold it over by thirds into a 10 cm x 30 cm rectangle. Chill for 30 minutes. Roll and fold again and leave to chill for 15 minutes. Repeat 3 more times until the dough is smooth. Roll out the dough to 32 cm x 20 cm, fold in each 20 cm edge to the centre, then fold in half like closing a book. Repeat this twice more. Wrap and chill for 2 hours.

Roll out the pastry to 3 mm thickness and cut into rectangles 5 cm x 10 cm. Place on a greased baking sheet and brush with beaten egg. Refrigerate for 20 minutes before baking in a preheated 220°C oven for about 15 minutes or until lightly browned and well risen. Allow pastry to cool and store in an airtight tin until required. Slice each pastry horizontally to make two thinner pieces.

Place the berries, castor sugar and lemon juice in a pot and bring to the boil. Simmer for two minutes. Allow the berry melange to cool and refrigerate.

To serve, place some berry melange on each plate. On top of this place one slice of pastry. Top this with plenty of cream. Wash, hull and slice the strawberries, and place on top of the cream. Next place another slice of pastry on top followed by some berry melange and more cream. Finish the mille feuille with one of the browned tops of the pastry and sprinkle liberally with icing sugar.

## HOWQUA DALE GOURMET RETREAT
### Northeastern Victoria

*Jellied tomato consommé with poached oysters*

*Soba noodle salad with prawns and squid seasoned with Thai herbs*

*Poached veal rolled with sweetbreads served with peas and Madeira sauce*

*Roast peaches layered with honey wafers and mascarpone cream*

---

HOWQUA DALE GOURMET RETREAT, VICTORIA
*Jellied tomato consomme with poached oysters*

# JELLIED TOMATO CONSOMMÉ WITH POACHED OYSTERS

### HOWQUA DALE GOURMET RETREAT

*36 oysters*
*150 ml champagne*
*crème fraîche*
*fresh salmon caviar*
*half continental cucumber, finely julienned*
*freshly snipped chives*
*Tomato Consommé*

IF POSSIBLE, open the oysters yourself and reserve the juice. Place the oysters in a stainless steel saucepan with the champagne. Bring to the boil over high heat then, as soon as the mixture reaches boiling point, drain the oysters and reserve the liquid. Strain the liquid through muslin until it is very clear.

Slowly add the reserved oyster juice and the strained liquid to the tomato consommé, tasting as you go to check for saltiness and adding additional salt, pepper and sugar to taste. Measure the consommé (for each 1 litre of consommé you need 6–7 leaves of gelatine). Soak the gelatine in cold water to soften for 5 minutes then drain.

Reheat 100 ml of the consommé in a saucepan over medium heat, add the gelatine and stir until dissolved. Stir back into the remaining consommé and cool completely. Pour about 75 ml of consommé into shallow European soup bowls. Chill until just 'set'.

Arrange 3 oysters in each bowl. Cover with another 75 ml of consommé and chill again for 46 hours or until set. Just before serving, place a spoonful of crème fraîche in the centre of the consommé, top with caviar and cucumber juliennes and scatter chives around the edge. Serves 12.

## TOMATO CONSOMMÉ

*3 kilograms vine-ripened tomatoes*
*2 stalks celery, chopped*
*2 cloves garlic, peeled and chopped*
*1–2 bird's eye chillies, chopped*
*6 cm piece fresh ginger, chopped*
*1 nugget fresh galangal, chopped*
*20 basil leaves*
*stalks and roots from 1 bunch coriander or chervil*
*2 stalks lemon grass, chopped*
*zest from 1 orange*
*salt, pepper and sugar, to taste*

Remove the core from the tomatoes and chop roughly. Combine with the remaining ingredients in a large bowl. Place, in small batches at a time, in a food processor and briefly process. Transfer the mixture to a large, stainless steel saucepan and bring to the boil over high heat. Reduce the heat and simmer for 15 minutes.

Set a large stainless steel 'chinois' over a clean pot and gently tip in the cooked pulp. Leave to drain for at least 1 hour without exerting any pressure. (The remaining pulp makes an excellent base for a very aromatic crustacean stock.)

*S*UMMER

35

# SOBA NOODLE SALAD WITH PRAWNS AND SQUID SEASONED WITH THAI HERBS

### HOWQUA DALE GOURMET RETREAT

36 large green prawns
olive oil
3 medium squid
1 packet soba noodles
1 cup garden mint leaves, finely julienned
1 cup fresh coriander leaves, finely julienned
12 Vietnamese mint leaves, finely julienned

DRESSING 1:
150 ml olive oil
2 cloves garlic, peeled
1–2 bird's eye chillies
1 lime, skin and pith removed
1 teaspoon sesame oil
2–3 tablespoons nam pla
1–2 tablespoons palm sugar

DRESSING 2:
1 teaspoon roasted blachan
2 cloves garlic, peeled
2 bird's eye chillies
10 white peppercorns
3 cm piece of fresh ginger, peeled
1 teaspoon salt
100 grams palm sugar
50 ml nam pla
50 ml fresh lime juice
300 ml coconut cream

DRESSING 3:
3 red or golden shallots, finely sliced
3 cloves garlic, finely sliced
1 small knob ginger, finely julienned
1 hot green chilli, finely julienned
2 tablespoons peanut oil
1 teaspoon sambal badjak or sambal oelek
1 teaspoon sesame oil
1 teaspoon blachan, roasted and crumbled
2 tablespoon nam pla
2–3 tablespoons palm sugar
100 ml tamarind juice

SHELL THE prawns and toss lightly in olive oil. Cover and refrigerate until needed. Skin the squid and slice into very fine rings or strips. Toss lightly in olive oil. Cover and refrigerate until needed.

DRESSING 1: Combine all of the ingredients in a food processor and blend until combined.

DRESSING 2: Combine all of the ingredients in a food processor and blend until combined. Transfer the mixture to a stainless steel saucepan and simmer over low heat for 10 minutes, stirring often. Set aside to cool.

DRESSING 3: Place the shallots, garlic, ginger and chilli in a saucepan and simmer in the peanut oil for 5 minutes or until aromatic. Add the remaining ingredients and simmer for a further 5 minutes, stirring to blend well. Set aside.

Cook the soba noodles in a large pot of boiling salted water until al dente. Drain without rinsing and immediately add enough of Dressing 1 to moisten. Cover and leave at room temperature.

Heat a wok or non-stick frying pan until smoking and add the squid a handful at a time. Toss until just cooked, which will take less than 1 minute. Continue to cook in small batches until all the squid is cooked, washing the wok between batches if necessary and reheating before adding the squid. When all of the squid is cooked, add enough of Dressing 3 to lightly moisten.

Cook the prawns under a grill or in a non-stick pan until tender. Just before serving, combine the cooked noodles and the cooked squid with the mint and coriander. Using an old-fashioned carving fork, twist the noodles into a nest shape and arrange in the centre of a serving plate. Garnish with the cooked prawns, a small spoonful of Dressing 2 and a scattering of Vietnamese mint. Serves 12.

# POACHED VEAL ROLLED WITH SWEETBREADS SERVED WITH PEAS AND MADEIRA SAUCE

## HOWQUA DALE GOURMET RETREAT

*1 kilogram veal sweetbreads*
*olive oil*
*3 kosher baby veal sirloins, thoroughly trimmed of all silver skin and membrane*
*dijon mustard*
*5 litres light veal stock*
*1 litre concentrated veal stock*
*300 ml madeira*
*1 kilogram fresh peas, shelled*
*butter*
*pepper*

COVER the sweetbreads with lightly salted cold water and refrigerate overnight. Drain the sweetbreads, cover with fresh cold water and leave to soak for a further 23 hours. Drain again, then thoroughly remove all fat, membrane and sinew. Pat dry.

Heat olive oil in a non-stick frying pan and cook the sweetbreads in a single layer for 15 to 20 minutes or until golden, crispy and tender. Drain on absorbent paper. Cover and refrigerate until needed (this step can be done 24 hours ahead).

An hour before serving, slice the veal fillets lengthwise at a 45° angle until you have a rectangle of meat and smear each fillet with 1 teaspoon of dijon mustard. Place a single layer of sweetbreads down the length of the fillets and roll up, tucking in the thin ends. Tie off with butcher's string.

Bring the light veal stock to a rolling boil in a saucepan large enough to hold the fillets in a single layer. Submerge the fillets then cook, covered, at a vigorous simmer for 5–8 minutes or until medium rare. Remove the fillets and wrap in foil, keeping in a warm place to rest for at least 5 minutes and up to 15 minutes.

Place the concentrated veal stock and madeira in a saucepan, bring to the boil and cook until it reaches a saucy consistency. Strain. Boil the fresh peas in a large pot of water until just cooked and still bright green. Drain. Return to the cooking pot and toss with a nugget of butter and some pepper.

Remove the string from the fillets and cut into eight discs. Place on serving plates, giving 2 discs per serve, and surround with the peas. Top with the sauce. Serves 12.

## ROAST PEACHES WITH HONEY WAFERS AND MASCARPONE CREAM

### HOWQUA DALE GOURMET RETREAT

*100 grams unsalted butter, softened*
*100 grams vanilla sugar*
*lime juice*
*1 large ripe but firm peach or nectarine per serve*
*Mascarpone Cream*
*Honey Wafers*
*Tuille Biscuits*

Cream the butter and vanilla sugar together and add lime juice to taste. Peel the peaches and cut into six or eight wedges. Place on baking parchment and paint with the lime butter. Roast in a 150°C oven, turning after 1 hour and painting again. Cook until caramelised. Retain the syrup left in the baking dish.

You can use either the honey wafers or the tuille biscuits for this dish. Put a dab of the mascarpone cream on each serving plate. Position a honey wafer on top and smear with some more of the cream. Arrange some of the peach segments on the cream, top with another wafer and dust with icing sugar. Drizzle the retained peach syrup around the edges.

### MASCARPONE CREAM

*4 egg yolks*
*120 grams vanilla sugar*
*120 grams castor sugar*
*500 grams mascarpone*

Cream the egg yolks and vanilla sugar together in a food mixer to a sabayon. Meanwhile, moisten the castor sugar with a little water, place in a saucepan and boil until it reaches 118°C on a sugar thermometer and forms a soft ball when dropped in cold water. Pour the syrup immediately over the sabayon and continue whisking until thick and cold. Whisk in the mascarpone until well combined. Cover and refrigerate.

### HONEY WAFERS

*150 grams butter*
*240 grams castor sugar*
*6 tablespoons aromatic honey*
*120 grams plain flour, sifted*
*1 teaspoon ginger*
*2 egg whites*

Cream the butter and sugar together. Mix in the honey, flour, ginger and egg whites and stir until combined. Form into thin circles on baking parchment and bake at 160°C for 7–8 minutes or until a deep golden brown.

CARRINGTON HOUSE, NEW SOUTH WALES
*Fresh figs poached in a lemon marmalade and dessert wine, served with sugared shortbread, page 41*

*S*UMMER

## CARRINGTON HOUSE
### Newcastle, New South Wales

•

*Malaysian shrimp and coconut milk laksa*

•

*Stacked chicken salad with fried wontons and a vindaloo dressing*

•

*Fresh figs poached in a lemon marmalade and dessert wine, served with sugared shortbread*

# MALAYSIAN SHRIMP AND COCONUT MILK LAKSA

### CARRINGTON HOUSE

*1 kg raw prawns*
*1 celery stalk, leaves discarded*
*1 onion, chopped*
*1 knob of garlic, chopped*
*500 gram can of whole tomatoes*
*water to cover*
*sesame oil*
*2 large onions, peeled and sliced*
*5 small hot chillies, chopped*
*3 garlic cloves, peeled and sliced*
*2.5 cm fresh ginger, peeled and chopped*
*1 teaspoon of fennel seeds*
*2 tablespoons of a fragrant curry powder*
*3 tablespoons Thai fish sauce*
*1 tablespoons sugar*
*3 cans coconut milk*
*bean sprouts*
*3 chicken breasts, thinly sliced*
*2 packets of fresh Hokkein Mee noodles*
*peanuts, roasted and chopped*
*coriander, chopped*

REMOVE the shells and heads from the prawns. Set the prawn meat aside. Simmer the prawn shells and heads together with the celery, onion, garlic knob, tomatoes and water for 1 hour to make a crustacean stock.

To make a Laksa, sauté or sweat the sesame oil, onions, chillies, garlic cloves, ginger and fennel seeds together. Stir often for 5 minutes and do not allow it to burn. Add the fragrant curry powder then the Thai fish sauce, sugar, coconut milk and 600 ml of crustacean stock and simmer for a further 15 minutes.

Sauté the peeled and de-veined prawns, putting them into large hot serving bowls with some bean sprouts.

Add the chicken breasts and noodles to the Laksa and simmer for 2 minutes.

Serve in the hot bowls and garnish with chopped roasted peanuts and coriander. Serves 6.

# STACKED CHICKEN SALAD WITH FRIED WONTONS AND A VINDALOO DRESSING

### CARRINGTON HOUSE

*1 whole roasted chicken, room temperature*
*mixed lettuce leaves, including radicchio*
*1 cup French dressing*
*2 teaspoons vindaloo curry paste*
*24 wontons, 3 per person*
*oil*

DISCARD the chicken skin and bones. Shred the leg meat and slice the breasts.

Chiffonnade or finely slice the lettuce leaves. Whisk the curry into the dressing and dress the chicken meat well in advance of serving. Fry the wonton sheets in hot oil until they are a light golden colour. Drain well.

Stack the wontons, lettuce and dressed chicken in that order on a plate finishing with the third wonton on top. Pour a little of the dressing onto the plate and decorate the top with two violas or something similar. Serves 8.

# FRESH FIGS POACHED IN A LEMON MARMALADE AND DESSERT WINE, SERVED WITH SUGARED SHORTBREAD

## CARRINGTON HOUSE

*3 lemons halved, seeded and sliced thinly horizontally*
*2 cups white sugar*
*2 cups water*
*375 ml dessert wine*
*16 whole figs*
*Sugared Shortbreads*
*45% fat cream*

PLUNGE the sliced lemons into boiled water and allow to steep for five minutes. Drain and repeat the process. This will remove some of the bitterness from the pith.

Next simmer the lemons in the sugar and water until the syrup is a golden caramel colour. Add the dessert wine and figs. Cook gently for 10 minutes covered. Cool and chill.

Serve the figs chilled with a Sugared Shortbread baton and unsweetened 45% fat cream.

## SUGARED SHORTBREADS

*100 grams pure icing sugar*
*150 grams unsalted butter, chopped*
*1 whole egg, beaten*
*250 grams plain flour*
*castor sugar*

In a food processor process the icing sugar until fine. Add the butter, egg and flour and process only until a ball has formed. Remove from the bowl and on a lightly floured bench knead the dough 3 or 4 times by hand. (The food processor will only mix the dough but will not knead it.)

Refrigerate the dough in a patty shape, covered in a plastic wrap until it is firm.

Roll out the dough to ½ cm thick. Cut into batons 9 cm long and 2 cm wide. Dust liberally with castor sugar before cooking at 170°C until golden brown. Shake off any excess sugar.

# Fine Food from Country Australia

**RED OCHRE GRILL**
Cairns, Queensland

•

*Crocodile fillet tempura, snow pea and chinois salad, Kakadu plum and wasabi dressing*

•

*Char-grilled wallaby topside medallions with quandong chilli glaze and choi sum*

•

*Lemon aspen and rosella flower ice-cream terrine, rum and coconut sabayon*

## CROCODILE FILLET TEMPURA, SNOW PEA AND CHINOIS SALAD, KAKADU PLUM AND WASABI DRESSING

RED OCHRE GRILL

*300 grams crocodile tail fillet*
*1 packet tempura batter mix*
*200 grams chinois salad mix*
*(chard, tatsio, legume sprouts)*
*20 snow peas*
*500 ml vegetable oil*
*200 ml Kakadu Plum Dressing*

Slice the crocodile fillet into thin strips (3 to 5 mm thick) across the grain, keep cold.

Mix the tempura batter mix according to the instructions on the box. Top and string the snowpeas. Wash and dry the salad mix. Toss the salad and the snow peas together and divide between 4 plates.

Heat the oil to 180°C, dip the crocodile strips into the batter, wiping the excess off on the side of the bowl. Fry until crisp and golden, about 3 minutes, remove and place on a paper towel. Place the pieces around the edge of the salad.

Put whole Kakadu plums between the crocodile strips and drizzle 30 ml of dressing over the salad but not the crocodile strips. Serve the remaining dressing as a dipping sauce. Serves 4.

### KAKADU PLUM AND WASABI DRESSING

*100 grams Kakadu plums*
*5 grams ginger, sliced*
*30 grams sugar*
*150 ml water*
*70 ml rice wine vinegar*
*10 grams wasabi powder*
*oil (peanut or sunflower)*

Simmer plums, ginger, sugar, water and vinegar slowly in a pot with a lid on until the plums are soft. Remove 20 plums and continue to simmer for 15 minutes. Cool and strain, pushing the plum meat through the strainer.

Whisk in a little oil and the wasabi powder. Put the reserved plums back into the dressing and refrigerate.

LUCINDA, TASMANIA
*Butternut pumpkin soup with spicy seared Tasmanian scallops, page 69*

*S*UMMER

43

## CHAR-GRILLED WALLABY TOPSIDE MEDALLIONS WITH QUANDONG CHILLI GLAZE AND CHOI SUM

##### RED OCHRE GRILL

*30 grams dried quandong halves*
*100 ml port wine*
*20 ml ketcup manis (sweet soy)*
*300 ml game glaze or good reduced veal stock*
*2 chillies (red hot)*
*800 grams wallaby topside*
*salt and pepper*
*8 pieces of choi sum (or similar)*

RECONSTITUTE the quandongs in sweetened water to cover. Bring to the boil and cool. Reduce port and ketcup manis by 60% in stainless steel saucepan, add the glaze and the finely sliced chillies. Reduce by 40% or until a good consistency. Add the drained poached quandongs and bring back to the boil and skim.

Char-grill the lightly seasoned wallaby to rare, remove and rest in a warm oven at 90°C for 5 to 10 minutes.

Blanch the choi sum for 2 minutes in water. Slice the wallaby onto warm plates, pour over the sauce and garnish with choi sum. Serves 4.

## LEMON ASPEN AND ROSELLA FLOWER ICE-CREAM TERRINE, RUM AND COCONUT SABAYON

##### RED OCHRE GRILL

*Lemon Aspen Ice-cream*
*Rosella Flower Ice-cream*
*Rum and Coconut Sabayon*

LINE A terrine mould with Go Between, ¾ fill with lemon aspen ice-cream and freeze. Fill the rest of the terrine with Rosella flower ice-cream and freeze. To serve turn out the terrines onto a chilled chopping board. Cut into slices 3 cm thick. Place onto chilled plates with sabayon poured around on the plate. Garnish with reserved rosella flowers. Serves 8 to 10.

### LEMON ASPEN ICE-CREAM

*200 grams lemon aspen*
*100 ml lemon juice*
*500 grams castor sugar*
*1 litre milk*
*12 egg yolks*
*1 litre cream*
*200 ml glucose*

Purée lemon aspen. Boil with lemon juice for 5 minutes. Add sugar and milk and warm through. Pour over the egg yolks, slowly whisking. Cook gently over a water bath until it reaches a light custard consistency. Strain, stir through the glucose and add the cream. Cool and churn in an ice-cream maker.

## ROSELLA FLOWER ICE-CREAM

*300 grams rosella flowers*
*250 grams water*
*300 grams sugar*
*8 egg yolks*
*500 ml milk*
*750 ml cream*

Boil rosella flowers in water for 10 minutes, reserve 10 flowers. Whisk the sugar and egg yolks together. Add milk and cook over a double boiler until light ribbons form. Add the rosella flowers. Cool then add cream that has been beaten to form soft peaks. Churn in an ice-cream maker.

## RUM AND COCONUT SABAYON

*4 egg yolks*
*75 grams castor sugar*
*220 ml coconut cream*
*30 ml Bundaberg rum*

Whisk egg yolks, sugar and coconut cream and rum over a double boiler until the sabayon forms.

# CHICKEN LIVER, HAZELNUT AND MUSHROOM PATÉ WITH BEETROOT CONFIT

### THE MOUNT INN

*4 onions, diced*
*8 rashers bacon, diced*
*1 head of garlic*
*1½ bunches thyme, finely chopped*
*black pepper, freshly ground*
*700 grams field mushrooms, diced*
*1 cup port*
*1 cup brandy*
*600 ml cream*
*400 grams hazelnuts*
*1 kg chicken livers*
*200 grams diced butter*
*1/2 cup brandy, extra*
*1 teaspoon sea salt*

SAUTÉ ONIONS and bacon well. Add minced garlic, thyme and black pepper. Add the mushrooms and cook until the mushrooms start to give up their juice. Add the port and brandy, then rapidly boil off the alcohol. Add the cream and nuts. Reduce over the heat to a thick sauce consistency. Set aside.

Sear the cleaned livers on a hot plate or in a frying pan leaving them pink. Place the livers in a processor and blend, adding small amounts of butter while the motor is running. Gradually add the extra brandy and salt. While the motor is running add a ¼ of the mushroom reduction and process well. Add the remaining mushroom and lightly process. Line a mould with paper. Turn the mixture into the mould and refrigerate. Use half measures for home use.

---

**THE MOUNT INN**
Blue Mountains,
New South Wales

•

*Chicken liver, hazelnut and mushroom paté with beetroot confit*

•

*Warm salad of duck breast, artichoke and sun-dried capsicum*

•

*Vanilla bean ice-cream with mango sorbet polka dots*

## WARM SALAD OF DUCK BREAST, ARTICHOKE AND SUN-DRIED CAPSICUM

### THE MOUNT INN

*4 preserved artichokes*
*8 duck breasts (2 per person)*
*rocket leaves, deveined*
*sun-dried capsicums, sliced*
*duck demi-glaze (reduced brown duck stock)*
*balsamic vinegar*

Roast the artichokes until they give up most of their oil. Sear the duck breasts on a hotplate and roast skin side down for 5 minutes in a hot oven. Rest in a warm place.

Combine the rocket and sundried capsicum slices in a bowl adding a little oil from the capsicums. Slice the duck breast finely and toss into the salad with plenty of boiling demi-glaze and balsamic vinegar. Serve at once with the artichokes.

## VANILLA BEAN ICE-CREAM WITH MANGO SORBET POLKA DOTS

### THE MOUNT INN

*Vanilla bean ice-cream*
*2 litres cream*
*1 litre milk*
*800 grams castor sugar*
*2 vanilla beans, split and scraped*
*24 egg yolks*

*Mango sorbet:*
*1 kg fresh mango pulp, blended*
*200 grams castor sugar*
*200 grams glucose*
*juice of 2 lemons*

Boil half of the cream, 1 litre of milk, half the sugar and the vanilla beans in a pot. Whisk the egg yolks with the remaining sugar and pour over the boiling milk through fine sieve whisking lightly. Cook over boiling water until it coats the back of a spoon. Whisk in the remaining cold cream. Chill and churn.

To make the sorbet, place all the ingredients in a pot and stir until the sugar and glucose have dissolved. This will not take long and the purée will barely be warm. Chill.

DAY ONE
Freeze a large work board and piping bag until frozen. Churn half of the mango sorbet and working quickly pipe 'logs' of mango sorbet onto the board and freeze overnight.

DAY TWO
Place a rectangular mould in the freezer until frozen. Churn the vanilla ice-cream. Add enough ice-cream to the mould so that it covers the bottom, then start laying the frozen logs of sorbet in the container alternating with the vanilla ice-cream. Finish with the vanilla ice-cream. Freeze overnight.

THE MOUNT INN,
NEW SOUTH WALES
*Vanilla bean ice-cream with mango sorbet polka dots*

$\mathscr{S}$UMMER

47

**FLUTES OF BROOKLAND VALLEY**
Margaret River Region,
Western Australia

•

*Sweet potato and marron fritters with grapefruit and coriander salsa*

•

*Fresh Vasse asparagus with quail eggs and anchovy and parmesan dressing*

•

*White Rock veal with parsley and bone marrow persillade on mashed parsnip and potatoes*

•

*Sweet Fonti ricotta fritters with Kununurra mangoes*

---

Day three

Freeze a large work board. Turn out the ice-cream onto the frozen board by dipping the mould in hot water first. (Using Gladbake paper over the frozen board makes handling the ice-cream easier.) Place the 'cake' in the freezer to firm. Churn half of the remaining mango sorbet and with a spatula put an even coat of sorbet on the top and halfway down the sides. Place the cake in the freezer for two hours until the top is set. Churn the rest of the sorbet. Invert the cake and cover the remaining sides and top with sorbet. Freeze until firm. Slice to serve. Allow the ice-cream to soften before slicing if the ice-cream becomes too hard.

# SWEET POTATO AND MARRON FRITTERS WITH GRAPEFRUIT AND CORIANDER SALSA

### FLUTES OF BROOKLAND VALLEY

*250 grams sweet potatoes*
*100 grams marron or prawns, shelled and deveined*
*1/2 cup self-raising flour*
*1/2 cup rice flour*
*generous pinch of ground turmeric*
*1 teaspoon sugar*
*generous pinch of salt*
*250 to 500 ml thick coconut milk*
*vegetable oil*
*lettuce leaves*
*mixed fresh herbs*
*Grapefruit and Coriander Salsa*

Peel the sweet potatoes and grate them coarsely. Squeeze the grated sweet potato to extract as much moisture as possible and drain. Slice the marron in half lengthwise and set aside.

Mix the self-raising flour, rice flour, turmeric, sugar and salt together in a bowl. Gradually add enough coconut milk to make a thick batter. Stir in the grated sweet potato and prawns, mixing well to distribute the marron evenly through the batter. If the mixture becomes too thick, add a little more coconut milk. It should be solid enough to hold its shape when being fired.

Heat enough oil over high heat in a wok or frying pan to deep fry the fritters. When the oil is hot, fry tablespoons of the batter, a few at a time, for 2–3 minutes on both sides or until golden brown on the outside and soft on the inside. Serve with soft lettuce, assorted fresh herbs and a bowl of Grapefruit andCoriander Salsa.

## GRAPEFRUIT AND CORIANDER SALSA

*2 grapefruits*
*375 ml olive oil*
*3 shallots, finely sliced*
*3 tablespoons chopped fresh coriander leaves*
*salt, to taste*

Peel the grapefruits, including the pith, and cut or pull apart into sections. Cut each section in half. Heat the olive oil in a heavy frying pan and fry the shallots over low heat for 5 minutes or until cooked. Add the grapefruit to the pan for the last 12 minutes of cooking. Transfer the salsa to a bowl and cool completely. Mix in the coriander and season with salt.

# FRESH VASSE ASPARAGUS WITH QUAIL EGGS AND ANCHOVY AND PARMESAN DRESSING

## FLUTES OF BROOKLAND VALLEY

*24 asparagus spears*
*8 hard-boiled quail eggs, halved*
*100 grams rocket leaves*
*1 egg*
*2 egg yolks*
*4 anchovy fillets, finely chopped*
*1 clove garlic, finely chopped*
*3 tablespoons shallot vinegar*
*250 ml sunflower oil*
*55 grams Parmesan cheese, grated*
*cracked pepper, to taste*

PEEL THE asparagus from the base to 5 cm from the top and discard the bottom 2.5 cm. Steam the asparagus until just slightly crisp and refresh in iced water. Remove from the water and pat dry.

Place the egg, egg yolks, anchovies, garlic and shallot vinegar in a food processor. Begin processing, slowly drizzling in the oil, then add the Parmesan cheese and cracked pepper.

Place the asparagus on a serving plate and top with the quail eggs and rocket leaves. Drizzle the dressing over the top.

# WHITE ROCK VEAL WITH PARSLEY AND BONE MARROW PERSILLADE ON MASHED PARSNIP AND POTATOES

## FLUTES OF BROOKLAND VALLEY

*2 pontiac potatoes*
*1 parsnip*
*50 grams unsalted butter*
*50 ml cream*
*salt and pepper, to taste*
*2 slices white bread, crust removed*
*50 ml milk*
*4 White Rock veal cutlets, frenched*
*oil*
*1 bunch parsley, washed and roughly chopped*
*100 grams bone marrow*
*1 clove garlic, crushed*
*salt and pepper, extra, to taste*
*4 heaped tablespoons pesto*
*4 large pieces of caul fat*

STEAM THE potatoes and parsnip whole, then peel and chop. Mash with the butter and cream and season. Set aside and keep warm.

Soak the bread in the milk. Seal the veal cutlets with a little oil in a frying pan over high heat, then remove from the heat and cool. Place the bread and milk mixture, parsley, bone marrow, garlic and extra salt and pepper in a food processor and blend until smooth.

Place the pesto on top of the cutlets, then wrap the caul fat over the cutlets with the stem underneath. Place in a roasting pan and cook in a 200°C oven for 10 minutes. Remove from the oven and rest on an airing rack.

Place a spoonful of the mash on each serving plate and top with a cutlet and a good house gravy. Serves 4.

## SWEET FONTI RICOTTA FRITTERS WITH KUNUNURRA MANGOES

*FLUTES OF BROOKLAND VALLEY*

*4 eggs*
*½ cup sugar*
*3 drops vanilla essence*
*500 grams fresh ricotta cheese*
*1 cup plain flour*
*2 teaspoons baking powder*
*oil*
*icing sugar*
*mangoes, half a mango per person*

Blend the eggs in a food processor until pale and fluffy. Blend in the sugar and vanilla essence. Add the ricotta cheese and blend again. Place the mixture in a bowl and add the combined sifted flour and baking powder gradually, folding it in with a rubber scraper or spatula. Cover the bowl and let stand for at least 1 hour.

Heat oil in a large pan over high heat. Test the oil by placing a few drops in a small square of bread (it is hot enough when the bread turns golden within 10 seconds).

Drop dessertspoonfuls of the batter into the hot oil, three or four at a time. Cook, turning with tongs, until golden on both sides. Remove from the oil and drain on absorbent paper.

Dust with icing sugar and serve hot with half a mango per person.

---

THE COTTAGE RESTAURANT, NEW SOUTH WALES
*Char-grilled corn-fed chicken with bell peppers, tomato with fresh basil linguini, page 53*

*S*UMMER

51

## THE COTTAGE RESTAURANT
### Hunter Valley, New South Wales

*Salad of cold marinated raw beef fillet with grilled eggplant and a herbed wine vinegar dressing*

*Plum sorbet*

*Char-grilled corn-fed chicken with bell peppers, tomato and fresh basil linguini*

*Freshly poached stone fruits with their sorbets*

# SALAD OF COLD MARINATED RAW BEEF FILLET WITH GRILLED EGGPLANT AND A HERBED WINE VINEGAR DRESSING

### THE COTTAGE RESTAURANT

*500 grams beef fillet middle piece, cleaned of sinew and fat*
*3 teaspoons freshly milled peppercorns*
*1 dessertspoon strong dijon mustard*
*1 dessertspoon fresh garlic olive oil*
*1 teaspoon freshly ground cardamom*
*1 dessertspoon coriander leaves, coarsely chopped*
*1 teaspoon freshly ground sea salt*
*30 ml brandy*
*1 tablespoon shallots, finely chopped*
*1 tablespoon fresh marjoram, oregano, thyme, rosemary, finely chopped*
*pinch of fresh lavender flowers*
*100 ml red wine, sherry or merlot*
*250 ml red wine vinegar*
*200 ml extra virgin olive oil*
*salt and pepper to season*
*2 medium eggplants, sliced*
*olive oil*

MIX PEPPERCORNS, mustard, garlic, olive oil, cardamom, coriander leaves and sea salt to a paste. Place the beef fillet on a sheet of aluminium foil and coat evenly with the mixture. Pour on the brandy and enclose. Chill overnight.

Sauté the chopped shallots in a little of the oil, add the fresh herbs and the red wine. Simmer for 2 minutes then add the wine vinegar and olive oil. Simmer for another 4 minutes and set aside to cool. Season the dressing with salt and pepper when cold.

Sprinkle the sliced eggplant with salt, set aside for half an hour, then rinse off and pat dry. Grill the eggplant slices under a hot griller until cooked.

Remove the beef fillet from the foil and scrape the excess marinade away. Slice into 12 pieces. Flatten the pieces out between plastic wrap and place a large plate on top.

Place grilled eggplant on each plate with beef fillet slices, spoon over the dressing. Serve with a crusty white loaf of bread. Serves 4.

# PLUM SORBET

### THE COTTAGE RESTAURANT

*500 ml water*
*300 grams plums, washed and stones removed*
*60 ml plum schnapps or plum brandy*

BOIL THE water with the plums in a saucepan. Remove any foam from the top of the pan as the plums cook. Blend the plums and water in a processor. Chill and mix with the liqueur. Freeze in a sorbet machine. Serve in chilled glasses.

# CHAR-GRILLED CORN-FED CHICKEN WITH BELL PEPPERS, TOMATO AND FRESH BASIL LINGUINI

## THE COTTAGE RESTAURANT

*2 x 1.3 kg fresh corn-fed chickens*
*olive oil*
*freshly ground black pepper*
*lemon juice*
*a rosemary sprig*
*½ onion*
*1 carrot*
*3 cloves garlic, crushed*
*10 peppercorns*
*parsley stalks*
*2 large red capsicums*
*2 large yellow capsicums*
*1 large green capsicum*
*1 kg large fleshy ripe tomatoes*
*1 medium Spanish onion, sliced*
*100 ml good olive oil*
*250 ml dry white wine (Semillon)*
*small bunch fresh sage, chopped*
*salt and pepper to taste*
*500 grams Fresh Basil Linguini*

REMOVE breast and legs, marinate with a little oil, fresh pepper, a squeeze of lemon and fresh sprig of rosemary.

Prepare a stock from the carcasses using the ½ onion, carrot, 3 cloves of crushed garlic, peppercorns and parsley stalks.

Quarter and seed the capsicums and lightly roast in oil, skin side down, until the skin has blackened. Peel away the skin and drain. Blanch the tomatoes in boiling water, refresh in cold water then peel the skins off. Cut the tomatoes in half, squeeze out the seeds and chop roughly. Sauté the sliced onion in olive oil, add the tomatoes and white wine and simmer for 10 to 15 minutes. Add the chopped sage and remove from the heat, season to taste.

Season the chicken, brush with oil and place in a medium heat grill, turn regularly and allow 10 to 15 minutes until cooked.

Toss the cooked Basil Linguini in a little hot water, olive oil, salt, pepper and fresh basil. Place the linguini in the middle of the plates with the grilled chicken on top and surround with the capsicum, tomato sauce and a fresh sprig of marjoram.

## FRESH BASIL LINGUINI

*50 grams durum wheat flour*
*2 tablespoons minced basil leaves*
*2 teaspoons salt*
*4 eggs*
*2 tablespoons olive oil*
*pepper*

Mix all the ingredients to a firm dough and allow to rest for 1 hour. Cut into pieces and work through a pasta machine to the second last setting. Allow to rest, dust with flour and pass through the cutter.

Place into a large pot of boiling salted water and bring to boil, remove and refresh under cold running water, allow to drain and set aside in a container with a sprinkle of salt and a little garlic oil.

# FRESHLY POACHED STONE FRUITS WITH THEIR SORBETS

## THE COTTAGE RESTAURANT

*4 small plums*
*4 small peaches*
*4 small nectarines*
*300 grams firm cherries*
*2 vanilla beans*
*1.5 litres water*
*500 grams castor sugar or raw sugar*
*Plum, Peach, Nectarine and Cherry Sorbet*

BLANCH THE peaches in a two litre pot of boiling water, when their skins loosen remove the peaches and place in cold water. Repeat the same process with the nectarines. Remove the skins and set aside.

To make a vanilla syrup bring the vanilla beans, 1.5 litres of water and the castor sugar to the boil and simmer for 5 minutes. Remove the vanilla beans and split lengthwise, scrape out and put this back into the syrup. Bring the syrup back to the boil and poach the peaches for about 4 to 5 minutes on simmer. When they are ready, remove and cover with a little syrup. Poach the nectarines as for the peaches. Poach the plums for about 3 minutes, then remove and cover with a little syrup. Poach the cherries in clusters for 3 minutes, remove and cover with syrup.

Allow all the fruits to chill in refrigerator. When the sorbets are finished serve on cold plates with a fruit selection with the four sorbets. Serves 4.

## SORBET

*500 ml water*
*300 grams fruit, plums or peaches or nectarines or cherries*
*60 ml schnapps or brandy*

To make the four individual sorbets, use this basic method. Remove the stones from the fruit. Boil the water with the fruit in a saucepan. Remove any foam from the top of the pan as the fruit cooks. Blend the fruit and water in a processor. Chill and mix with the liqueur. Freeze in a sorbet machine.

---

THE MOUNT INN,
NEW SOUTH WALES
*Chicken liver, hazelnut and mushroom paté with beetroot confit, page 45*

*S*UMMER

# Fine Food from Country Australia

**BAWLEY POINT GUEST HOUSE**
South Coast,
New South Wales

- Iced cucumber soup
- Nonya chicken in coconut gravy with lacy pancakes
- Peach brulée

## ICED CUCUMBER SOUP

**BAWLEY POINT GUEST HOUSE**

*2 potatoes*
*3 large cucumbers*
*butter*
*1 litre chicken stock*
*1 cup parsley, chopped*
*2 sprigs mint*
*salt and pepper, to taste*
*thickened cream*

Peel and slice the potatoes and cucumbers. Place in a saucepan with butter and sauté until soft but not brown.

Add the chicken stock and parsley and cook until soft. Add the mint and stir to blend. Season to taste.

Push through a sieve, then place in the refrigerator until chilled. Serve with a swirl of thickened cream and a slice of cucumber or fresh mint.

## FRESH MINT CHUTNEY

*1½ cups mint leaves*
*1 medium onion, chopped*
*2 tablespoons sugar*
*3 small red or green chillies, chopped*
*2 tablespoons vinegar (approximately)*

Place the mint leaves, onion, sugar and chillies in a food processor and blend. Add sufficient vinegar to form a paste. Store and seal in sterilised jars.

## NONYA CHICKEN IN COCONUT GRAVY WITH LACY PANCAKES

**BAWLEY POINT GUEST HOUSE**

*2 slices leugkaus (galangal)*
*2 medium onions, chopped*
*3 cloves garlic, chopped*
*5 cm piece fresh ginger, chopped*
*6 red chillies, chopped*
*3 stalks lemon grass, chopped*
*3 tablespoons oil*
*½ teaspoon turmeric powder*
*1 x No. 16 chicken, cut into 10 pieces*
*2 tins coconut milk*
*2 daun salaun leaves*
*Lacy Pancakes*

Soak the leugkaus in hot water until tender. Drain and chop.

Grind the onion, garlic, ginger, chillies, lemon grass and leugkaus in a mortar and pestle until it forms a paste.

Heat the oil in a wok and gently fry the ground ingredients for about 5 minutes. Add the turmeric powder and the chicken pieces and stir fry for another 5 minutes or until the chicken is well coated. Add the coconut milk and daun salaun leaves and cook gently until the chicken is cooked and the gravy is thick and golden (this dish is better well cooked than undercooked).

## LACY PANCAKES

1 cup coconut milk
1¼ cups water
1½ cups plain flour
½ teaspoon salt
3 eggs, well beaten
oil

Combine the coconut milk and water in a bowl. Sift the flour and salt into a food processor, add the eggs and coconut milk mixture and process. Allow to stand for 5 minutes.

Lightly brush a heated omelette pan with oil. Hold a perforated ladle over the pan with one hand and pour one small ladle of batter into it with the other. Quickly rotate the perforated ladle around the pan. Cook until nicely set but not brown. Remove and keep warm. Repeat until all the batter is used.

## PEACH BRULÉE

### BAWLEY POINT GUEST HOUSE

2 peaches
1 tablespoon slivered almonds
½ teaspoon cinnamon
½ tablespoon glace ginger, finely chopped
6 egg yolks
3 tablespoons sugar
1 teaspoon vanilla essence
600 ml cream
castor sugar

Peel and slice the peaches and place in the bottom of soufflé dishes. Sprinkle the almonds, cinnamon and glace ginger evenly over the peaches.

Blend the egg yolks, sugar and vanilla essence together in a food processor.

Heat the cream until it is quite hot but not boiling, then add to the egg mixture and process until blended.

Return the blended mixture to a saucepan and stir over low heat until it thickens. Pour the mixture over the peaches and allow to cool in the refrigerator.

Before serving, sprinkle each brulée with castor sugar and place under a hot grill until the sugar melts. Serves 8.

## FILLET OF SMOKED TROUT WITH WATERMELON PICKLE

### THE PARLOUR AND PANTRY

1 whole smoked trout
fresh dill, to garnish
1 slice of watermelon

Remove the head from the fish. Lay the fish down flat on a bench and, using a sharp knife, very gently slice the trout in a horizontal direction starting in the back of the head and slicing through to the tail. This will give you 2 fillets.

---

**THE PARLOUR AND PANTRY**
Northeastern Victoria

•

*Fillet of smoked trout with watermelon pickle*

•

*The Parlour and Pantry's char-grilled rump of lamb*

•

*Macadamia nut tart*

Very carefully remove the bones from both fillets, leaving the fish still attached to the skin. Place the fillets on a serving plate with the skin side up. Starting at the head end, gently peel back the skin, leaving it coiled up at the tail end but still attached.

Spoon some Watermelon Rind Pickle onto the plate and drizzle over some of the watermelon pickle juice. Garnish with fresh dill and serve at room temperature with a wedge of fresh watermelon and fresh bread. Serves 2.

## STEPHANIE'S WATERMELON RIND PICKLE

*1 kg watermelon rind*
*¼ cup salt*
*1 litre water*
*1 kg sugar*
*600 ml white wine vinegar*
*600 ml water, extra*
*1 lemon, thinly sliced*
*1 tablespoon cinnamon bark*
*1 teaspoon whole cloves*
*1 teaspoon allspice berries*

Cut the rind, leaving just a blush of pink, and trim into 6 x 1 cm even pieces. Soak the rind overnight in the combined salt and water. Drain the rind, put in a saucepan and cover with cold water. Bring to a simmer and cook for about 30 minutes, or until the head of a pin easily pierces the skin. Drain.

Combine the remaining ingredients in a saucepan and bring to a simmer. Cook for 20 minutes. Add the rind, bring to a rapid boil and cook until the rind is translucent. Fill a hot, clean jar with the rind and syrup and leave for about 14 weeks.

This recipe can be varied with the addition of 12 slices of ginger to the syrup, or 125 ml of Grenadine if you prefer a pink pickle.

# THE PARLOUR AND PANTRY'S CHAR-GRILLED RUMP OF LAMB

### THE PARLOUR AND PANTRY

*1 lamb rump, trimmed*
*assorted coloured summer vegetables: red and yellow capsicum, eggplant, zucchini, red onions, chopped and whole mushrooms*
*balsamic vinegar*
*fresh herbs, chopped*

THE MEAT can be marinated in your favourite marinade for up to 1 week if desired. Heat a char-grill for a good 10 minutes. Place the rump on the grill plate and char well on all sides. Turn down the heat and continue to cook the rump until just pink. Remove to a warm oven or barbecue and allow to rest for a good 10 minutes. Slice.

Cook the vegetables on the char-grill until nicely charred. Splash over some vinegar to refresh and place in a salad bowl.

THE PARLOUR AND PANTRY,
VICTORIA
*The Parlour and Pantry's char-grilled rump of lamb*

*S*UMMER

Heat a serving plate and spoon about 50 ml of warm Capsicum Coulis (see recipe following) onto it. Place the lamb slices on top of the coulis and sprinkle over Preserved Lemon. Garnish with the herbs and serve with the bowl of warm vegetables. Serves 12.

## CAPSICUM COULIS

50 ml olive or vegetable oil
2 onions, chopped
3 cloves garlic, chopped
4–5 red capsicums, chopped and seeded
50 grams sugar
80 ml vinegar, white wine or sherry
500 grams fresh or tinned tomatoes, chopped
100 grams tomato paste
juice and zest of 1 lemon
juice and zest of 2 oranges
1 bay leaf
10 grams salt
5 peppercorns
500 ml vegetable stock

Heat the oil in a stainless saucepan. Add the onions and garlic and sauté until soft but not coloured. Add the capsicums and sweat. Add the sugar, vinegar, tomatoes and tomato paste and cook for 2 to 3 minutes. Add the lemon and orange juice and zest, bay leaf, salt, peppercorns and stock. Simmer, covered, on low heat for 20 minutes, stirring regularly. Add more stock or water if the mixture becomes too dry. Remove from the heat, purée and strain. Adjust the seasoning if necessary.

Serve with sautéed calamari, or as a base for various cream sauces and mayonnaises, sour cream and Hollandaise sauce.

## PRESERVED LEMON

15 lemons, just picked
750 grams rock salt
1 bay leaf, chopped
1 cinnamon stick, chopped
coriander seeds
good-quality olive oil

Cut the lemons almost the whole way through but leaving intact by 1 cm at the base. Pack rock salt into the cavity and reshape the lemons. Place into a sterilized jar, layering the spices as you go. Sprinkle over any leftover salt. Press down hard on the lemons to extract as much juice as possible. Cover and place in a cool place for 1 week. Cover the lemons completely with the olive oil and seal the jar. When ready to use, remove the lemons from the jar and rinse with water. Cut off and discard the flesh, leaving only the rind. Dice or cut into strips as required.

## MACADAMIA NUT TART
### THE PARLOUR AND PANTRY

*30 grams butter*
*200 grams golden syrup*
*3 eggs*
*125 grams brown sugar*
*1 teaspoon ground cinnamon*
*½ teaspoon ground nutmeg*
*150 grams unsalted macadamia nuts*
*1 x 24 cm sweet pastry shell*

Place the butter and golden syrup in a saucepan and cook over medium heat until melted. Beat the eggs and sugar together until creamy, then add the cinnamon and nutmeg and beat until combined.

Put the pastry shell into a buttered baking dish. Scatter the nuts over the pastry shell, pour the mixture in and bake at 160°C for 30 to 40 minutes or until set. Serves 10.

## PINK SNAPPER WITH THAI FLAVOURS
### LOUISA'S RESTAURANT

*10 ml ginger juice*
*10 ml garlic juice*
*20 ml lime juice*
*200 ml carrot juice*
*100 ml coconut milk*
*1 small red chilli, chopped*
*1 small piece lemon grass, chopped*
*80 grams jasmine rice*
*500 grams pink snapper fillet (cut into 4)*
*oil*
*10 grams coriander, roughly chopped*
*5 grams basil, roughly chopped*
*5 grams mint, roughly chopped*
*10 grams butter*
*Thai fish sauce*

Combine the ginger, garlic, lime and carrot juices, coconut milk, chilli and lemon grass in a bowl. Cook the rice in boiling salted water and strain.

Place the fish fillets and a little oil in a non-stick pan and cook over high heat, browning the fish on one side then turning it over and browning the other side.

Add the juice mixture, bring to the boil, reduce the heat and simmer until the fish is cooked. Add the chopped herbs and whisk in the butter. Season with the fish sauce.

Remove the fish from the sauce and place on top of the rice. Pour the sauce over and garnish with a little fried leek and carrot strips. Serves 4.

---

**LOUISA'S RESTAURANT**
Bunbury,
Western Australia

•

*Pink snapper with Thai flavours*

•

*Emu fillet with bitter chocolate and red wine sauce*

•

*Strawberry crepe Rasputin*

# EMU FILLET WITH BITTER CHOCOLATE AND RED WINE SAUCE

### LOUISA'S RESTAURANT

*600 grams emu inner fillet*
*extra virgin olive oil*
*4 sprigs thyme*
*80 grams onion, diced*
*20 grams garlic, chopped*
*1 teaspoon cracked black peppercorns*
*350 ml red wine*
*500 ml veal stock*
*500 ml chicken stock*
*5 grams good-quality dark chocolate*
*10 grams butter*
*salt and pepper, to taste*
*Spatzellie*

Trim the emu fillet of any sinew and cut into 4 steaks, keeping any trimmings. Cover the emu with oil, add the thyme and set aside for 2 hours. Remove the thyme and reserve.

Place the emu trimmings, onion and garlic in a heavy-based pan and cook over high heat. Add the reserved thyme, peppercorns and red wine and cook until the liquid has almost evaporated.

Add the veal stock and cook further until reduced by two-thirds. Add the chicken stock and cook again until reduced by two-thirds. Strain.

Whisk in the chocolate a little at a time, tasting as you go. You don't want to overpower the sauce, just give a hint of chocolate. Whisk in the butter and add salt and pepper to taste. Keep warm.

Remove the emu from the oil, place in a saucepan and cook over high heat until medium rare. Remove from the heat and put in a warm place to rest for 8 minutes. Slice thinly.

Place the emu on four serving plates around some Spatzellie. Pour the sauce around and garnish with some young vegetables. Serves 4.

## SPATZELLIE

*100 grams plain flour*
*1 egg*
*50 ml milk*
*nutmeg*
*salt and pepper, to taste*
*10 grams butter*
*Parmesan cheese*

Place the flour, egg, milk and nutmeg in a bowl and mix until just combined and it forms a paste.

Over a pot of boiling salted water, push the paste through the holes of a colander and boil for 2 minutes. Strain and toss with the salt and pepper, butter and Parmesan cheese. Serves 4.

The Parlour and Pantry,
Victoria
*Macadamia nut tart,
page 61*

*S*UMMER

63

**ARCOONA**
Deloraine,
Northern Tasmania

•

*Blackeyed peas and spinach with Ashgrove Pepperberry cheese over brioche*

•

*Pan-seared Atlantic salmon darne with hot summer greens and wattle seed dressing*

•

*Raspberries in Cointreau with Arcoona's lavender ice-cream*

## STRAWBERRY CREPE RASPUTIN
### LOUISA'S RESTAURANT

*1 clove garlic*
*100 grams unsalted butter*
*100 grams castor sugar*
*pinch of English mustard*
*ground black pepper*
*juice and zest of 1 lemon*
*juice and zest of 1 orange*
*15 ml Benedictine*
*15 ml vodka*
*250 grams strawberries*
*8 thin crepes*

MASH the garlic clove and wipe all over the base of a heavy-based sautéing pan. Discard. Place the butter and sugar in the pan and cook over low heat until the mixture caramelises.

Add the mustard, pepper and lemon and orange juices and zest. Cook over medium heat until the mixture reduces to a syrupy consistency.

Add the strawberries and flame with the Benedictine and vodka. When the flames subside, spoon the strawberries onto the crepes and wrap. Pour the sauce over. This dish is best served with cream and vanilla ice-cream. Serves 4.

## BLACKEYED PEAS AND SPINACH WITH ASHGROVE PEPPERBERRY CHEESE OVER BRIOCHE
### ARCOONA

*200 grams blackeyed peas*
*olive oil*
*2 Spanish onions, chopped*
*1 bunch English spinach*
*salt and pepper, to taste*
*3 brioche, sliced and toasted*
*200 grams grated Ashgrove Pepperberry cheese*
*carrot swirls, to garnish*
*broadleaf parsley, to garnish*

SOAK THE peas overnight in water. Strain. Place in a saucepan of boiling salted water and simmer for 1 hour or until tender. Drain and pat dry.

Place the oil in a saucepan big enough to hold all the ingredients and sauté the onions until softened but not browned.

Remove the stems from the spinach and chop the leaves into chunky pieces. Blanche in boiling water for 1 minute. Strain and refresh in cold water. Drain. Add to the saucepan with the onions.

Toss the peas into the spinach and onion mix and stir to heat through. Season with the salt and pepper and keep warm.

Cut the brioche into 2.5 cm slices, toast and sprinkle with the cheese. Melt under a hot grill.

Serve the peas and spinach on warm platters topped with 2 slices of the brioche per serve. Garnish with carrot swirls and broadleaf parsley.

# PAN-SEARED ATLANTIC SALMON DARNE WITH HOT SUMMER GREENS AND WATTLE SEED DRESSING

### ARCOONA

*olive oil*
*2 Spanish onions, chopped*
*100 grams broccoli, chopped*
*100 grams snow peas, topped and tailed*
*100 grams green zucchini, julienned*
*100 grams spinach, chopped*
*100 grams sun-dried tomatoes, chopped*
*18 Spanish olives*
*100 grams fetta cheese, crumbled*
*salt and pepper, to taste*
*300 ml olive oil*
*100 ml balsamic vinegar*
*salt and pepper, to taste*
*2 teaspoons wattle seeds, roasted and ground*
*2 teaspoons Dijon mustard*
*1 clove garlic, crushed*
*Atlantic salmon fillets, boned and skinned (200 grams per serve)*
*snow pea sprouts, to garnish*

PLACE THE olive oil in a wok and gently fry the onions. Toss in the broccoli, snow peas, zucchini and spinach and stir fry for 3 minutes. Add the tomatoes and olives and warm for 2 minutes. Remove from the heat and add the fetta cheese. Season to taste.

Combine the 300 ml of olive oil with the balsamic vinegar, salt and pepper, wattle seeds, Dijon mustard and garlic in a jar and shake vigorously.

Pan fry the salmon fillets in olive oil for approximately 5 minutes.

Arrange the hot summer greens on hot serving plates, top with the salmon and drizzle the vinaigrette over to taste. Garnish with snow pea sprouts.

# RASPBERRIES IN COINTREAU WITH ARCOONA'S LAVENDER ICE-CREAM

### ARCOONA

*1 kg fresh raspberries*
*150 ml Cointreau*
*300 ml milk*
*600 ml full cream*
*1 cup sugar*
*6 florets of lavender flowers, stems removed*
*10 egg yolks*

SOAK THE raspberries in the Cointreau for 1 hour.

Place the milk, cream, sugar and lavender flowers in a saucepan and heat gently. Do not boil. Remove from the heat and allow to infuse overnight. The next day, strain the lavender flowers from the mixture.

Gently reheat the milk mixture. Beat the egg yolks in a bowl,

**NEWTOWN HOUSE RESTAURANT**
Margaret River Region, Western Australia

•

*Yabbie tails in an Asian marinade with mango, coriander, mint and buckwheat noodles*

•

*Beef fillets with roast tomato, baby eggplant and tapenade*

•

*Quinces in syrup with prune and cognac ice-cream and shortcrust shards*

---

add 1 cup of the warm milk mixture and mix well. Place the eggs in the saucepan with the remaining milk mixture and beat well. Stir constantly over a simmering heat for approximately 15 minutes or until the mixture coats the back of a wooden spoon. Do not allow to boil. Cool.

Freeze in an ice-cream maker, or place in the freezer and whisk at regular intervals until soft and frozen. Serve with the raspberries.

## YABBIE TAILS IN AN ASIAN MARINADE WITH MANGO, CORIANDER, MINT AND BUCKWHEAT NOODLES

### NEWTOWN HOUSE RESTAURANT

*125 grams buckwheat noodles*
*250 ml olive oil*
*100 ml fish sauce*
*1 tablespoon mint, chopped*
*1 tablespoon coriander, chopped*
*1 tablespoon chilli, chopped*
*1 tablespoon basil, chopped*
*1 tablespoon garlic, chopped*
*40 x 80 grams yabbies*
*2 medium mangoes*
*1 small red onion, peeled and thinly sliced*
*coriander, garnish*
*mint, garnish*

Cook the buckwheat noodles in boiling salted water. Refresh in cold water and drain well.

Combine the olive oil, fish sauce, mint, coriander, chilli, basil and garlic to make a marinade and mix with the noodles.

Cook the yabbies in boiling salted water. Refresh in cold water and drain. Remove the heads and shells from 32 yabbies. Remove the tail shell only from the 8 remaining yabbies, reserve these for garnish. Add the 32 cleaned tails to the marinade and leave for two hours.

Take the sides off the mangoes and peel and slice. Fan equal portions of mango on 8 plates. Remove any excess mango from the seed and chop. Add to the marinade. Place equal portions of noodle mix on the fanned mango. Garnish with the reserved whole yabbies, onion rings and roughly chopped coriander and mint. Serves 8.

---

ARCOONA, TASMANIA
*Pan-seared Atlantic salmon darne with hot summer greens with wattle seed dressing, page 65*

*S*UMMER

67

## BEEF FILLETS WITH ROAST TOMATO, BABY EGGPLANT AND TAPENADE

NEWTOWN HOUSE RESTAURANT

4 Roma tomatoes
1 sprig basil, chopped
2 cloves garlic, chopped finely
olive oil
salt and cracked black pepper
4 baby eggplant
8 pieces beef fillet (150 grams each)
1 bunch rocket leaves
Tapenade
200 ml beef demi-glaze (reduced beefstock)
20 ml balsamic vinegar, or to taste

Slice the tomatoes and sprinkle with basil, garlic, cracked black pepper and a drizzle of olive oil. Roast in a moderate oven. Cut the eggplant lengthwise and roast in the same way. Grill or sauté the steaks to desired doneness and set aside to rest.

Heat the demi-glaze and when hot add the balsamic vinegar.

Spread the top of each steak with some tapenade, then add the roast tomatoes and eggplant. Place in an oven for a few minutes. Pour the sauce over, and finish with fresh rocket. Serves 8.

### TAPENADE

500 grams black olives, de-seeded
2 garlic cloves, peeled
50 grams capers in vinegar
100 grams anchovies in oil
3 tablespoons olive oil
ground black pepper

Combine the ingredients for the tapenade in a food processor until finely chopped and well combined. Store in the refrigerator until needed. (Will last for three months — if you can stop yourself from eating it! Great on Italian bread with a cold dry white wine.)

## QUINCES IN SYRUP WITH PRUNE AND COGNAC ICE-CREAM AND SHORTCRUST SHARDS

NEWTOWN HOUSE RESTAURANT

4 large quinces (1 kg)
250 grams sugar
1 lemon, rind and juice
1 cinnamon stick
10 cloves
water, to cover
shortcrust pastry, for pastry shards
castor sugar
Prune and Cognac Ice-cream
cream

Peel, core and slice the quinces thinly. Place them in a saucepan with the sugar, lemon and cinnamon and cloves. Cover with water, and simmer until the quinces are tender, approximately 1 hour. Remove the quinces from the pan and reduce the remaining liquid to a syrup. Strain, pour over the quinces and refrigerate.

Make your favourite shortcrust pastry and roll thinly. Cut the pastry into long triangles (approximately 16 cm long with a base of 2.5 cm). Place on a baking sheet, sprinkle with castor sugar and bake until golden brown.

Place one or two scoops of ice-cream (or a square if you have a rectangular mould) on the serving plates, top with quinces in syrup. Add a little fresh whipped cream and arrange three shortbread triangles in a tee-pee effect and dust with icing sugar. The ice-cream, pastry shards and quinces in syrup can all be prepared in advance.

## PRUNE AND COGNAC ICE-CREAM

*20 unpitted prunes*
*30 ml cognac*
*6 egg yolks*
*200 grams sugar*
*250 ml milk*
*½ vanilla bean cracked*
*350 ml cream*

Chop the prunes and steep in cognac for 1 hour. Combine the egg yolks with the sugar and whisk until a pale straw colour is achieved. Bring the milk to the boil with the vanilla bean. Set aside for a few minutes to allow the vanilla flavour to permeate. Strain and add to the yolk mixture. Whisk until well combined. Return to the saucepan and cook until the custard coats the back of the wooden spoon. Place in the refrigerator until well chilled. Whip the cream and add to the custard mixture. Fold in the prunes and the cognac. Put into a container and freeze. Stir occasionally as it freezes to ensure the prunes are evenly distributed.

## BUTTERNUT PUMPKIN SOUP WITH SPICY SEARED TASMANIAN SCALLOPS

### LUCINDA

*1 large butternut pumpkin, peeled and seeded*
*2 brown onions, chopped*
*1 teaspoon cracked black pepper*
*1 carrot, peeled and chopped*
*good-quality chicken stock*
*salt and pepper, to taste*
*1 teaspoon sesame oil*
*250 grams Tasmanian scallops*
*1 teaspoon cumin*
*1 teaspoon coriander*
*1 teaspoon curry powder*
*1 teaspoon chilli powder*
*200 ml King Island cream*
*chives, chopped*

Place the pumpkin, onions, pepper, carrot and enough stock to cover in a large pot. Bring to the boil, reduce the heat and simmer until tender. Blend in a food processor until smooth, then season.

Heat the sesame oil over high heat in a wok. Place the scallops and spices in the wok and sear all over. Portion the scallops out into bowls and pour the soup over. Garnish with the cream and chives. Makes 2 litres.

---

LUCINDA
North Coast, Tasmania

•

*Butternut pumpkin soup with spicy seared Tasmanian scallops*

•

*Ocean trout on wilted spinach, roasted capsicum and tapenade*

•

*Orange and almond cake*

## OCEAN TROUT ON WILTED SPINACH, ROASTED CAPSICUM AND TAPENADE

### LUCINDA

*1 teaspoon olive oil*  
*200 grams ocean trout fillet*  
*1 red capsicum*  
*10–12 spinach leaves*  
*1 sprig of lemon thyme*  
*Tapenade*  
*Lemon Thyme Butter Sauce*

Brush the olive oil over the trout. Char grill, so that a crisscross pattern forms on the skin, until medium-rare, then set aside in a warm place. Place the capsicum over an open gas flame until black. Cool in water, peel, clean, seed and slice into strips.

Heat a wok and cook the spinach until wilted. Stir in the butter sauce. Arrange the spinach on a serving plate with capsicum around it, place the fish on top of the spinach and top with some tapenade (see Tapenade recipe page 68) and lemon thyme sprig.

## LEMON THYME BUTTER SAUCE

*100 ml lemon juice*  
*100 ml white wine*  
*3 sprigs of lemon thyme*  
*1 teaspoon cracked black pepper*  
*½ onion, diced*  
*100 ml cream*  
*200 grams cold butter, diced*

Place all of the ingredients except the butter in a saucepan. Cook over medium heat until reduced by one-third. Remove from the heat and stir in the butter until melted. Strain and keep warm.

## ORANGE AND ALMOND CAKE

### LUCINDA

*3 small oranges*  
*375 grams whole almonds, skinned*  
*1½ teaspoons baking powder*  
*9 eggs*  
*325 grams castor sugar*  
*juice and zest of 6 oranges*  
*juice of 1 lemon*  
*¾ cup castor sugar*  
*125 ml water*  
*icing sugar*  
*King Island cream*

Boil the oranges in enough water to cover for 1 hour or until soft. Remove, cool and purée in a food processor. Place the almonds and baking powder in a food processor and process until fine. Beat the eggs and sugar together until thick. Gently fold the orange purée and almond mixture into the egg mixture. Pour the mixture into a greased 28 cm springform tin and bake at 180°C for about 1 hour. Remove from the oven, rest for 5 minutes then remove from the tin and cool.

Combine the juice and zest of 6 oranges, lemon juice, castor sugar and water in a saucepan, bring to the boil then reduce the heat and simmer until the mixture is syrupy.

Cut the cake into wedges and dust with icing sugar. Spoon the syrup over and serve with dollops of King Island cream.

## SALAD OF LOCAL YABBIES WITH SUNNYBRAE SOFT-DRIED TOMATOES, BASIL AND BEANS

SUNNYBRAE COUNTRY RESTAURANT

*18 large live yabbies*
*15 very ripe Roma tomatoes*
*salt and pepper, to taste*
*extra virgin olive oil*
*dried garlic*
*chilli*
*250 grams small butter beans*
*250 grams small green beans*
*1 bunch basil*
*salt, extra, to taste*
*Vinaigrette*

CHOOSE LARGE, fresh yabbies with claws large enough to eat the sweet flesh they contain.

Cut the tomatoes in half and season very lightly with salt and pepper. Dry to a consistency similar to a dried apricot, that is, soft but not wet, in a dehydrator or in a very slow oven (120°C) on a wire rack with the oven door open. Marinate in extra virgin olive oil, dried garlic and chilli and refrigerate. The tomatoes will keep for 6–8 weeks in a cold refrigerator. When ready to use, remove from the marinade.

Wash the beans and basil. Fill two large pots with water and heat to boiling point. Season with salt. Cook the beans until soft but do not refresh. Place into the vinaigrette while hot — they will absorb the flavour of the vinaigrette.

Plunge the yabbies in rolling boiling water for 45 seconds. Do not refresh. Allow to cool until they are able to be handled, then peel and remove the intestine (this is the same as deveining prawns). Add to the bean and vinaigrette mixture with the soft-dried tomatoes.

Pour on a serving plate, leaving the mixture as it falls, and serve at room temperature or slightly warmed. Provide a finger bowl for the claws. Serves 6.

## VINAIGRETTE

*30 g olive oil*
*2 cloves garlic, crushed*
*sea salt and freshly cracked pepper, to taste*
*1 teaspoon white vinegar*
*juice of ½ lemon*
*basil, chopped*

Combine the olive oil, garlic, salt and pepper and cover with the lemon juice, vinegar and basil.

---

**SUNNYBRAE COUNTRY RESTAURANT**
Southern Coast, Victoria

•

*Salad of local yabbies with Sunnybrae soft-dried tomatoes, basil and beans*

•

*Corn-fed chicken with tiny garden leeks, thyme and verjuice*

•

*Mulberry pudding with white peach sorbet*

## CORN-FED CHICKEN WITH TINY GARDEN LEEKS, THYME AND VERJUICE

### SUNNYBRAE COUNTRY RESTAURANT

*3 x No. 10 corn-fed chickens, boned and halved*
*salt and pepper, to taste*
*1 small bunch thyme, chopped*
*150 ml reduced chicken stock*
*18 small garden leeks or asparagus in season, julienned (save the tops for the stock)*
*1 stick celery, julienned*
*½ carrot, julienned*
*30 ml verjuice (such as Maggie Beer's)*

Season the chicken halves. Place in a large, heat-proof baking dish and sear on both sides over high heat. Sprinkle with the thyme. Place in a 175°C oven for about 10 minutes, after which time they should be nearly completely cooked. Add the stock, leeks and julienne of celery and carrots. Cook in the oven for a further 10 minutes with about 1 cm of reduced stock in the baking tray.

Remove the chicken and leeks and deglaze the remaining stock and vegetables with the verjuice. This should give a light but very flavoursome sauce to ladle over the chicken. This dish can be served with a potato and leek gallette.

## CHICKEN STOCK

*2 onions, roughly chopped*
*3 sticks celery, roughly chopped*
*3 carrots, roughly chopped*
*2 cloves garlic, chopped*
*2 bay leaves*
*1 sprig thyme, chopped*
*3 chicken carcasses*

Clean and chop the retained leek tops. Place them with the other vegetables, garlic, bay leaves and thyme in a baking tray. Place the chicken carcasses on top and roast in a 190°C oven until lightly browned.

Place in a large stockpot with enough water to cover (there should be about three times the volume of water to the solid ingredients). Bring to the boil and boil for 1 minute. Skim the top, reduce the heat and simmer for 4 hours. Remove from the heat and strain. Cool in the refrigerator overnight.

Skim the fat from the top, place back on the stove and simmer over medium heat until reduced by three-quarters. The result should be a full-flavoured, not too thick stock.

# MULBERRY PUDDING WITH WHITE PEACH SORBET

## SUNNYBRAE COUNTRY RESTAURANT

*10 ml cassis*
*800 grams fresh mulberries*
*60 grams sugar*
*juice of 1 lemon*

*½ brioche loaf or sliced white bread*
*Peach Sorbet*

Place the cassis, mulberries, sugar and lemon juice in a heavy-based stainless steel saucepan and cook over low heat until the mulberries start to give up their juices. Be careful not to overcook.

Cut the brioche to line a terrine. Dip the brioche into the mulberry mixture, then line the terrine with it. Pour the mulberry mixture on top, top with brioche and cover with plastic wrap. Put a weight on top of the plastic wrap and place in the refrigerator overnight.

Unmould, cut into slices and serve with a scoop of peach sorbet.

## PEACH SORBET

*water*
*sugar*
*lemon verbena*
*½ vanilla bean*

*10 ripe white peaches*
*lemon juice*
*50 grams icing sugar*

Combine the water, sugar, lemon verbena and vanilla bean in a saucepan and cook over low heat until warm. Very lightly score the peaches and dip into the sweet water for a few seconds. Peel and remove the flesh. Place in a food processor with the lemon juice and icing sugar and blend until smooth. The result should not be too sweet as the sorbet will not set properly.

Put through a very fine sieve and process in an ice-cream machine. If you do not have an ice-cream machine, place in a food processor bowl and process every 30 minutes until a smooth consistency is achieved.

## FRANKLIN MANOR
### West Coast, Tasmania

*Warm quail salad and sweet potato game chips*

•

*Baked Tasmanian salmon*

•

*Passionfruit curd tart with King Island cream*

# WARM QUAIL SALAD AND SWEET POTATO GAME CHIPS

### FRANKLIN MANOR

1 small butter lettuce
1 small fellice lettuce
1 small minuette lettuce
1 small coral lettuce
4 boneless quail
salt and pepper, to taste
500 ml cottonseed oil
1 large sweet potato, sliced
25 ml redcurrant jelly
50 ml red wine vinaigrette
20 ml olive oil

PREHEAT the oven to 190°C. Wash the lettuce leaves and drain. Quarter the quails and season with salt and pepper.

Place the cottonseed oil in a medium-sized frying pan and heat to 180°C. Cook the sweet potato slices in the oil until golden brown. Drain on absorbent kitchen paper.

Place the quails and the olive oil in a heat-proof casserole dish and brown on both sides. Cook in the oven for 3 minutes. Place back on the stove and add the redcurrant jelly and red wine vinaigrette. Cook until heated through.

Toss the quails and sweet potato chips through the lettuce leaves. Garnish with chopped parsley, chives and chervil. Serves 4.

# BAKED TASMANIAN SALMON

### FRANKLIN MANOR

4 Tasmanian salmon pieces
1 large onion, roughly chopped
4 small fennel bulbs, roughly chopped
50 ml vermouth
2 lemons, sliced
70 grams semi sun-dried tomato
1 clove garlic
white pepper
tarragon leaves, to garnish
Fish Stock

PREHEAT the oven to 190°C for 10–15 minutes.

Sauté the butter, onion, fennel and vermouth in a saucepan. Add the lemons, sun-dried tomato, garlic and pepper, then remove from the heat and set aside to cool.

Spray a baking tray with vegetable spray and lay 2 of the fish pieces skin side down on it. Divide the filling in half and place evenly on one side of each fish piece, then place the uncovered fillet over the filling. Cook for 15 minutes.

To serve, place some of the filling on the serving plates and pour the stock over, then place the fish pieces on top. Garnish with tarragon leaves if desired. Serves 4.

FRANKLIN MANOR,
TASMANIA
*Baked Tasmanian salmon*

*S*UMMER

## FISH STOCK

*100 grams butter*
*1 medium onion*
*4 fish heads and their bones*
*6 parsley stems*
*3 peppercorns*
*juice of 1 lemon*
*1 bay leaf*
*1 litre cold water*
*250 ml cream*
*salt and pepper, to taste*
*tarragon, garnish*
*lemon zest, garnish*
*butter*

Melt the butter in a saucepan and sauté the onion. Add the reserved fish bones, parsley, peppercorns, lemon juice, bay leaf and water. Bring to the boil, reduce the heat and simmer for 20 minutes.

Strain through a cloth and place back on the heat. Bring to a simmer, then add the cream and salt and pepper. Cook, stirring, until a roux forms. Just before serving, add the tarragon, lemon zest and a dob of butter.

## PASSIONFRUIT CURD TART WITH KING ISLAND CREAM

FRANKLIN MANOR

*4 cups plain flour*
*1 cup icing sugar*
*350 grams butter*
*juice of 2 passionfruit*
*45 grams butter, extra*
*40 grams icing sugar, extra*
*6 passionfruit*
*50 ml Advokaat*
*1 egg yolk*
*100 ml King Island cream*

SIFT THE flour and icing sugar together. Rub together with the butter until crumbly. Add the passionfruit juice, then knead to form a smooth dough. Rest for 20 minutes or longer.

Line four 9 cm fluted quiche tins with the pastry. Bake blind at 300°C for 15 minutes.

Place the extra butter in a small saucepan and melt over medium heat. Add the extra icing sugar, pulp of 4 passionfruit, Advokaat and egg yolk. Stir until it has the consistency of thick cream. Set aside to cool.

Fold the cream through and place into the pastry case. Spoon the remaining passionfruit pulp over.

# Summer

## CHILLED WATERMELON SOUP WITH FRESH SPICES, SOUR CREAM AND CRISP GINGER THREADS

### PEREGIAN PARK HOMESTEAD RESTAURANT

*500 ml sweet wine (such as sauterne)*
*1 tablespoon rich brown sugar*
*1 teaspoon fresh ginger juice*
*zest of 1 lemon, grated*
*1 teaspoon freshly grated nutmeg*
*½ teaspoon ground allspice*
*½ teaspoon cloves*
*½ teaspoon ginger*
*½ teaspoon cinnamon*
*pinch of black pepper*
*watermelon*
*fresh ginger, very finely julienned*
*vegetable oil*
*6 tablespoons sour cream or crème fraiche*
*fresh mint, very finely julienned*

Place the wine, sugar, ginger juice, lemon zest and spices in a stainless steel saucepan and simmer for 5 minutes. Chill. Blend enough watermelon to produce 2 litres of liquid (don't overblend, you want some texture to the soup). Add to the wine mixture and chill well. Deep fry the ginger in vegetable oil heated to 180°C.

Serve the soup in chilled bowls topped with sour cream, crispy ginger threads and mint. Serves 6.

## LOCAL REDCLAW CRAYFISH AND SCALLOPS WITH FRESH BAMBOO SHOOTS AND CARROT JULIENNE IN LIME-SCENTED JUS

### PEREGIAN PARK HOMESTEAD RESTAURANT

*1 kg tomatoes, roughly chopped*
*Poaching Stock, make two days ahead*
*12 medium redclaw crayfish*
*Lime-scented Jus*
*24 large scallops*
*100 grams unsalted butter*
*juice from 1 lime*
*75 grams carrot, cut in 4 cm juliennes*
*75 grams fresh bamboo shoots, cut in 4 cm juliennes*
*salt and pepper, to taste*
*zest from 1 lime*
*chervil leaves*

One day in advance, place the tomatoes in a strainer lined with muslin and set over a bowl to catch the clear juice.

Place the strained poaching stock in a saucepan, bring to the boil and blanch the crayfish for 10 seconds. Remove the crayfish and, when cool, peel off the heads and shells. Reserve the carcasses for the jus.

Bring the jus liquid to a simmer in a large saucepan. Cut the crayfish flesh in half lengthwise, and gently poach with the scallops

---

**PEREGIAN PARK HOMESTEAD RESTAURANT**
Sunshine Coast, Queensland

•

*Chilled watermelon soup with fresh spices, sour cream and crisp ginger threads*

•

*Local redclaw crayfish and scallops with fresh bamboo shoots and carrot julienne in lime-scented jus*

•

*Quail smoked over paperbark leaves and orange rind with Peregian Park greens*

•

*Ginger ice-cream and strawberry sorbet-layered terrine with fresh berries and strawberry coulis*

in the jus for 1 minute or until just opaque, making sure the scallops are still plump and rare in the middle. Remove the seafood and keep warm.

Pour off all but 500 ml (the remainder can be frozen for use in other dishes) and bring to a light simmer. Gently whisk in the butter, then add the carrot and bamboo shoots. Cook over low heat for 1 minute to wilt the vegetables, then add the lime juice. Return the seafood to the sauce, season with the salt and pepper and cook until heated through. Remove the seafood and vegetables, arranging them in a layered pile in the centre of wide, shallow bowls. Pour the jus over the seafood, and scatter over the lime zest and chervil leaves. Serves 6.

## POACHING STOCK

*1 onion, diced*
*2 celery stalks, diced*
*½ head of garlic, chopped*
*1 leek, diced*
*2 star anise*
*4 carrots, diced*
*1 stalk lemon grass, chopped*
*finger of fresh ginger, diced*
*1 bay leaf*
*sprig each of parsley, chervil, thyme and coriander*
*1½ litres water*
*200 ml dry white wine*

Make the poaching stock two days in advance. Combine all of the ingredients in a stainless steel saucepan and simmer over low heat for 30 minutes. Cool, cover and refrigerate for 2 days, then strain through muslin.

## LIME-SCENTED JUS

*50 ml vegetable oil*
*150 grams green prawn heads and shells (optional)*
*50 ml Chinese rice wine*
*3 shallots, diced*
*4 cloves garlic, sliced*
*½ carrot, diced*
*½ stalk celery, diced*
*1 stalk lemon grass, sliced*
*5 mm piece ginger*
*½ teaspoon black peppercorns*
*clear tomato juice*
*150 ml dry white wine*
*2 kaffir lime leaves, chopped*
*sprig each of thyme and chervil*

Heat half of the vegetable oil in a frying pan and sauté the reserved crayfish carcasses and prawn heads and shells until they change colour. Add the rice wine and deglaze the pan.

In another frying pan, heat the remaining oil and sauté the shallots, garlic, carrot, celery, lemon grass, ginger and peppercorns until aromatic. Add to the crayfish shells along with the remaining ingredients, then simmer gently until the mixture has a full but delicate flavour. Strain out the solids and pass the liquid through muslin.

MOUNT LOFTY HOUSE
MERCURE GRAND HOTEL,
SOUTH AUSTRALIA
*Grilled bluefin tuna with mulloway brandade, roasted red capsicums and crispy fried golden shallots, page 84*

*S*UMMER

79

# QUAIL SMOKED OVER PAPERBARK LEAVES AND ORANGE RIND WITH PEREGIAN PARK GREENS

### PEREGIAN PARK HOMESTEAD RESTAURANT

6 jumbo quails
prickly ash (in a dry pan toast 1 teaspoon szechwan peppercorns with 3 teaspoons salt, then grind together)
12 fresh young paperbark leaves
6 slices lesser galangal
zest of 1 orange
Smoking Mix
orange chilli oil (optional)
200 grams beanshoots
½ continental cucumber, halved, seeded and finely sliced
3 shallots, thinly cut
coriander leaves
purple cabbage, very finely julienned
assorted fresh leaves: mizuria, rocket, tat soi, beetroot leaves, chrysanthemum leaves
Orange and Mustard Vinaigrette

ONE DAY in advance, pat the quails dry inside and out, rub the outside of the birds with prickly ash and sprinkle some into the cavities. Place 2 paperbark leaves, 1 slice of galangal and a strip of orange zest into each cavity, cover and refrigerate overnight.

Place the Smoking Mix in a large wok. Insert a round rack to fit just below the rim of the wok. Place the quails on the rack, allowing space between each bird, and seal with an inverted wok of the same diameter. Place over a medium to high gas flame and smoke for approximately 10 minutes. If the quails are a good golden colour but are not cooked (they should be pink inside), then remove the rack to a 180°C oven for 2–5 minutes. Rest the quail and brush with an orange chilli oil if desired. Cut the quails on either side of the backbone with kitchen scissors, separate the breast and legs and remove the breast bones.

Toss the beanshoots, cucumber, shallots, coriander leaves and a small amount of purple cabbage with the assorted leaves and a small amount of Orange and Mustard Vinaigrette (see recipe). Alternate with the quail on a serving plate to form a stack, drizzle with more vinaigrette and sprinkle with more coriander. Serve with 2 to 4 rounds of Pickled Lotus Root. Serves 6.

## SMOKING MIX

10 fresh young paperbark leaves, crushed
½ cup jasmine rice
¼ cup rich brown sugar
3 pieces cinnamon bark
zest of 1 orange
2 tablespoons fragrant tea
2 teaspoons szechwan peppercorns

Combine all of the ingredients in a bowl.

## ORANGE AND MUSTARD VINAIGRETTE

*2 teaspoons dijon mustard*
*50 ml fresh, strained orange juice*
*1 tablespoon balsamic vinegar*
*50 ml pickling juice*
*1 tablespoon light soy sauce*
*good pinch of prickly ash*
*1 cup peanut oil*

Blend all of the ingredients in a bowl and slowly incorporate the peanut oil.

## PICKLED LOTUS ROOT

*375 ml Japanese rice vinegar*
*pinch salt and pepper*
*pinch dried chilli flakes*
*2 teaspoons julienned ginger*
*2 teaspoons julienned lemon rind*
*1 tablespoon lemon juice*
*⅓ cup sugar*
*3 lotus roots*

Simmer all of the ingredients except the lotus roots in a stainless steel or glass saucepan until the sugar dissolves. Peel the roots and slice into thin rounds, then place in a sterilised glass jar. Pour over the hot liquid, cool, cover and refrigerate. Leave for 2 days. The lotus roots will last for several months if refrigerated.

## GINGER ICE-CREAM AND STRAWBERRY SORBET-LAYERED TERRINE WITH FRESH BERRIES AND STRAWBERRY COULIS

### PEREGIAN PARK HOMESTEAD RESTAURANT

*150 ml water*
*125 ml sugar*
*2/3 cup finely chopped green ginger*
*500 ml milk*
*5 egg yolks*
*1/2 cup sugar*
*500 ml cream*
STRAWBERRY SORBET:
*300 grams sugar*
*1 tablespoon glucose syrup*
*250 ml water*
*500 ml strawberry purée, strained lemon juice, to taste*
*200 ml strained strawberry coulis sweetened with sugar syrup*
*300 grams fresh berries: strawberries, raspberries and blueberries*

TO MAKE the ginger ice-cream, place the water, sugar and green ginger in a stainless steel saucepan, bring to the boil and simmer for 10 minutes. Place the milk in a saucepan and bring to the boil, then add the ginger mixture, take off the heat and set aside until cool.

Whisk the egg yolks and sugar together in a bowl. Reheat the milk mixture, then quickly whisk in the egg mixture. Cook over low heat until it reaches 84°C (if it exceeds this temperature it will curdle), stirring constantly. Remove from the heat and strain. Put

**MOUNT LOFTY HOUSE, MERCURE GRAND HOTEL**
Adelaide Hills, South Australia

*Caramelised vine-ripened tomato tart with goat's cheese and basil oil*

•

*Grilled bluefin tuna with mulloway brandade, roasted red capsicums and crispy fried golden shallots*

•

*Mango and macadamia nut tart, mango and passionfruit mousse and mango sorbet in a tuille biscuit*

---

the strained ginger pieces in a food processor and blend, then add to the milk mixture with the cream. Refrigerate, then when cold churn in an ice-cream machine.

To make the sorbet, place the extra sugar, glucose syrup and 250 ml of water in a saucepan and cook over a medium heat until the sugar dissolves. Cool. Reheat with the strawberry purée until it reaches 11 on a saccharometer, add the lemon juice then churn in an ice-cream machine.

Line a terrine mould with plastic wrap and fill with alternate layers of ginger ice-cream and strawberry sorbet, freezing between the layers. Cut into 1½ cm slices.

Place a small round of strawberry coulis to one side of a large serving plate. Sit a pile of assorted berries on the centre of the coulis, and lay a slice of terrine in the middle. Serves 6.

## CARAMELISED VINE-RIPENED TOMATO TART WITH GOAT'S CHEESE AND BASIL OIL

MOUNT LOFTY HOUSE, MERCURE GRAND HOTEL

*16 tomatoes, organically grown and vine ripened*
*olive oil*
*garlic*
*salt and pepper, to taste*
*basil leaves*
*100 grams sugar*
*50 ml champagne vinegar*
*50 ml water*
*puff pastry*
*goat's cheese (such as Woodside)*
*purple basil sprigs, to garnish*

BLANCH THE tomatoes in boiling salted water for 10 seconds, refresh in iced water. Peel the tomatoes, cut into quarters, remove the seeds and dry out in a 100°C oven for 30 minutes.

Blend the olive oil, garlic, salt and pepper and basil leaves in a food processor until combined. Set aside.

Place the sugar, champagne vinegar and water in a saucepan and cook over medium heat until the sugar dissolves. Pour the caramel into the bottom of four ramekins. Pile the tomato quarters neatly on top of the caramel.

Cut the puff pastry to fit the top of the ramekins, and spread with the goat's cheese. Sit the cheese side of the pastry down on the tomato and bake at 180°C for 20 minutes or until golden. Turn out on a serving plate and garnish with the purple basil and basil oil. Serves 4.

---

MOUNT LOFTY HOUSE MERCURE GRAND HOTEL, SOUTH AUSTRALIA
*Caramelised vine-ripened tomato tart with goat's cheese and basil oil*

*S*UMMER

# GRILLED BLUEFIN TUNA WITH MULLOWAY BRANDADE, ROASTED RED CAPSICUMS AND CRISPY FRIED GOLDEN SHALLOTS

### MOUNT LOFTY HOUSE, MERCURE GRAND HOTEL

*4 x 150 grams fresh bluefin tuna steaks*
*GARNISH:*
*premium-quality olive oil*
*garlic, chopped*
*tomatoes, dice*
*salt and pepper, to taste*
*roasted red capsicum juice*
*MULLOWAY BRANDADE:*
*red capsicums*
*olive oil*
*shallots*
*plain flour*
*oil*

Season the capsicums, brush with olive oil and cook in a 180 to 190°C oven until brown. Remove from the oven, cool, then peel and deseed. Cut the capsicums into strips.

Peel and slice the shallots into rings, then sprinkle lightly with flour. Deep fry until golden.

Char-grill the tuna until lightly cooked. Shape the brandade into quenella shapes. Serve garnished with the red capsicum strips and fried shallots. Serves 4.

## MULLOWAY BRANDADE

*⅔ cup salt*
*⅓ cup sugar*
*chopped parsley stalks*
*200–250 grams mulloway fillet*
*milk*
*garlic cloves*
*potatoes, peeled and chopped*
*salt, pepper and cayenne pepper, to taste*
*olive oil*
*fresh lemon juice*
*salt and pepper, to taste*

Combine the salt, sugar and parsley stalks in a bowl. Salt the mulloway fillet in the mixture for 3–5 hours, depending on the size of the fillet.

Simmer the mulloway fillet in milk until tender, drain and flake the flesh. Cook the garlic cloves in milk until soft, drain and purée. Reserve the milk. Cook the potatoes in boiling salted water, then pan through a drum sieve.

Combine the flaked mulloway, potato and garlic purée and mix thoroughly with a wooden spoon. Add some of the reserved milk to smooth the mixture. Add the seasoning and enough olive oil to balance the flavours. Finish with a few drops of lemon juice.

# MANGO AND MACADAMIA NUT TART, MANGO AND PASSIONFRUIT MOUSSE AND MANGO SORBET IN A TUILLE BISCUIT

### MOUNT LOFTY HOUSE, MERCURE GRAND HOTEL

*60 grams butter*
*60 grams sugar*
*1 egg*
*30 grams plain flour*
*60 grams desiccated coconut*
*60 grams macadamia nuts, chopped*
*puff pastry (home-made or frozen)*
*1 mango, peeled and sliced*
*egg wash*
*icing sugar*
*mint sprigs*
*Mango Sorbet*
*Tuille Biscuits (see recipe page 257)*

CREAM the butter and sugar toget5her, then stir in the egg. Fold the flour, coconut and nuts through. Cut the puff pastry into rounds and spread with the frangipani. Arrange the sliced mango on top of the frangipani, brush the edges with egg wash and bake at 180°C until the pastry is golden. Place the pastry rounds on plates, sprinkle with icing sugar and garnish with the mint. Serve with Mango Sorbet in Tuille Biscuits.

## MANGO SORBET IN A TUILLE BISCUIT

*100 grams sugar*
*100 ml water*
*200 grams mango purée*
*30 ml white rum*

Place the sugar and water in a saucepan and cook over medium heat until the sugar has dissolved. Cool. Combine the sugar syrup, mango purée and white rum in a bowl then place in an ice-cream machine. Churn. Otherwise, place in bowl in the freezer and whisk quickly every 30 minutes until frozen.

Make up the tuille biscuit recipe (page 257) and spread the mixture out in large circles on a baking tray. Bake at 180°C until golden. Rest each circle over the back of a small cup until it cools. To serve, spoon the sorbet into the tuille biscuits.

## MANGO AND PASSIONFRUIT MOUSSE

*6 gelatine leaves*
*water*
*200 grams mango purée*
*50 ml passionfruit juice, panned*
*1 basic sponge cake*
*500 ml cream*
*75 grams sugar*
*100 ml passionfruit juice, extra*
*1 gelatine leaf, extra, soaked in water*

Soak the gelatine leaves in water until soft. Place the mango purée and passionfruit juice in a saucepan and heat over medium heat. Add the gelatine leaves, remove from the heat and chill in the refrigerator until it almost sets. Cut the sponge cake to fit the

**SEVEN SPIRIT BAY**
Cobourg Peninsula,
Northern Territory

•

*Prawn and sweet potato flat cakes*

•

*Coral trout with ginger and black beans*

•

*Banana spring rolls with lime syrup*

bottom of moulds. Whip the cream, then fold the mango mixture through. Spoon quickly into the sponge-lined moulds and refrigerate until set.

Heat the sugar with the extra passionfruit juice over a medium heat then add the extra gelatine leaf. Carefully spoon on top of the mousse.

# PRAWN AND SWEET POTATO FLAT CAKES
### SEVEN SPIRIT BAY

*juice of 6 limes*
*1 tablespoon fish sauce*
*4 tablespoons brown sugar*
*1 tablespoon lemongrass*
*1 tablespoon sweet soy sauce*
*¼ cup water*
*16 large tiger prawns, peeled with tail left on*

*1 golden kumara sweet potato, peeled and cooked*
*1 tablespoon chilli, finely sliced*
*2 tablespoons coriander, chopped*
*¼ cup rice flour*
*4 eggs, lightly whisked*

TO MAKE a sauce, place the lime juice, fish sauce, brown sugar, lemongrass, soy sauce and water in a pot and simmer until it has reduced by half.

Cut the prawns in half (not all the way through) and lightly beat each side until it has spread to double in size.

Combine the sweet potato, chilli, coriander and garlic. Place the potato mixture in the centre of the prawns and fold the sides to the centre. Coat in rice flour and dip in egg.

Heat a pan with oil and shallow fry for 20 minutes on each side. Serve 4 per serve with the dripping sauce. Serves 4.

# CORAL TROUT WITH GINGER AND BLACK BEANS
### SEVEN SPIRIT BAY

*4 coral trout fillets sliced into 2 cm long strips (two per person)*
*1 cup rice, cooked*
*¼ cup beans, sliced*
*¼ cup red capsicum, sliced*
*¼ cup shallots, sliced*
*2 tablespoons fresh ginger, chopped*
*2 tablespoons black bean paste*

*3 tablespoons mirin*
*2 eggs*
*500 ml seafood stock*
*2 tablespoons white shiro miso*
*2 limes*
*salt and black pepper*
*shallots*
*pink peppercorns*

ROLL THE trout fillets like a wheel and place a skewer through them. Sauté together in a pan the cooked rice, beans, capsicum, shallots, ginger and black bean paste. Cool then add the mirin and eggs. Mix well and shape into rice cakes. Set aside.

PROSPECT HOUSE,
TASMANIA
*Blueberry tart served warm with mixed berry sauce, page 89*

$\mathcal{S}$UMMER

**PROSPECT HOUSE**
Richmond,
Southeast Tasmania

•

*King island double brie coated with crushed cashew nuts and oven baked on a blueberry coulis*

•

*Medallions of wallaby*

•

*Blueberry tart served warm with mixed berry sauce*

Place the seafood stock and miso in a pan and simmer for 10 minutes, do not boil. Set aside. Pan fry the coral trout in oil, season and squeeze lime juice over the top. Finish in a moderate to hot oven for 10 minutes.

Shallow fry the rice cakes until crisp but not overcooked. Place the miso broth in the base of the plates with 2 rice cakes and 2 wheels of fish. Garnish with shallots and peppercorns. Serves 4.

## BANANA SPRING ROLLS WITH LIME SYRUP

### SEVEN SPIRIT BAY

*4 limes, zest and juice*
*3 tablespoons palm sugar*
*½ cup water*
*½ cinnamon stick*
*2 bananas, finely diced*
*2 limes, juiced*
*¼ cup brown sugar*
*8 wonton sheets*
*1 egg*
*125 grams water*
*250 grams sugar*
*4 limes, segmented*
*cream rosettes*

To make the sauce place the lime zest and juice, palm sugar, water and cinnamon stick together in a saucepan and reduce by half.

Mix together in a bowl the banana, brown sugar and lime juice. Take a wonton sheet and place 1 tablespoon of the banana mixture at the edge of the sheet. Brush the remainder of the sheet with egg, roll and place on a tray. Make up the remaining wontons in the same way. Cover with a clean damp cloth.

Make a toffee using a heavy based saucepan with the water and sugar. Cook until the sugar has caramelised. Dip lime segments into the toffee and cool on a rack with greaseproof paper.

Using fresh oil, cook the wontons for approximately 2 minutes at 160°C. Pour warm sauce over the wontons and serve with caramelised lime and cream rosettes. Serves 4.

## KING ISLAND DOUBLE BRIE COATED WITH CRUSHED CASHEW NUTS OVEN BAKED ON A BLUEBERRY COULIS

### PROSPECT HOUSE

*1 wheel of King Island double brie cheese*
*500 grams unsalted cashew nuts*
*1 egg*
*flour*
*500 grams Tasmanian blueberries*
*2 tablespoons sugar*
*lemon juice*

Cut a wheel of brie into 12 wedges. Crush the cashew nuts. Coat the brie with beaten egg and flour then cashew nuts.

Simmer the blueberries, sugar and lemon juice in a saucepan until very soft. Blend in a processor.

Bake the brie for 4 to 5 minutes in a hot oven until it turns golden brown and starts to melt. Place the heated blueberry coulis on the serving plates. Place the brie onto the coulis. Serves 12.

## MEDALLIONS OF WALLABY
### PROSPECT HOUSE

*medallions of wallaby, preferably topside or porterhouse*
*mixed herbs (fresh thyme, basil, sage, rosemary,, chives)*
*cracked black pepper*
*olive oil*
*red and green capsicum, thinly sliced*
*black olives, chopped*
*fresh mushrooms, sliced*
*red wine*
*reduced stock*

CUT THE wallaby into serving size medallions. Encrust with mixed herbs and cracked black pepper. Pan fry the wallaby with olive oil. Add olives, capsicum, mushrooms and red wine. Place in a hot oven for 3 to 4 minutes. Add a small quantity of reduced stock and serve.

## BLUEBERRY TART SERVED WARM WITH MIXED BERRY SAUCE
### PROSPECT HOUSE

*450 grams castor sugar*
*500 grams softened butter*
*9 fresh eggs*
*650 grams self-raising flour*
*1 kg Tasmanian blueberries*
*Berry Sauce*
*King Island pure cream*

BEAT THE sugar and the butter slowly until white and fluffy. Add the eggs one at a time then the flour. Place in 2 large well greased flan tins. Place 500 grams of blueberries evenly over the top of each flan. Bake in a moderate oven at 180°C for 1 hour.

Serve the tart warm with some Berry Sauce and King Island pure cream.

### BERRY SAUCE

*300 grams strawberries*
*300 grams raspberries*
*300 grams blueberries*
*lemon juice*
*sugar*

Place all the berries in a saucepan and simmer with a dash of lemon juice and sugar until soft.

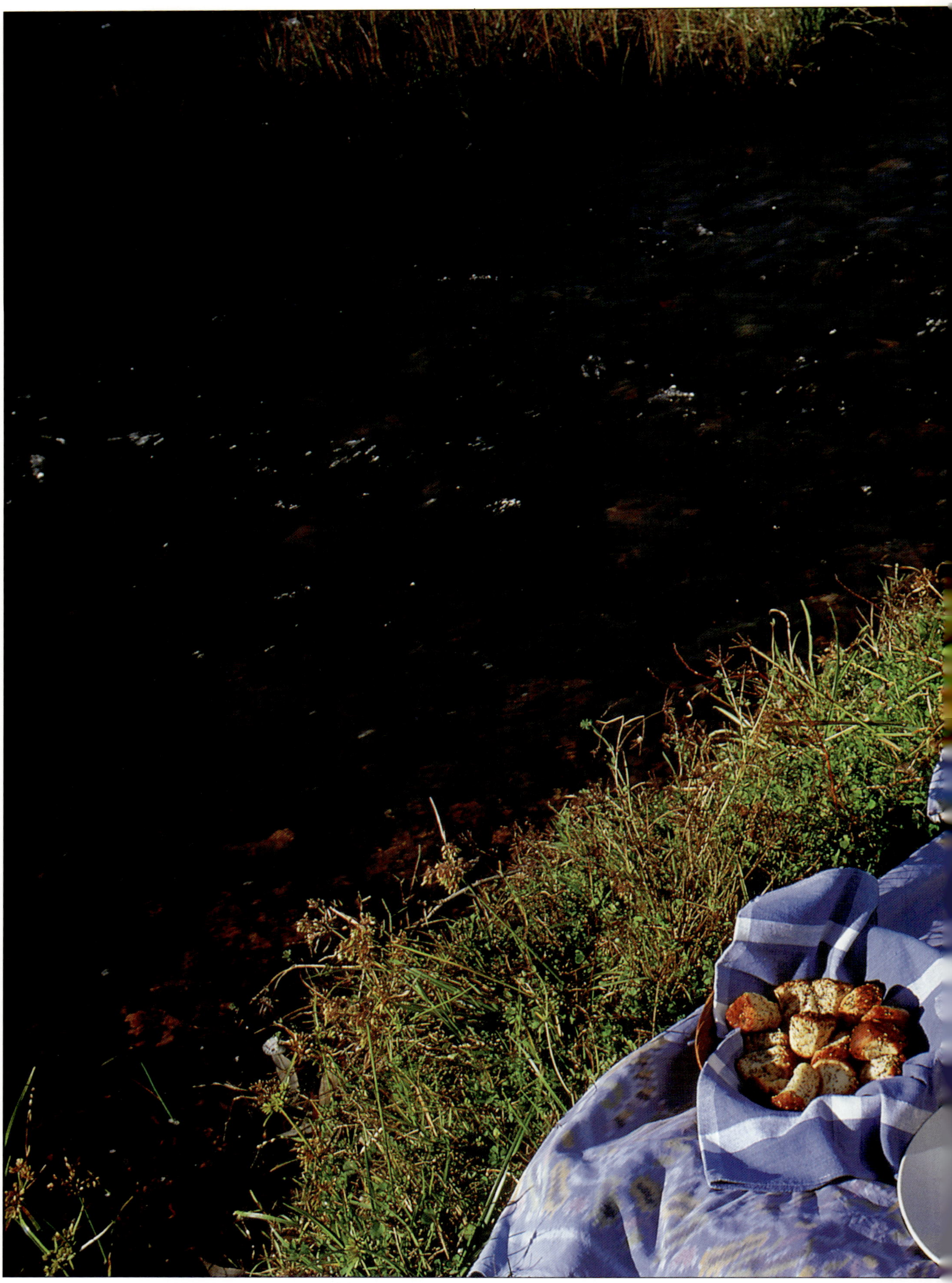

# Autumn

**SAN SOLERO BAY**
Cox Peninsula,
Northern Territory

•

*Crab and golden nugget pumpkin mulligatawny soup*

•

*Paperbark barramundi fillet*

•

*Cinnamon and macadamia nut soufflé with blue gum honey ice-cream*

# CRAB AND GOLDEN NUGGET PUMPKIN MULLIGATAWNY SOUP

### SAN SOLERO BAY

*100 grams yellow mung beans*
*1 large mud crab*
*2 cups pumpkin pieces, steamed and diced*
*1 apple, peeled, cored and chopped*
*1 onion, peeled and chopped*
*1 stick cinnamon*
*1 pinch turmeric*
*pinch mustard seeds*
*500 ml chicken stock*
*125 ml reduced shellfish stock*
*250 ml cream*
*fried shallots*
*coriander leaves*

WASH AND soak the mung beans for 2 hours. Steam the mud crab, crack and remove all the meat and reserve. Bring to the boil in a large pot the pumpkin, apple and onion then add the cinnamon, turmeric, mustard seeds, chicken stock, shellfish stock and mung beans. Reduce and simmer for approximately 1 hour. Purée the soup and return to the heat to boil. Add the cream, season and simmer briefly. Place the mud crab into the soup to heat through briefly. Serve garnished with fried shallots and coriander leaves.

# PAPERBARK BARRAMUNDI FILLET

### SAN SOLERO BAY

*1 bunch lemon grass*
*8–10 grams paperbark*
*300 grams barramundi fillet*
*60 grams basil pesto*
*pinch lemon myrtle, ground*
*pinch native mint, ground*
*pinch sea salt*
*pinch ground pepperleaf*
*50 grams macadamia nuts, crushed*
*2 lemon wedges*
*1 piece banana leaf*

PLACE THE lemon grass sticks, approximately 12 to 15 pieces, on to damp paperbark. Place the barramundi fillet on the lemon grass and spread the pesto on the fish. Sprinkle lemon myrtle and native mint on the pesto. Season with sea salt and ground pepperleaf. Shape the crushed or roughly chopped macadamia nuts over the fish. Cook in a hot oven of approximately 180–190°C for about 12 minutes. When cooked place the whole piece on the serving plate with lemon wedges and appropriate garnishes. The paperbark will not burn in the oven as it has natural non-burning agents.

# CINNAMON AND MACADAMIA NUT SOUFFLÉ WITH BLUE GUM HONEY ICE-CREAM

### SAN SOLERO BAY

*200 ml milk*
*200 grams butter*
*80 grams sugar*
*40 grams plain flour*
*3 to 5 egg yolks*
*1 teaspoon ground cinnamon*
*2 tablespoons crushed macadamia nuts, lightly roasted*
*4 egg whites*
*icing sugar*
*Blue Gum Honey Ice-cream*

Combine the milk, butter and half of the sugar in a saucepan and bring to the boil. When boiling add the plain flour. Stir until a light crust forms on the inside of the pan. Take the pan off the heat and add the egg yolks, one at a time, stirring constantly. Add the cinnamon and macadamia nuts to the custard base and set aside. Make a meringue by beating together the egg whites and the remainder of the sugar. Combine the two egg mixtures. Grease the soufflé moulds and coat the inside with sugar. Add the soufflé mix and bake at 180°C for 15 to 20 minutes. Dust with icing sugar and serve immediately with Blue Gum Honey Ice-cream.

## BLUE GUM HONEY ICE-CREAM

*1 litre vanilla ice-cream base*
*80 ml blue gum honey*

Mix blue gum honey with vanilla ice-cream base and churn.

# ROAST BLACK GENOA FIGS WITH PANCETTA AND GIPPSLAND BLUE CHEESE

### DARLEYS RESTAURANT, LILIANFELS

*350 ml thickened cream*
*140 grams Gippsland blue cheese*
*8 black Genoa figs, quartered*
*16 thin slices of pancetta*
*½ bunch watercress leaves*
*25 ml balsamic vinegar*
*freshly ground black pepper, to taste*

Place the cream in a heavy-based saucepan and cook over medium heat until reduced by half. Put 90 grams of the blue cheese in a food processor and pour in the warm cream. Blend for 30 seconds until smooth. Keep the sauce at room temperature until ready to serve.

Place ¼ teaspoon of the remaining cheese on each fig quarter. Cut the pancetta slices in half and wrap each segment of fig with a piece of pancetta. Cook the figs under a very hot grill for

---

**DARLEYS RESTAURANT, LILIANFELS**
Blue Mountains, New South Wales

•

*Roast black genoa figs with pancetta and Gippsland blue cheese*

•

*Pepper-crusted venison with saffron noodle pancakes, glazed baby beetroot and roast shallots*

•

*Grilled nectarines on almond meringue with amaretto ice-cream*

2 minutes, or until the pancetta starts to lightly colour. Dress the watercress leaves with the vinegar.

To serve, pour a little of the sauce in the centre of a serving plate. Place the watercress leaves on top, surround with the warm figs and garnish with a few turns of freshly ground black pepper. Serves 4.

## PEPPER-CRUSTED VENISON WITH SAFFRON NOODLE PANCAKES, GLAZED BABY BEETROOT AND ROAST SHALLOTS

DARLEYS RESTAURANT, LILIANFELS

*400 grams golden shallots or baby onions*
*vegetable oil (you need three lots)*
*1 bunch baby beetroot*
*50 grams dijon mustard*
*20 grams cracked black peppercorns*
*100 grams soft white breadcrumbs*
*4 trimmed 4-bone racks of venison or 4 venison loins*
*salt and pepper, to taste*
*25 grams freshly grated Parmesan cheese*
*300 ml reduced venison stock*
*Saffron Noodles*

Peel the shallots and roast in the vegetable oil in a 180°C oven for about 25 minutes or until soft. Cut the tops off the baby beetroot, wash and then plunge into boiling salted water for 6 minutes. Refresh under cold running water, then rub off the skins. Mix the mustard with the peppercorns and 50 grams of the breadcrumbs.

If using racks, remove the bones (this step is optional), season and seal the venison meat in a hot frying pan with vegetable oil. Spread a little of the mustard mixture on the back of each venison rack and place into a 230°C oven for 25 minutes. The venison should still be pink at this stage, but you can cook it for longer if you prefer it more well done. Be sure to rest the meat for at least 15 minutes in a warm place before serving.

While the meat is cooking, mix together the Saffron Noodles, the remaining breadcrumbs and the Parmesan cheese. Divide the mixture into four. Heat a small frying pan with a little vegetable oil over medium heat, then gently fry the noodle mixture until crisp. Flip over and fry the other side. Keep the pancakes warm until ready to serve.

Place the beetroot and venison stock in a saucepan and boil over high heat for 5 minutes or until the beetroot is well glazed. Add the shallots and simmer over medium heat for another 2 minutes.

To serve, place a saffron noodle pancake in the centre of a plate, put the venison rack on top and surround with the beetroot and shallots. Spoon a little of the shiny venison glaze over the top. Serves 4.

DARLEYS RESTAURANT, LILIANFELS, NEW SOUTH WALES
*Pepper-crusted venison with saffron noodle pancakes, glazed baby beetroot and roast shallots*

*A*UTUMN

## SAFFRON NOODLES

*1 tablespoon olive oil*
*1 teaspoon saffron threads*
*250 grams plain flour*
*50 grams gluten flour*
*3 large eggs*

Gently warm the olive oil and saffron threads over a very low heat. Remove from the heat and set aside to cool.

Place the saffron threads and the remaining ingredients in a food processor and blend until the mixture forms a firm ball. Remove from the processor and cover with plastic wrap. Refrigerate for 1 hour.

Cover the work surface with rice flour or a mixture of fine semolina and flour to stop the noodles sticking while rolling and cutting. Divide the dough into 6 or 7 pieces, roll out with a rolling pin then pass through a pasta machine as fine as it will go. Cut the dough into noodles. Hang over a broom handle until ready to cook.

This quantity makes much more than you need for the venison, but it is difficult to successfully make a smaller batch. Enjoy leftover noodles with a little fresh tomato sauce, artichoke hearts and a few black olives.

## GRILLED NECTARINES ON ALMOND MERINGUE WITH AMARETTO ICE-CREAM

### DARLEYS RESTAURANT, LILIANFELS

*3 egg whites*
*65 grams icing sugar*
*65 grams ground almonds*
*500 grams raspberries (fresh or frozen)*
*300 grams castor sugar*
*500 ml milk*
*250 ml cream*
*6 egg yolks*
*125 grams sugar*
*125 ml Amaretto*
*4 ripe nectarines or peaches*
*castor sugar, extra*

Using an electric mixer, whisk the egg whites until frothy. Slowly add the icing sugar, continuing to whisk until stiff, then fold in the ground almonds.

Pipe the meringue into rings on non-stick parchment paper using a 1 cm plain or fancy piping tube. Cook in a 100°C oven for 2 hours. They are cooked when the top and the bottom of the meringue are firm. Store in a cool, dry place until needed.

Place the raspberries and the castor sugar in a saucepan and simmer over low heat for 1 hour. Pass the sauce through a fine sieve and place in the refrigerator to cool.

Place the milk and cream in a saucepan and bring to the boil.

Whisk the egg yolks and sugar together, pour on the hot milk mixture and whisk together. Return the mixture to the saucepan and cook, stirring all the time, over a very low heat for 5 minutes or until the mixture is thick enough to coat the back of a spoon. Do not let the mixture boil. Pass through a sieve and set aside to cool. Add the Amaretto and churn in an ice-cream machine. Store in the freezer.

Cut the nectarines in half, remove the stone and sprinkle the cut side with a little castor sugar. Cook under a hot grill for 3–4 minutes or until they begin to colour.

Pour a little raspberry sauce on a serving plate, place a meringue ring on top and rest half a nectarine on the meringue. Serve with a ball of Amaretto ice-cream in the nectarine where the stone was. Serves 8.

**THORN PARK COUNTRY HOUSE**
Clare Valley,
South Australia

*Vegetable and beef samosas*

*Leather jackets with ginger and lime in coconut milk*

*Banana pudding with toffee sauce*

## VEGETABLE AND BEEF SAMOSAS
### THORN PARK COUNTRY HOUSE

*1 onion, finely chopped*
*2 cloves garlic, chopped*
*1 tablespoon fresh ginger, chopped*
*1 tablespoon whole cumin seed*
*1 tablespoon whole coriander seeds*
*1 tablespoon ground turmeric*
*2 tablespoons garam masala*
*2 bird's-eye chillies, finely chopped*
*75 grams clarified butter or ghee*
*250–300 grams ground beef, lamb or kid*
*1 carrot, very finely diced*
*1 large potato, finely diced*
*1 cup peas, fresh or frozen*
*250 ml stock*
*1 tablespoon plain flour*
*Samosa Pastry*

SAUTÉ THE onion and spices in the butter over a high heat, then add the beef and cook for 5 minutes or until coloured. Add the vegetables and stock, reduce the heat and simmer, covered, for 15–20 minutes. Sprinkle over the flour and stir in to thicken. Set aside to cool.

Place a teaspoon of filling into the centre of each pastry round, brush the edges lightly with a little water and fold over and press together. Crimp with your fingers or roll the edge to make an airtight parcel.

Deep-fry the parcels in hot oil for 2 to 3 minutes or until golden brown. Drain on absorbent paper and serve with a fruit and tomato chutney or relish. To make vegetarian samosas, delete the beef and add some additional vegetables such as chopped green beans, sweet potatoes and corn.

## SAMOSA PASTRY

3 cups plain flour
2 tablespoons roasted cumin seeds
60 grams clarified butter or ghee
250 ml warm water

Sift the flour, add the cumin seeds and rub in the butter. Add enough water to make a firm dough. Knead for 5 minutes or until smooth, then leave to rest for 15–20 minutes.

Divide into several pieces and roll out to about a 2–3 mm thickness. Cut into 7–10 cm rounds with a cookie cutter.

## LEATHER JACKETS WITH GINGER AND LIME IN COCONUT MILK

### THORN PARK COUNTRY HOUSE

2–3 onions, thinly sliced
125 ml peanut oil
1 tablespoon galangal, finely chopped
1–2 tablespoons ginger, finely julienned
3 cloves garlic, finely chopped
1 tablespoon ground turmeric
4 green bird's-eye chillies, finely sliced
zest of 1 lime
6 lime leaves
juice of 1 lime
1 tablespoon palm sugar or brown sugar
400 ml thick coconut milk or cream
2 tablespoons fish sauce
200 ml fish stock
1 kg leather jacket pieces, skinned and boned
½ cup coriander leaves

Sauté the onions in the oil until soft but not coloured. Add the galangal, ginger, garlic, turmeric, chillies, lime zest and lime leaves. Cook for 2–3 minutes to infuse the flavours, then add the lime juice, sugar, coconut milk, fish sauce and fish stock. Simmer for 35 minutes. The dish may be prepared to this stage a few hours in advance.

Just before serving, bring the sauce to the boil, add the fish and cook until the fish is tender. Add the coriander and serve with steamed rice and stir-fried green vegetables. Serves 6.

THORN PARK COUNTRY HOUSE, SOUTH AUSTRALIA
*Banana pudding with toffee sauce, page 100*

*A*UTUMN

**THE WILD OLIVE**
Barossa Valley,
South Australia

•

*Feuilletée of sweetbreads and wild mushrooms with an orange butter sauce*

•

*King George Whiting baked on a bed of creamy fennel fondue scented with saffron*

•

*Gratin of spiced poached pears with quince wine sabayon*

## BANANA PUDDING WITH TOFFEE SAUCE
### THORN PARK COUNTRY HOUSE

*3–4 ripe bananas*
*water*
*2 tablespoons banana liqueur*
*1 teaspoon vanilla essence*
*250 grams butter*
*1 cup castor sugar*
*4 eggs*
*125 grams plain flour*
*1 teaspoon baking powder*
*150 grams butter, extra*
*150 grams brown sugar*
*300 ml cream*
*1 teaspoon vanilla essence, extra*

MASH THE bananas with a little water and cook for a few minutes over low heat. Add the liqueur and vanilla essence, remove from the heat and set aside to cool.

Cream the butter and sugar together and add the eggs one at a time, beating well between each addition. Sift the flour with the baking powder and fold into the egg mixture. Add the banana mixture and mix well.

Butter and flour a 20 cm springform cake tin. Pour the mixture in and bake at 180°C for about 40 minutes or until the pudding is firm and cooked in the centre. (The pudding can be made well in advance and reheated before serving.)

Melt the extra butter in a saucepan, then add the brown sugar and cook over a low heat until the sugar has dissolved. Stir in the cream and extra vanilla essence. Cook the toffee sauce for 2–3 minutes until thick and any sugar lumps have dissolved.

Serve the pudding with the toffee sauce. Serves 6–8.

## FEUILLETÉE OF SWEETBREADS AND WILD MUSHROOMS WITH AN ORANGE BUTTER SAUCE
### THE WILD OLIVE

*1 kg sweetbreads*
*300 ml white wine*
*1 kg wild mushrooms*
*500 grams puff pastry*
*2 egg yolks*
*600 ml orange juice*
*100 ml cream*
*200 grams butter, chopped*
*100 grams shallots, sliced*
*1 tablespoon butter, extra*
*salt and pepper, to taste*
*parsley, chopped (optional)*

SOAK THE sweetbreads in water overnight, strain, then place in a saucepan with fresh salted water and 100 ml of the wine. Bring to the boil, reduce the heat and simmer for 1 minute. Refresh in cold water. Clean off any sinew and nerves and place on absorbent paper to dry. Cut into 2 cm cubes.

Clean the mushrooms, preferably with damp absorbent paper as washing them will cause them to absorb water. Discard the stalks and cut the mushroom caps into thick slices.

Preheat the oven to 220°C. Roll out the pastry and, using a sharp knife, cut it into 5 x 10 cm rectangles. Beat the egg yolks and brush over the tops of the pastry shapes. Bake on a baking tray until puffed and golden brown. This step can be done a few hours beforehand.

Place the remaining wine and the orange juice in a saucepan and cook over medium heat until reduced by three-quarters. Strain and return to the pot. Add the cream and heat over medium heat (but do not boil). Whisk in the butter.

Cut the pastry in half lengthwise with a serrated knife. Heat the extra butter in a pan until hot, then add the sweetbreads and salt and pepper. Cook on high heat until they start to colour, then add the shallots and mushrooms more salt and pepper and the parsley. Sauté until everything is golden brown and smells delicious.

Place the bottom half of the pastry on a serving plate, pile with the sweetbread and mushroom mixture and pour over some of the orange sauce. Place the pastry lid on top. Serves 10.

## KING GEORGE WHITING ON A BED OF CREAMY FENNEL FONDUE SCENTED WITH SAFFRON

### THE WILD OLIVE

*5 fennel bulbs, thinly sliced*
*2 tablespoons butter*
*salt and pepper, to taste*
*½ teaspoon saffron tips*
*500 ml cream*
*10 whole King George whiting*
*salt and pepper, extra, to taste*
*butter, extra*
*2–3 sprigs savoury, chopped*
*2–3 sprigs dill, chopped*
*200 grams shallots, sliced*
*700 ml white wine*

PLACE THE fennel bulbs and butter in a large saucepan and season with the salt and pepper. Cook over a low heat for 5 minutes or until the fennel starts to soften. Sprinkle over the saffron tips and pour in the cream, then cook for a further 5 minutes or until the cream thickens slightly.

Clean and scale the whiting. Remove the backbone by slicing down through the back and working against the bones to the front. Leave the head and tail on. If you prefer fillets, cook for less time than stated here. Season the whiting inside and out with the extra salt and pepper.

Preheat the oven to 200°C. Butter a large baking tray with the extra butter, then scatter the herbs and shallots over. Arrange the fish in the tray, stomach down, and cover the bottom of the tray with the wine. Bake the fish for 20 minutes. Arrange the fennel fondue on a serving plate and place the fish on top. Serves 10.

## ADAMS OF NORTH RIDING
### St Andrews, Victoria

*Pressed terrine of sunripened tomatoes and mozzarella cheese*

*Stuffed saddle of rabbit on roasted garlic and wild mushroom risotto*

*Pumpkin ginger tart brûlée with iced mascarpone ice-cream*

# GRATIN OF SPICED POACHED PEARS WITH QUINCE WINE SABAYON
### THE WILD OLIVE

*1 litre water*
*500 grams castor sugar*
*1 cinnamon stick*
*2 star anise*
*3 cloves*
*10 black peppercorns*
*1 vanilla bean, split lengthwise*
*5 cardamom pods*
*10 beurre bosc pears*
*1 lemon*
*Sabayon*

COMBINE ALL of the ingredients except for the pears, lemon and Sabayon in a saucepan, bring to the boil and simmer for 2–3 minutes.

Peel the pears and rub with the lemon to prevent discolouring. Leave whole and place in the poaching liquid. Poach over low heat for about 20 minutes, depending on the ripeness of the pears, turn off the heat and allow to cool in the liquid.

Cut the pears in half lengthwise and remove the cores. Slice thinly and arrange around a serving bowl. Spoon the Sabayon over the pears, then place under a salamander or hot grill and cook until golden brown. Serve immediately. Serves 10.

### SABAYON

*4 egg yolks*
*150 grams sugar*
*300 ml quince wine*
*250 ml cream*

Place the egg yolks, sugar and wine in a stainless steel bowl and whisk continuously over a pot of simmering water until the mixture thickens and holds a figure eight. Remove from the heat and continue whisking until cool. Whip the cream until stiff and fold into the cooled sabayon.

# PRESSED TERRINE OF SUNRIPENED TOMATOES AND MOZZARELLA CHEESE
### ADAMS OF NORTH RIDING

*15 sunripened tomatoes*
*100 ml good olive oil*
*salt and pepper*
*1 bunch basil*
*500 grams mozzarella*
*50 ml tomato juice*
*50 ml good olive oil, extra*
*25 ml red wine vinegar*
*2 teaspoons sugar*
*salt and pepper*

BLANCH AND peel the tomatoes. Cut them into four and take out their centres. Square up the sides of the tomato fillets. Toss in oil and seasoning. Slice the mozzarella thinly. Toss the basil leaves in oil and seasoning.

ADAMS OF NORTH RIDING, VICTORIA
*Pressed terrine of sunripened tomatoes and mozzarella cheese*

*A*UTUMN

Line a terrine with plastic wrap. Place a layer of tomatoes in the terrine, then cheese, then basil. Continue making layers till the terrine is full. Cover and weight overnight in the refrigerator.

To make a dressing mix together the tomato juice, extra olive oil, wine vinegar, sugar and salt and pepper, do not emulsify.

# STUFFED SADDLE OF RABBIT ON ROASTED GARLIC AND WILD MUSHROOM RISOTTO

### ADAMS OF NORTH RIDING

10 rabbit saddles
100 grams pork lard, minced
300 grams pork mince
100 grams rabbit livers, minced
salt and pepper
200 grams crepenette
Roasted Garlic and Wild
Mushroom Risotto

Bone the rabbit saddles, keeping the kidneys aside. To make a farce, mix together the pork lard, pork mince and livers, season with salt and pepper. Roll the rabbit saddles individually in crepenette with the farce and livers in the middle. Hold together with string. Season and roast in an oven for 15 minutes. Slice and serve on Roasted Garlic and Wild Mushroom Risotto. Serves 10.

## ROASTED GARLIC AND WILD MUSHROOM RISOTTO

40 garlic cloves, unpeeled
4 tablespoons olive oil
20 grams dried mushrooms
400 grams wild mushrooms, sliced
1 cup shallots, chopped
2 tablespoons thyme, chopped
1½ cups Arborio rice
½ cup white wine
4 cups chicken stock
2 cups spinach leaves, sliced
⅓ cup parmesan cheese

Roast, peel and chop the garlic (¼ cup). Soak, drain and slice the dried mushrooms. Fry the fresh mushrooms and add to the sliced dried mushrooms.

Sauté the shallots in oil until golden, then add the thyme. Add the rice and stir. Next add the wine and cook until almost evaporated. Mix in the garlic and 3½ cups stock, bring to the boil. Simmer until the rice is tender, stirring occasionally. Add the mushrooms and spinach. Stir in the parmesan cheese to finish. Serves 10.

# PUMPKIN GINGER TART BRÛLÉE WITH ICED MASCARPONE ICE-CREAM
## ADAMS OF NORTH RIDING

1½ cups plain flour
¼ cup castor sugar
pinch salt
2 tablespoons crystal ginger, finely chopped
100 grams unsalted butter, cubed
2½ tablespoons iced water
3 large eggs
1¾ cups pumpkin purée
1 cup light brown sugar
1 teaspoon ground ginger
½ teaspoon ground cinnamon
⅛ teaspoon nutmeg
pinch salt
¾ cup milk
¾ cup cream
Iced Mascarpone

To make the ginger tart pastry, blend the flour, sugar, salt and ginger in a processor. Add the cubes of butter and blend. Add the water and continue to blend. Knead quickly, wrap in plastic wrap and refrigerate for 30 minutes. Makes 6 small tarts.

Lightly whisk the eggs and beat in the pumpkin purée and brown sugar being careful not to over-beat. Add the ground ginger, cinnamon, nutmeg and salt. Whisk in the milk and cream.

Roll out the pastry and line 6 small tart pans, then chill. Scrape in the pumpkin filling. Bake for 10 minutes in a preheated oven at 230°C. Reduce the oven to 180°C and bake for another 45 to 50 minutes or until the tarts are set. Refrigerate. To serve, sprinkle with sugar and caramelise under a griller. Makes 6 small tarts. Serve with Iced Mascarpone Ice-cream.

## ICED MASCARPONE ICE-CREAM

2 egg yolk
85 grams icing sugar
225 grams mascarpone
few drops vanilla essence
200 ml orange juice, reduced

Beat the egg yolks with the icing sugar. Gradually whisk in the mascarpone. Flavour with the vanilla essence and reduced orange juice. Churn in an ice-cream machine.

**ARTHURS RESTAURANT**
Mornington Peninsula, Victoria

•

*Flinders mussels with a gratin of sandcrab meat*

•

*Roast sirloin of kangaroo*

•

*Poached yellow peaches served with a fig cream flavoured with kirsch*

# FLINDERS MUSSELS WITH A GRATIN OF SANDCRAB MEAT

**ARTHURS RESTAURANT**

*1 kg mussels*
*150 ml white wine*
*1 white onion, peeled*
*rock salt*
*40 grams butter*
*40 grams flour*
*250 ml fish stock or stock of cooked mussels*
*100 ml double cream*
*2 tablespoons virgin olive oil*
*200 grams sandcrab meat (out of their shell)*
*2 tablespoons of chopped tips of wild fennel (can be substituted with dill)*
*½ cup parmesan cheese*

Scrape the mussels and remove their beards, then wash them vigorously under running water before draining.

Heat the white wine with the finely diced onion in a saucepan big enough to hold the mussels. Add the mussels and quickly bring to the boil. Cover the saucepan until all the mussels have opened. The mussels will need to be shaken several times during this process. Cooking time is about 3 to 5 minutes.

Drain the mussels from their stock and remove the top half of their shells. Place the mussels on a large baking tray on a bed of rock salt.

Make a roux from the butter and flour and add the fish stock or mussel juice and gently cook for 10 to 12 minutes. Add the cream and continue to cook until you have a smooth veloute sauce.

In a separate frying pan heat the olive oil and gently warm up the crabmeat, season before adding the creamy veloute plus the chopped fennel. Cover each mussel with the crab mixture, sprinkle with parmesan and broil in a hot oven until coloured. Serve immediately. Serves 4.

# ROAST SIRLOIN OF KANGAROO

**ARTHURS RESTAURANT**

*4 pieces of kangaroo sirloin, approximately 150–180 grams each*
*1 punnet shelled fresh peas, approximately 150 grams*
*24 to 32 pearl onions or continental shallots, peeled*
*60 grams butter*
*2 tablespoons sherry or red wine vinegar*
*2 tablespoons honey*
*1 cup green lentils, precooked*
*250 ml brown beef stock or kangaroo stock*

Remove all sinews from the sirloin. Boil the peas in salted water until just tender. Glaze the pearl onions or shallots gently in ⅔ of the butter in a saucepan until lightly coloured, then add the vinegar and honey and cook further until just tender and well glazed.

**Lake House, Victoria**
*A warm salad of slow cooked chicken coated in Moroccan spices, page 109*

$\mathcal{A}$UTUMN

Roast the sirloin in hot preheated frying pan or baking dish. Remove the sirloin from the pan once it has been well seared but still really pink. Remove the excess fat from the pan and add the beef or kangaroo stock. Gently warm the lentils and peas in this stock.

To serve place the lentils and peas in the middle of plates, slice the meat and place over the vegetables. Garnish with glazed onions. Serves 4.

## POACHED YELLOW PEACHES SERVED WITH A FIG CREAM FLAVOURED WITH KIRSCH

### ARTHURS RESTAURANT

*4 large clingstone peaches*  
*500 ml sugar syrup*  
*1 lemon*  
*1 vanilla bean, split*  
*250 grams fresh figs*  
*150 grams sugar*  
*150 ml cream, for whipping*  
*2 tablespoons kirsch*  
*1 punnet strawberries*

PEEL AND gently poach the peaches in the sugar syrup together with the outer peel of ½ the lemon, juice of the whole lemon and the vanilla bean. Continue to poach until the flesh is soft and easy to prick with a fork. Allow the peaches to cool in the syrup. Remove when cool.

Peel the figs and cook to a purée consistency in the remaining lemon juice and sugar. Pass through a moulis or fine sieve and allow to cool.

To assemble place a peach in the middle of each plate. Whip the cream and lightly blend in the fig purée and half the kirsch. Coat the peaches generously with the fig cream and surround the peaches with fine slices of strawberries drizzled with the remaining kirsch.

# A WARM SALAD OF SLOW COOKED CHICKEN COATED IN MOROCCAN SPICES

## LAKE HOUSE

*4 chicken fillets*
*½ teaspoon ground coriander*
*½ teaspoon cardamom*
*vinaigrette made with 400 ml oil and 200 ml wine vinegar, salt and pepper*
*½ cup cooked chick peas*
*¼ teaspoon dried chilli flakes*
*3 cups vegetable oil, for cooking*
*1½ cups chicken stock*
*1½ cups cous cous*
*3 stalks parsley, finely chopped*
*1 egg yolk*
*1 cup mild natural yoghurt*
*150 grams baby spinach leaves*
*4 quarters Middle-eastern preserved lemons*

Remove the skin and any sinews from the chicken. Combine the coriander, cumin and cardamom and rub the spices thoroughly into the chicken fillets. Refrigerate overnight.

Pour a little of the vinaigrette over the chick peas and add a little chilli. Also refrigerate overnight.

Heat the oil in a saucepan. Place the chicken fillets in a baking dish large enough for the fillets to fit side by side. Cover completely with the warm oil. Place in a low preheated oven at 130°C and cook until just firm to the touch. The chicken should be just cooked through. Remove from the oil and pat dry with kitchen paper.

Heat the chicken stock to boiling point. Put the cous cous in a bowl and pour over the chicken stock. Set aside for a few minutes until the cous cous has absorbed all the liquid. Stir through the parsley with a little vinaigrette and salt and pepper to taste.

Whisk the egg yolk and slowly pour in half a cup of vinaigrette, beating all the time. Add the yoghurt and season to taste.

Finely slice the chicken across the grain. Place a mound of cous cous onto the centre of each plate. Toss the spinach leaves ad chicken slices in some vinaigrette and pile a small heap onto the cous cous. Sprinkle some of the dressed chick peas over the top and around the salad. Spoon some yoghurt dressing onto each salad and top with finely diced preserved lemon. Serves 6.

---

## LAKE HOUSE
### Central Victoria

•

*A warm salad of slow cooked chicken coated in Moroccan spices*

•

*Braised rabbit with green lentils and sweet potato ravioli*

•

*Lace biscuits, layered with fresh local berries served with lavender and honey ice-cream.*

# BRAISED RABBIT WITH GREEN LENTILS AND SWEET POTATO RAVIOLI

## LAKE HOUSE

*3 small rabbits*
*⅓ cup flour, seasoned with salt and pepper*
*oil and butter, for frying*
*3 onions, chopped*
*450 ml dry white wine*
*300 ml beef or poultry stock*
*a bouquet garni*
*150 grams bacon or kaiserfleisch, diced*
*2 cups green lentils, cooked*
*2 tomatoes, peeled, seeded and diced*

IF YOU wish to serve a whole foreleg per person as well as some of the braised meat you will need 3 small rabbits. There will be a considerable amount of braised rabbit left which can be eaten on its own or used on other pasta as a sauce, or in a risotto.

Trim the rabbits of their kidneys, liver, lungs and any fat or sinew. Neatly remove the forelegs, cutting through the shoulder joints. Chop the remainder of the rabbits into pieces, approximately the size of the legs.

Roll all the rabbit pieces in the seasoned flour. Melt a little butter and oil in a heavy based pot. Brown the chopped onion. Remove it from the pot and then brown the rabbit pieces two or three at a time. Return the onion and all the rabbit back to the pot. Add the wine and stock, scraping up all the sediment from the bottom of the pan. Add the bouquet garni. Bring to the boil, reduce the heat to simmer for approximately 1½ hours or until very tender.

Pan fry the bacon until it has rendered most of its fat. Drain on kitchen paper. When the rabbit is cooked, remove the pieces from the sauce. If necessary reduce the sauce until it is a good consistency with a strong flavour.

When the rabbit has cooled, remove the flesh from the bones, leaving the legs intact. Shred the flesh into long pieces and put it back into the sauce. Add the bacon, cooked lentils and diced tomato. Reheat and adjust the seasoning. Replace the legs in the pot and continue to gently cook until they are heated through. Serve one braised leg per person together with the meaty sauce over the Sweet Potato Ravioli.

## SWEET POTATO RAVIOLI

*1 kg sweet potato*
*salt and pepper*
*nutmeg*
*250 grams flour*
*2 eggs*
*butter, salt and pepper*

Peel and chop the sweet potato into large pieces and cook in the oven at 180°C until tender, about 30 minutes. Remove from the

LAKE HOUSE, VICTORIA
*Braised rabbit with green lentils and sweet potato ravioli*

*A*UTUMN

111

oven and pass the sweet potato through a sieve. Season with salt and pepper and a pinch of nutmeg.

Make a pasta combining the flour and the eggs. Knead into a ball and then roll through a pasta machine into sheets. Cut out circles of about 10 cm in diameter.

Place a small amount of sweet potato slightly off centre in each circle. Fold the dough over. Press down the edges to make sure the dough is well sealed using a little egg glaze or water if necessary.

Plunge the ravioli into boiling salted water and cook for 4–5 minutes. Remove the ravioli with a slotted spoon, one by one taking care not to break the pasta. Toss with a little butter, salt and pepper.

## LACE BISCUITS, LAYERED WITH FRESH LOCAL BERRIES, SERVED WITH LAVENDER AND HONEY ICE-CREAM

### LAKE HOUSE

*160 grams butter*
*70 grams golden syrup*
*1 tablespoon brandy*
*140 grams plain flour*
*125 grams castor sugar*
*500 ml milk*
*6 egg yolks*
*80 grams sugar*

*150 ml honey*
*100 ml double cream*
*lavender oil, few drops*
*1 kg mixed fresh berries, raspberries, blueberries and blackberries*
*icing sugar*

To make the biscuits, melt the butter and pour in the golden syrup. Blend together and add the brandy. Stir in the flour and castor sugar, making sure the mixture is smooth. Refrigerate till smooth and thick.

On a baking tray lined with parchment paper, place small round balls of the mixture ( a scant teaspoon of each) at least 6 cm apart. When positioned, press the top of each ball down with your thumb, to flatten slightly.

Bake at 160°C for about 8 minutes or until the biscuits are a pale caramel colour.

Remove the tray from the oven and rest the biscuits for a moment until they are set and are easy to remove with a lifter. Allow to cool. Store the biscuits in an airtight container.

To make the ice-cream, bring the milk to the boil. Whisk together the yolks, sugar and honey until very pale. Pour on the hot milk, whisking quickly. Pour the mixture into a saucepan and cook over a medium heat, stirring with a wooden spoon. When the custard starts to coat the spoon, pour it into a bowl and let it cool down completely. Fold in the cream and refrigerate.

When it is ready to churn, remove from the refrigerator and add stir through the lavender oil. Taste and adjust the flavour if necessary. Churn and store in the freezer.

Pick through the berries discarding any under-ripe or imperfect ones. Combine them in a bowl and dust lightly with icing sugar if more sweetness is desired. Stir through very gently to ensure minimal bruising.

Layer three biscuits per person with berries inbetween the layers. Scatter a few more berries over the plate. Dust the whole plate with icing sugar and serve immediately with two quenelles of ice-cream.

## SCALLOP LASAGNE WITH GREEN PEA SAUCE AND ROAST CAPSICUM
### LOUISA'S RESTAURANT

1 red capsicum
50 ml extra virgin olive oil
salt and pepper, to taste
80 grams onion, chopped
50 grams butter
50 grams pancetta, thinly sliced
200 grams sweet green peas
200 ml fish stock
25 large Esperance scallops, roe removed
salt and pepper, extra, to taste
butter, extra
6 sheets lasagne, cooked and cut into 8 cm circles (12 circles are needed)

ROAST THE capsicum whole in a very hot oven or over a gas flame until the skin is charred all over. Place in a plastic bag, seal and leave for 10–15 minutes until cool. Remove from the bag and scrape away the skin. Cut in half, remove the seeds and cut into thin strips. Heat the olive oil in a fry pan over medium heat and cook the capsicum until tender. Season with salt and pepper and set aside in the oil.

Place the onion, 10 grams of the butter and 1 slice of pancetta in a saucepan and sweat over a medium heat until the onion is soft but not brown. Add the peas and cook for 3 minutes. Remove 1 tablespoonful of peas and reserve for the garnish.

Add the fish stock, bring to the boil, turn down the heat and simmer for 2 minutes. Pour the mixture into a food processor, add 1 scallop and blend until very smooth.

Add the remaining butter and blend again. Season to taste and strain through a fine mesh strainer. Keep warm but do not reheat or you will lose the bright green colour.

Place the remaining pancetta and extra butter in a heavy-based frying pan and cook over high heat. When cooked, add the scallops and brown very quickly on both sides.

Warm the lasagne circles in a little water and drain. Place a spoonful of pea sauce in the centre of four serving plates. Place a

---

**LOUISA'S RESTAURANT**
Bunbury,
Western Australia

•

*Scallop lasagne with green pea sauce and roast capsicum*

•

*Stuffed pig's trotter, sautéed of lamb kidney and braised ox tongue*

•

*Apple, pear, banana and date tart*

circle of lasagne on top, add 3 scallops, a slice of pancetta and some roast capsicum. Place another circle of lasagne on top and repeat. Place a third circle on top with a slice of roast capsicum over it and scatter a few peas around. Serves 4.

## STUFFED PIG'S TROTTER, SAUTÉ LAMB KIDNEYS AND BRAISED OX TONGUE
### LOUISA'S RESTAURANT

*4 pig's trotters, soaked in cold water overnight*
*2 large onions*
*2 carrots*
*2 sticks celery*
*1 head garlic*
*250 grams corned ox tongue*
*olive oil*
*100 ml Madeira wine*
*100 ml white wine*
*1 litre chicken stock*
*1 sprig thyme, chopped*
*2 sage leaves*
*1 Kalahari truffle*
*100 grams shiitake mushrooms*
*300 grams chicken breast*
*butter*
*salt and pepper, to taste*
*nutmeg*
*1 egg*
*200 ml cream*
*4 lamb kidneys, cut in half and marinated in olive oil and bay leaves overnight*
*2 bay leaves*
*10 grams butter, extra*

THOROUGHLY clean the trotters and remove any hair. Cut open from the underside and remove all the bones except the toes.

Dice 1½ onions and the carrots, celery and garlic. Place half of this mixture in a saucepan with the ox tongue and cover with cold water. Bring to the boil, reduce the heat and simmer, covered, for 2½ hours. Remove from the stove and cool in the pan.

Place the trotter bones and the remaining onion mixture in a heat-proof casserole dish and brown in a little oil over high heat. Add the Madeira and white wine, lower the heat and simmer until the mixture has reduced by two-thirds. Add the chicken stock, thyme, 1 sage leaf and the trotter skins, bring to the boil, cover and cook in a 160°C oven for 3 hours. Remove from the oven and cool in the stock.

Finely dice the remaining ½ onion and the truffle. Roughly dice the mushrooms and 100 grams of the chicken breast. Place the onion in a saucepan with a little butter and sweat until soft but not brown. Add the diced chicken and half of the mushrooms. When cooked, add the truffle and salt and pepper to taste, remove from the heat and allow to cool.

Remove the tongue from its cooking liquid and peel the skin away. Cut into 5 slices. Dice one slice and add to the chicken mushroom mixture.

Place the remaining chicken breast, salt, pepper and nutmeg to taste and remaining sage leaf in a food processor and blend for 1

HOWQUA DALE GOURMET RETREAT, VICTORIA
*Moulded trifle with rhubarb bavarois, poached pears and quinces, page 121*

*A*UTUMN

115

minute. Add the egg and blend for a further minute. Gradually add the cream, blending between additions. Remove from the food processor and add enough of the mushroom mixture to bind it all together.

Remove the trotter skins from the stock and lay down flat on 4 pieces of kitchen foil, skin side down. Divide the stuffing between the skins. Roll up like a sausage and twist the ends.

Strain the stock into a saucepan and cook over a high heat until it has reduced to a sauce consistency.

Steam the stuffed trotter skins in a steamer for 15–20 minutes until the stuffing is cooked.

Place the kidneys and bay leaves in a saucepan and sauté over high heat. Add the 4 remaining slices of tongue and the remaining mushrooms. Cook until both sides of the tongue have browned, drain off any fat and deglaze the pan with Madeira. Add the sauce, simmer for 1 minute, remove the bay leaves and whisk in the extra butter.

Place the trotters on 4 serving plates with a kidney and 1 slice of tongue per plate and pour the sauce over. Serve with mashed potato. Serves 4.

## APPLE, PEAR, BANANA AND DATE TART

### LOUISA'S RESTAURANT

*shortcrust pastry*
*50 grams butter*
*1 apple, peeled and sliced*
*1 pear, peeled and sliced*
*juice and zest of 1 lemon*
*pinch cinnamon*
*150 grams castor sugar*
*100 grams dates, chopped*
*2 bananas, sliced*
*4 eggs*
*125 ml cream*

Line a 22 cm flan ring with the pastry.

Place the butter, apple, pear, lemon juice and zest, cinnamon and 50 grams of the sugar in a heavy-based saucepan and cook over medium heat until just tender but not mushy. Strain, retaining the liquid.

Scatter the dates over the base of the pastry in the flan ring. Pile the apple and pear on top, then scatter the bananas over.

Whisk the eggs with the remaining sugar. Add the cream and the reserved liquid. Pour over the fruit in the flan ring. Bake in a 200°C oven for 30 minutes. Serve warm with fresh cream.

# DOUBLE-BAKED CORN SOUFFLÉS WITH CRAB POTS

### HOWQUA DALE GOURMET RETREAT

*3–4 large blue swimmer crabs (½ a crab per serve)*
*1 cup fresh corn kernels*
*1 cup tomato, skinned, seeded and cubed*
*1–2 tablespoons spring onion, finely chopped*
*1–2 tablespoons fresh ginger, finely chopped*
*1–2 tablespoons chervil, finely chopped*
*1–2 tablespoons parsley, finely chopped*
*2 tablespoons lime juice*
*2 tablespoons fish sauce*
*2 tablespoons mirin*
*2 tablespoons sesame oil*
*2 tablespoons tamarind juice*
*1 tablespoon peanut oil*
*Crab Stock*
*Corn Soufflé*

As Alice Waters sagely remarked, the sweetness of corn has a special affinity with crab; both are in their prime in autumn. This corn soufflé, based on the model of the traditional soufflé suisse, is from Cher Panisse.

Remove the crab meat from the carcasse and the legs, reserving the shells. Combine the crab meat with the corn kernels, tomato, spring onion, ginger, chervil and parsley. Season with the lime juice, fish sauce, mirin, sesame oil, tamarind juice and peanut oil. Pack into ramekins, and bake in a water bath at the same time as the rebaking of the corn soufflés.

Place the reheated soufflés on serving dishes and surround with the crab stock. Set the crab pots alongside. Serves 6 to 8.

## CRAB STOCK

*peanut oil*
*6 tomatoes, chopped*
*splash of cognac or Chinese rice wine*
*ginger, to taste*
*spring onion trimmings*
*1 vanilla bean, split*
*white wine, to taste*
*cream, to taste*

In a large stockpot, heat a film of peanut oil to smoking and toss in the reserved crab shells, stirring until toasted. Add the tomatoes and continue tossing until caramelised. Deglaze with the cognac, add the ginger, spring onion trimmings and vanilla bean and just cover with cold water and some white wine (not too dry).

Bring to a bare simmer and cook for 2–3 hours. The stock will end up being very clear. Strain, replace in a saucepan, bring to the boil and cook until reduced. Add the cream.

---

**HOWQUA DALE GOURMET RETREAT**
Northeastern Victoria

•

*Double-baked corn soufflés with crab pots*

•

*Roast squab with wild mushroom risotto*

•

*Moulded trifle with rhubarb bavarois, poached pears and quinces*

## CORN SOUFFLÉ

*1½ cups corn kernels*
*250 ml milk*
*40 grams butter*
*generous pinch Maldon sea salt*
*¼ teaspoon freshly ground white pepper*
*pinch cayenne pepper or paprika*
*few drops tabasco*
*¼ cup plain flour*
*3 whole large eggs, separated*
*cornmeal*

Place 1 cup of the corn kernels and the milk in a food processor and blend until very smooth. Press through a sieve into a clean saucepan. Add the butter, salt, peppers and tabasco and heat over a low heat. Once the butter has melted, slowly add the flour and continue to whisk vigorously for a couple of minutes until smooth and thick. Cool, then whisk in the egg yolks and the remaining corn kernels. Remove from the heat. Beat the egg whites and fold into the mixture.

Butter 6–8 soufflé dishes and lightly dust with fine cornmeal. Pour the mixture into the soufflé dishes, set in a water bath and bake at 180°C for 40 minutes or until puffed and golden. Cool, unmould and set upright on a baking tray lined with silicon paper. Reheat at 250°C until hot and slightly swollen, then lightly coat with the crab stock.

## ROAST SQUAB WITH WILD MUSHROOM RISOTTO

### HOWQUA DALE GOURMET RETREAT

*10 or 12 x 450 gram squab (1 per serve)*
*2 large carrots, chopped*
*2 large brown onions, chopped*
*6 cloves garlic*
*2 celery stalks, chopped*
*2 veal shanks, sawn through*
*1–2 pig's trotters, cleaned*
*100 grams dried mushrooms*
*olive oil*
*cracked white pepper*
*cognac*
*Wild Mushroom Risotto*

THE BEST squab in Australia comes from Glenloth in the Mallee.

Trim the squabs of the head, neck, wing tips and legs. Roast the trimmings with the carrots, onions, garlic and celery in a frying pan until golden. Transfer to a large stockpot and add the veal shanks, pig's trotters and mushrooms. Cover with cold water, bring to the boil and strain the surface. Reduce the heat to a simmer and cook for 8–10 hours. Strain, cool and refrigerate overnight. Skim off the fat layer, bring back to the boil and cook until the flavour is concentrated.

Smear the squab breasts with olive oil and some cracked white pepper and cognac. Cover and refrigerate overnight. Remove from the refrigerator and bring to room temperature. Brown the squab

HOWQUA DALE GOURMET RETREAT, VICTORIA
*Roast squab with wild mushroom risotto*

*A*UTUMN

in a non-stick frying pan over high heat until the breast skin is golden and crispy. Place in a baking dish and roast in a 240°C oven for 6–7 minutes. Remove to rest in a warm place for 5–10 minutes. Carve off the breasts and serve on top of the risotto. Serves 10–12.

## WILD MUSHROOM RISOTTO

*1.5 kg mixed wild mushrooms (such as saffron milk caps, boletus, lepista nuda, Swiss brown), uniformly diced*
*butter and oil*
*50 grams unsalted butter, extra*
*50 ml olive oil, extra*
*2 red onions, finely sliced*
*3 bird's eye chillies, seeded and julienned*
*3 cloves garlic, finely chopped*
*600 grams arborio rice (preferably Carnavoli)*
*200 ml light red wine*
*1 litre squab stock (approximately)*

Sauté the mushrooms in butter and oil in small batches over very high heat until well coloured and cooked through. Drain, reserving the juices, and transfer to a colander. In a deep-sided frying pan or wok, heat the extra butter and oil. Add the onions, chillies and garlic and simmer over low heat for 15 minutes or until caramelised. Add the rice and stir to coat thoroughly.

Increase the heat and add the red wine — it should sizzle and 'sing'. Stir until all of the wine is absorbed, then reduce the heat to medium and add a ladleful of hot, concentrated squab stock, stirring until all of the liquid has evaporated. Continue cooking until the rice is nearly cooked through, adding a ladleful of squab stock at a time. Add the mushrooms and the reserved juice in the last 5 minutes. The rice should be only just cooked and creamy, with the grains separated.

# MOULDED TRIFLE WITH RHUBARB BAVAROIS, POACHED PEARS AND QUINCES

### HOWQUA DALE GOURMET RETREAT

*3 large eggs*
*60 grams castor sugar*
*60 grams plain flour, sifted*
*2 pears*
*cloves*
*red wine syrup*
*2 pears, extra*
*water*
*sugar*
*orange peel*
*cinnamon*
*1 vanilla pod*
*2 quinces*
*water, extra*
*sugar, extra*
*cloves, extra*
*star anise*
*100 ml sugar syrup*
*6 gelatine leaves, soaked for 5 minutes in cold water and drained*
*600 ml sparkling burgundy*
*1 tablespoon lime juice*
*sugar syrup, extra*
*liqueur*
*Rhubarb Bavarois*

Place 1 egg in a food mixer and beat for 5 minutes. Add another egg and beat for 5 minutes. Repeat with the remaining egg. Gradually add the castor sugar and beat until a very stable foam forms. Gently fold in the flour. Pour the batter onto a parchment-lined baking tray and bake at 180°C for approximately 20 minutes or until firm. Cool and cut in 1 cm thick slices to fit a mould.

Poach the pears with the cloves in a red wine syrup. Poach the extra pears in a sugar syrup made from equal quantities of water and sugar and flavoured with the orange peel, cinnamon and vanilla pod. Poach the quinces in a sugar syrup made from equal quantities of water and sugar and flavoured with the cloves and star anise. Drain all of the fruit, reserving the liquid, and cut into even-sized cubes. Place the 100 ml of sugar syrup in a saucepan, heat over a low heat then add the gelatine and cook until dissolved. Add the sparkling burgundy to this and set aside to cool.

Place the reserved fruit juices in a saucepan and cook over medium heat until reduced. Strain.

Line the mould with a double layer of baking parchment. Scatter the base with the diced fruit, then pour over the sparkling burgundy mixture and place in the refrigerator to set. Pour in the rhubarb bavarois and smooth the surface. Moisten the sponge slices with some sugar syrup mixed with any liqueur. Position over the Rhubarb Bavarois. Return to the refrigerator and cool for a minimum of 4 hours. Invert the moulded trifle, cut into squares and serve with the reserved fruit juices.

## THE MOUNT INN
Blue Mountains,
New South Wales

•

*Jerusalem artichoke soup*

•

*Rainbow trout with pine forest mushrooms*

•

*Baked apple with almond praline ice-cream*

## RHUBARB BAVAROIS

1 bunch rhubarb, washed and finely chopped
1 tablespoon water
80 grams castor sugar
4 large egg yolks
100 grams sugar
30 ml milk
6 gelatine leaves soaked in cold water for 5 minutes and drained
420 grams sugar, extra
140 ml water, extra
8–9 egg whites (you need 250 grams)
80 grams castor sugar, extra
350 grams whipped cream (whip the cream until soft peaks form before weighing)

Cook the rhubarb with the water, stirring often, over medium heat until tender and dry. Weigh out 600 grams and combine with the castor sugar.

Whisk the egg yolks and sugar together in a bowl. Place the milk in a saucepan and bring to the boil. Pour over the egg yolks and return the mixture to the saucepan. Cook over low heat until the custard coats the back of a spoon. Stir in the gelatine immediately until dissolved, then keep whisking until cool. Whisk in the rhubarb.

Place the extra sugar and extra water in a saucepan, bring to the boil and cook until it reaches 118°C on a sugar thermometer. Whisk the egg whites until firm peaks form, then beat in the extra castor sugar. With the beaters still running, pour in the sugar syrup. Continue whisking until cold and very glossy. Weigh out 250 grams (freeze the remainder for a later date). Carefully fold with the cream into the rhubarb.

## JERUSALEM ARTICHOKE SOUP

### THE MOUNT INN

1 kg jerusalem artichokes
1 litre clear poultry stock, duck or chicken
cream
prosciutto, sliced thinly

Peel and wash the artichokes. Place in a pot and just cover with rich clear brown poultry stock. Boil the artichokes until very tender. Blend well in a processor and add a dash of cream. Very lightly grill thin slices of prosciutto and lay them on top of the served soup.

*The Mount Inn, New South Wales*
*Rainbow trout with pine forest mushrooms, page 124*

AUTUMN

123

## RAINBOW TROUT WITH PINE FOREST MUSHROOMS

### THE MOUNT INN

*1 large rainbow trout*  
*2 knobs butter*  
*black pepper*  
*1 small Spanish onion, diced*  
*olive oil*  
*4 pine forest mushrooms, sliced*  
*rich fish stock, reduced*  
*1 tablespoon lemon juice*  
*sea salt and black pepper*  
*1 bunch rocket leaves*

FILL THE cavity of the trout with a knob of butter, black pepper and diced Spanish onion. Heat a large teflon pan capable of fitting into the oven. Rub the fish with olive oil and brown very quickly so the skin becomes crisp. (It is important the fish is quickly browned on the first side. The browned skin becomes a 'lid' to steam the fish without overcooking the flesh.) Turn over immediately and add the mushrooms, a dash of olive oil and a knob of butter. Allow the mushrooms to absorb the oil and add plenty of reduced rich fish stock, lemon juice, sea salt and black pepper. Place the pan in a hot oven for 10 minutes.

Serve the fish on the plate, crisp skin side up. Add a handful of rocket to the mushrooms. Put a lid on the pan and simmer. Peel the skin off the fish and pour over the mushrooms and rocket.

'Modern' fish stocks are usually made with white fish because of the low oil content. But putting warm trout or salmon stock through an oil filter and reducing it very quickly works wonders.

## BAKED APPLE WITH ALMOND PRALINE ICE-CREAM

### THE MOUNT INN

*½ cup water*  
*1 cup castor sugar*  
*6 granny smith apples*  
*2 granny smith apples, extra*

MAKE A toffee by boiling the water and the sugar together until light brown. Line dariole moulds with the light toffee. Peel, core and finely slice the granny smith apples. Stack the slices neatly back to the shape of an apple and place into the moulds. Bake at 180°C for 2 to 4 hours until golden. It is important the apples don't boil in the moulds. Check them regularly and turn the oven down if they begin to boil.

Make a clear apple sauce with the apple scraps and the addition of some extra chopped apples. Use some of the leftover toffee to colour and sweeten the sauce. Put the sauce through a jelly bag. When the apples are cooked, fill the dariole moulds with apple sauce. Turn out to serve.

## VANILLA BEAN ICE-CREAM

*1 litre cream*
*½ litre milk*
*200 grams castor sugar*
*1 vanilla bean, split and scraped*
*12 egg yolks*

Boil half of the cream, all of the milk, half the sugar and the vanilla bean in a pot. Whisk the egg yolks with the remaining sugar and pour over the boiling milk through a fine sieve, whisking lightly. Cook over boiling water until the custard coats the back of a spoon. Whisk in the remaining cream. Fold the broken Almond Praline through the ice-cream. Chill and churn.

## ALMOND PRALINE

*100 grams almonds*          *280 grams sugar*

Chop the almonds coarsely. Place the sugar in a heavy based pan and cover with enough water to wet the sugar. Cook over a medium heat and boil until the sugar turns golden brown.

Lay the chopped almonds on a lightly oiled tray and pour the caramel over the nuts. Cool and crush the praline.

## PORK AND PIGEON RILLETTES WITH ARISTOLOGIST PICKLED MONTMORENCY CHERRIES

THE URAIDLA ARISTOLOGIST

*1 kg belly pork*          *2 pigeons*
*salt, pepper, spices, thyme, bay leaf*

CUT THE pork into cubes and cook in a heavy pan with herbs and spices, covered with water for approximately 4 hours. Strain the meat from the liquid and shred, using forks, into an even mass of fibres. Reduce the remaining cooking juices and add to the rillettes.

Braise the pigeons until very tender but not dry. When cool enough to handle pull the meat from the bones, chop roughly and fold into the pork rillettes. Reduce and add the strained cooking juices as well. Store in a ceramic pot in the refrigerator with a layer of lard covering. Serve with pickled cherries or other pickles and fresh crusty bread.

---

**THE URAIDLA ARISTOLOGIST**
Adelaide Hills, South Australia

•

*Pork and pigeon rillettes with Aristologist pickled montmorency cherries*

•

*Coda alla vaccinara - oxtail stew with celery*

•

*Raised quince tart*

## CODA ALLA VACCINARA — OXTAIL STEW WITH CELERY

### THE URAIDLA ARISTOLOGIST

*2 kg oxtail, cut into pieces*
*1 carrot*
*1 leek*
*1 stick celery*
*sprig of thyme*
*2 bay leaves*
*salt and pepper*
*125 grams streaky bacon, chopped*
*1 onion, finely chopped*
*2 cloves garlic, finely chopped*
*3–4 tablespoons olive oil*
*2 sprigs marjoram, chopped*
*250 ml dry white wine*
*1 kg tomatoes, peeled and chopped*
*good pinch nutmeg*
*1 teaspoon cinnamon*
*1 kg celery hearts*
*2 tablespoons raisins*
*2 tablespoons pinenuts*

TRIM THE fat and wash the oxtail. Cover with water in a large pan, bring to the boil, simmer for 10 minutes, then drain and throw the water out. Return the oxtail to the pan, cover with water, bring to the boil and remove all the scum. Add the carrot, leek and celery, thyme and bay leaves. Season and simmer for 3 hours. Lift out the oxtail with a slotted spoon and keep the stock for later.

In another pan, fry the bacon, onion and garlic in oil till the bacon fat has melted, and the onion is golden. Add the marjoram and put in the oxtail pieces. Turn them over, then pour in the wine. Add the tomatoes, salt, pepper, nutmeg and cinnamon and simmer for an hour or until the meat is so tender that it comes off the bone, adding a little of the stock when necessary.

In the meantime cut the celery hearts into large pieces and cook in salted boiling water until tender but still crisp. Drain and put them in with the oxtail. Add raisins and pinenuts and cook for 10 minutes more. Serve hot.

## RAISED QUINCE TART

### URAIDLA ARISTOLOGIST

*⅓ cup milk, extra for egg wash*
*1 envelope of instant yeast*
*2 cups plain flour*
*4 tablespoons castor sugar*
*9 tablespoons unsalted butter, cut into small bits*
*½ teaspoon salt*
*2 eggs plus one yolk for wash*
*2 tablespoons water*
*1 kg quinces*
*600 grams sugar*

GENTLY heat the milk until it feels just warm to the touch of the fingertip, then stir in the dried yeast and leave to develop and dissolve. Assemble in a large mixing bowl the sifted flour, castor sugar, butter and salt. Work the ingredients together with the tips of the fingers, or mix these ingredients in the food processor. Add

THE URAIDLA ARISTOLOGIST, SOUTH AUSTRALIA
*Coda alla vaccinara - oxtail stew with celery*

*A*UTUMN

## THE COTTAGE RESTAURANT
Hunter Valley,
New South Wales

*Sautéed deboned quail with pecans on a witlof and orange salad*

*Fresh quince sorbet*

*Braised rabbit in shiraz with brandied prunes, spinach dumplings and buttered turnips*

*Warm apple feiuilletée with lemon double cream*

the eggs, lightly beaten, with water, plus the warm milk-yeast mixture. The dough should be kept between 21°C to 24°C. (At a warmer temperature, the butter would melt and ooze out of the dough.) Leave to rise for 3 hours, during which time it will double or triple in bulk, then stir down with a wooden spoon, roll into a ball, cover, and leave to refrigerate at least 4 hours, or preferably overnight.

When chilled, roll out the dough to fit a buttered 25 cm springform pan or flan ring, then leave it to rise for another 2 hours, again at a temperature of 21°C to 24°C. Shortly before the end of the 2 hour rising time, preheat the oven to 100°C. Bake blind at 110°C. Remove aluminium foil and dried pulses after approximately 10 minutes. Lower temperature to 200°C. Brush the sides with the egg yolk and milk wash and continue baking for approximately another 10 minutes or until pastry is lightly golden.

Wash and peel the quinces and cut into eighths. Cut out all the woody core. Place in a poaching pan, cover with water and add the sugar. Poach until tender and lift out of the syrup with a slotted spoon. Reduce the syrup to the consistency of jelly. Leave to cool. Place the quinces in the tart case and spoon the partially set jelly over them. Refrigerate briefly to set the jelly properly. Serve with lots of rich cream.

## SAUTÉED DEBONED QUAIL WITH PECANS ON A WITLOF AND ORANGE SALAD

### THE COTTAGE RESTAURANT

*4 extra large fresh dressed quail*
*olive oil*
*1 dessertspoon fresh rosemary*
*1 teaspoon fresh French lavender flowers*
*salt and freshly milled pepper*
*250 grams witlof*

*3 oranges (navel preferably)*
*150 grams shelled pecans*
*50 ml lemon juice*
*50 ml wine vinegar*
*200 ml light olive oil*
*salt and pepper*
*zest of 1 lemon*

Take a sharp knife and remove the spine of the quail, fold open and proceed to remove all the small breast bones and leg bones. Place the quail on a clean tray with the oil, herbs and pepper. Cover with plastic wrap and place in the refrigerator.

Separate and wash the witlof, shake off excess water. Peel and segment the oranges. Roughly chop the pecans and place in a bowl.

Mix the lemon juice, wine vinegar, light olive oil, salt, pepper and lemon zest together in a blender and stand at room temperature.

Preheat a grill and brush the quails with extra oil, salt and pepper and place on the grill. Turn the quail every 2 minutes and cook for 8 minutes.

Arrange the witlof on the plates with the orange segments. Place the grilled quails on the witlof, garnish with chopped pecans, pour over some lemon dressing and serve.

## FRESH QUINCE SORBET

### THE COTTAGE RESTAURANT

*300 grams quince segments, peeled and seeded*
*300 grams castor sugar*
*600 ml water*
*juice and zest from ½ a lemon*

BRING ALL the ingredients to the boil, stir regularly until the quinces are well cooked.

Purée in a blender, pass through a sieve, then chill. Prepare in a sorbet machine then serve in chilled glasses.

## BRAISED RABBIT IN SHIRAZ WITH BRANDY PRUNES, SPINACH DUMPLINGS AND BUTTERED TURNIPS

### THE COTTAGE RESTAURANT

*150 grams seedless D'Agen prunes*
*300 ml white wine*
*200 ml of good brandy or Armagnac*
*small cinnamon stick*
*2 fresh rabbits, skinned and gutted*
*salt and pepper*
*flour, for dusting*
*200 ml oil*
*1 medium onion, peeled*
*3 bacon rashers*
*1 medium carrot, peeled and diced*
*3 large cloves garlic, peeled and crushed*
*20 peppercorns, crushed*
*100 grams mushrooms, washed and sliced*
*1 tablespoon mixed fresh garden herbs, chopped*
*2 bay leaves*
*1 clove*
*2 tablespoons flour*
*1 bottle good Hunter Shiraz*
*1 litre good stock, beef or veal*
*Spinach Dumplings*
*Buttered Turnips*
*parsley, chopped*

PLACE THE prunes and the white wine in a plastic container with a lid. Put the prunes in a microwave and cook on high for 5 minutes. Remove and pour in the brandy, add the cinnamon and replace the lid. Allow to stand for 1 hour.

Chop the rabbits into four pieces each, making sure all the legs are separated. Season with salt and pepper and dust with flour, then brown the pieces in hot oil.

Remove half the oil and sauté the onion in the remainder,

adding the bacon and the carrot, garlic and peppercorns when the onion is well coloured. Add the mushrooms, herbs, bay leaves and clove and sauté a little more.

Lightly dust the pan with 2 tablespoons of flour and roast for 2 minutes over a gentle heat. Add the red wine and the stock and stir until boiling. Remove any excess fat and place the rabbit pieces in the liquid. Simmer with the lid on for 40 minutes, stirring occasionally. After 40 minutes test the legs, they should give a slight pressure. If not yet done, allow the rabbit to simmer for a further 10 minutes, then move the pot to the side of the stove.

To serve, remove the rabbit pieces from the pot and place a portion on each plate. Spoon the sauce over. Surround with 3 to 4 Spinach Dumplings and 4 to 5 prunes. Serve with Buttered Turnips and sprinkle with a little chopped parsley to finish.

## SPINACH DUMPLINGS

*2 bunches English spinach, washed*  
*½ loaf day-old white bread*  
*200 ml hot milk*  
*4 medium eggs, lightly beaten*  
*salt, pepper and nutmeg*

BLANCH and refresh the spinach and squeeze out excess moisture. Finely chop the spinach. Remove the crusts and dice the white bread. Dry out in a moderate oven for 7 to 8 minutes.

Place the bread and spinach in a bowl. Pour on the hot milk and the eggs. Season and work to a firm mixture, allow to stand for 10 minutes to soak up any liquid.

Bring a medium sized pot of water to the boil with ample salt. Form the dumplings, one at a time, with wet hands, moulding them firmly to about a large walnut size. Place in the simmering water for 5 minutes. Remove and place on a tray to keep warm, making sure they are covered.

## BUTTERED TURNIPS

*2 medium turnips, peeled and diced*  
*½ tablespoon butter*  
*salt and pepper*  
*little water*  
*1 stock cube*

Sweat the turnips in butter with the seasoning, add a little water and the stock cube and cover with a lid. Cook slowly, adding a little water if necessary.

THE COTTAGE RESTAURANT, NEW SOUTH WALES
*Braised rabbit in shiraz with brandied prunes, spinach dumplings and buttered turnips, page 129*

$\mathcal{A}$UTUMN

## LUCINDA
### North Coast, Tasmania

*Panfried duck livers with pancetta*

*Provincial style rock fish soup*

*Warm apple and brandy cake with cinnamon and honey ice-cream*

# WARM APPLE FEUILLETÉE WITH LEMON DOUBLE CREAM

### THE COTTAGE RESTAURANT

*4 small golden delicious apples*
*125 grams sugar*
*60 grams cornflour*
*500 ml milk*
*3 egg yolks*
*½ vanilla bean*
*1 packet of butter puff pastry, or ½ kg fresh puff pastry*
*250 grams King Island cream*
*1 dessertspoon icing sugar*
*zest and juice of 1 lemon*
*½ cup apricot confiture*

PEEL, CORE and lightly poach the apples in a little water. Set aside to cool in the liquid. Dissolve the cornflour in 100 ml of liquid from the poached apples. Combine the sugar, cornflour and 100 ml of milk and whisk with the egg yolks. Place 400 ml of the milk in a stainless saucepan and bring to the boil with the vanilla bean. Pour the milk over the cornflour mixture and whisk. Return to the saucepan and bring to the boil stirring constantly. Allow to boil for 1 minute, then remove the vanilla bean and pour the mixture into a bowl to cool. Brush a light film of oil over the pastry cream to prevent a skin forming.

Mix together the King Island cream, icing sugar and lemon and place in the refrigerator for 1 hour before serving.

Roll the puff pastry to 5 mm thickness and cut out using a saucer as a guide. Spread with a dessertspoon of pastry cream, fan the sliced apples on the pastry and bake in a hot oven, 225°C for 12 to 15 minutes. Remove and brush with hot apricot confiture. Accompany with a good spoonful of lemon cream.

# PANFRIED DUCK LIVERS WITH PANCETTA

### LUCINDA

*1 teaspoon olive oil*
*250 grams duck liver*
*5 slices pancetta*
*20 leaves baby spinach*
*¼ cup pinenuts, roasted*
*1 beetroot, julienned*
*1 teaspoon dijon mustard*
*⅓ cup vinegar*
*⅔ cup olive oil*
*1 teaspoon cracked black pepper*
*1 teaspoon red onion, diced*

HEAT THE oil in a frying pan, add the liver and cook until medium. Remove from the pan and keep warm. Add the pancetta to the pan and cook until brown all over. Add the spinach, pinenuts and beetroot and cook for 1 minute. Combine the mustard, vinegar, oil, pepper and onion in a bottle and shake well. Deglaze the pan with some of the dressing. Place the spinach mixture on a serving plate, place the warm livers on top and spoon over more dressing.

# Autumn

## PROVINCIAL-STYLE ROCK FISH SOUP
### LUCINDA

*1 onion, diced*
*1 carrot, diced*
*1 stick celery, diced*
*1 teaspoon olive oil*
*3 saffron stamens*
*100 grams scallops*
*100 grams market fish, roughly chopped*
*6 prawns*
*1 squid tube, sliced*
*6–8 mussels*
*2 cloves garlic*
*1 litre good-quality fish stock*
*3 slices French bread stick*
*olive oil, extra*

FRY THE onion, carrot and celery in the olive oil over medium heat in a frying pan. Add the saffron stamens, scallops, fish, prawns, squid, mussels and one of the garlic cloves and cook until the seafood is opaque. Add the fish stock and simmer until the fish and mussels are cooked. Rub the French bread stick slices with the remaining garlic and extra olive oil then char-grill. Pour the soup into serving bowls and serve with the bread.

## WARM APPLE AND BRANDY CAKE WITH CINNAMON AND HONEY ICE-CREAM
### LUCINDA

*150 grams butter*
*260 grams castor sugar*
*3 eggs*
*3 teaspoons brandy*
*225 grams self-raising flour, sifted*
*4 apples, peeled and sliced*
*1 teaspoon cinnamon*
*1 teaspoon sugar*
*Honey Ice-cream*

CREAM the butter and castor sugar together, then add the eggs one at a time, beating well between each addition. Stir in the brandy then fold in the flour. Pour the mixture into a greased 28 cm springform tin, top with the apple slices then dust with the cinnamon and sugar. Bake at 180°C for 1 hour. Rest for 5 minutes then remove from the tin. Serve in wedges with Honey Ice-cream.

### HONEY ICE-CREAM

*1 litre cream*
*2 vanilla beans, split*
*100 ml glucose*
*2 teaspoons honey*
*200 grams sugar*
*10–12 egg yolks*
*2 teaspoons cinnamon*

Bring the cream, vanilla beans, glucose and honey to the boil in a saucepan. Remove from the heat. Cream the sugar and egg yolks together. Pour into the cream mixture with the cinnamon. Return the saucepan to the heat and cook until the mixture coats the back of a spoon. Cool and churn in an ice-cream machine.

**LEEUWIN ESTATE**
Margaret River,
Western Australia

•

*Seared scallops on a bush tomato and bunya nut pizza with a wild basil pesto*

•

*Grilled field mushrooms with caramelised roasted garlic and baby Spanish onions*

•

*Pemberton emperor trout, grilled over bok choy and English spinach with a light soy, ginger and orange dill beurre blanc*

•

*Apple and polenta pie with a Leeuwin Estate 'brut' ice-cream*

**THE COTTAGE RESTAURANT, NEW SOUTH WALES**
*Sautéed deboned quail with pecans on a witlof and orange salad, page 128*

# SEARED SCALLOPS ON A BUSH TOMATO AND BUNYA NUT PIZZA WITH A WILD BASIL PESTO

LEEUWIN ESTATE

*Bunya Nut Pizza Dough*
*¼ cup bush tomato, diced and seeded*
*2 tablespoons olive oil*
*8 plump juicy scallops*
*Wild Basil Pesto*
*bunya nuts, crushed*
*chives, chopped*

ROLL OUT 8 pizza bases to approximately 5 cm in diameter and 10 mm in thickness. Place a little diced bush tomato on each base and bake on a floured tray in a pre-heated oven 220°C for 10 to 15 minutes until baked.

Heat the olive oil in a pan over a medium heat and quickly sear the scallops, cooking until only half cooked. (The heat in the scallops once they are seared will continue cooking the scallops to the desired texture leaving the scallops juicy and moist on the inside yet still cooked enough to enjoy.) Remove the scallops from the pan and place one on each pizza.

Arrange the pizzas on 8 warm plates and drizzle a little of the Wild Basil Pesto on and around the pizzas, garnish with crushed bunya nuts and chopped chives.

The unusual wild Australian ingredients in this dish can be obtained from Bush Tucker Supplies. The wild basil pesto can be obtained from this supplier ready made.

## BUNYA NUT PIZZA DOUGH

*115 grams wholemeal flour*
*7.5 grams yeast*
*1 tablespoon warm milk*
*120 ml warm water*
*100 grams bunya nuts, crushed*
*1 tablespoon dried bush tomato crushed*
*2 tablespoons olive oil*
*200 grams plain flour*
*½ teaspoon salt*

Mix together the wholemeal flour, yeast, milk and water and prove for 10 to 15 minutes. Add all other ingredients and knead to make a smooth dough. Prove until double in size, it is then ready to use.

## BUSH BASIL PESTO

*½ bunch bush basil (normal basil if wild basil not available)*
*¼ cup parmesan cheese*
*¼ cup pinenuts*
*¼ cup toasted almond flakes*
*½ cup olive oil*
*1 clove garlic*
*salt and black pepper to taste*

Combine all the ingredients in a food processor and blend to a smooth paste. Add some warm fish stock or water to thin out to a consistency a little thicker than a dressing.

*A*UTUMN

## GRILLED FIELD MUSHROOMS WITH CARAMELISED ROASTED GARLIC AND BABY SPANISH ONIONS

### LEEUWIN ESTATE

*16 field mushrooms, washed*
*16 whole cloves garlic*
*2 tablespoons olive oil*
*1 sprig rosemary*
*16 baby red Spanish onions, peeled*
*salt*
*cracked black pepper*
*75 grams honey*
*50 ml good red wine, Cabernet Sauvignon*
*rosemary*
*chives, chopped*

CUT THE stems from the field mushrooms leaving them flush with the cap of the mushroom.

Peel the garlic cloves and place in a roasting pan with olive oil and a rosemary sprig. Roast in a hot oven 220°C for approximately 10 to 15 minutes until the garlic softens. Remove the garlic once it is cooked and set aside.

In the roasting pan heat the remaining oil from the garlic and sauté the whole baby onions until they turn a light golden colour. Add the honey and caramelise the onions (until the honey bubbles and takes on a caramel like appearance and smell). Add the garlic and red wine to the pan and bake in a hot oven 220°C until the onions are tender and soft (15 to 20 minutes), keep warm.

Brush the field mushrooms with a little olive oil and season with salt and pepper. Grill on a char-grill for 2 minutes on each side.

Arrange the baby onions and garlic on each plate, drizzle with a little of the caramelised juices and top with field mushrooms, allow 2 mushrooms per person. Garnish with rosemary and chopped chives. Serves 8.

# PEMBERTON EMPEROR TROUT, GRILLED OVER BOK CHOY AND ENGLISH SPINACH WITH A LIGHT SOY, GINGER AND ORANGE DILL BEURRE BLANC

### LEEUWIN ESTATE

*1 Pemberton emperor trout*
*1 bunch English spinach*
*1 bunch bok choy*
*75 ml Late Harvest Riesling*
*30 ml orange juice*
*1½ cm ginger, finely chopped*
*1 clove garlic, crushed*
*fresh dill, to personal taste*
*20 ml (1 tablespoon) light soy sauce*
*30 ml pouring cream*
*250 grams unsalted butter, softened*
*black pepper and salt*
*olive oil*
*butter, extra*
*chives, chopped*

FILLET ONE emperor trout and remove any bones from the fillets with a pair of tweezers. Cut into portions.

Pick over and wash the English spinach, removing any stems and leaving only the tender leaves. Wash the bok choy and finely slice the stems leaving the leaves whole.

To make the beurre blanc, reduce together in a heavy saucepan the wine, orange juice, ginger, garlic and dill until about 40 ml of liquid is left. Add the soy sauce and cream and bring to the boil. Remove from the heat and whisk in the softened butter in small pieces one at a time, only adding more when the last piece has been incorporated. Season with black pepper.

Season the trout portions with freshly milled black pepper and salt. Pan fry in olive oil until the flesh turns from opaque to a translucent texture when parted slightly.

Sauté the English spinach and bok choy in a little extra butter and season, leaving a little crispness in the bok choy stems.

Arrange the bok choy and English spinach on the serving plates, place the pan fried trout on top and garnish with the beurre blanc and chopped fresh chives.

## APPLE AND POLENTA PIE

### LEEUWIN ESTATE

*1 cup polenta*
*4 cups milk*
*rind of 1 lemon*
*sugar to taste*
*1 full teaspoon butter*
*1 cup sultanas*
*1 cup cream*
*2 apples, skinned and sliced finely*
*½ cup golden syrup or treacle*

MIX THE polenta with the cold milk, lemon rind, sugar, butter and sultanas, bring to the boil and keep mixing for approximately

**ELLIMATTA GUEST HOUSE AND RESTAURANT**
Central Victoria

•

*A warm salad of roast quail and pan fried duck livers with goat's cheese croutons*

•

*Steamed seafood with braised fennel and green pea butter*

•

*Glazed Harcourt apples with cinnamon ice-cream*

10 minutes or until the spoon can open a road through the polenta. Remove the lemon rind and add the cream.

Grease a spring form pan and pour the mixture in. Lay the apples on the top then pour over the golden syrup. Cook in an 180°C oven for about 45 minutes. Let the polenta cool before removing from the spring form pan.

## LEEUWIN ESTATE 'BRUT' ICE-CREAM

*225 grams castor sugar*
*4 egg yolks*
*200 ml 'Brut' champagne (or any good quality champagne)*
*600 ml cream, semi-whipped to ribbon stage*

Place the castor sugar in a saucepan with enough water to just cover the sugar. Boil the sugar until it forms a thick syrup.

In a mixer, whisk the egg yolks until they are pale and creamy. Slowly pour the sugar syrup into the egg yolks whilst mixing all the time, continue mixing until cool and double in volume. Fold in the cream and then the champagne. Pour the ice-cream mixture into a suitable container and freeze overnight.

## A WARM SALAD OF ROAST QUAIL AND PAN FRIED DUCK LIVERS WITH GOAT'S CHEESE CROUTONS

ELLIMATTA GUEST HOUSE AND RESTAURANT

*6 quails*
*12 duck livers (use only the larger flat side)*
*24 white bread croutons, 4 cm rounds*
*200 grams goat's cheese*
*12 hard-boiled quail eggs (boiled for 4 minutes)*
*12 cherry tomatoes*
*250 grams salad mix, washed*
*200 grams pinenuts, toasted*
*100 ml good-quality vegetable oil*
*50 ml white wine vinegar*
*1 egg yolk*
*½ teaspoon French mustard*
*1 teaspoon finely chopped fresh garlic*
*salt and white pepper, to taste*

BONE THE quails out from the back, removing all bones except the wing and leg shank bones.

Preheat the oven to 180°C. In a large pan or roasting tray, seal and season the quails over a high heat, then place in the oven and cook for 2 minutes. At the same time, pan fry the duck livers over high heat for approximately 30 seconds on each side or until they are firm but not hard to the touch and they are pink. Set aside the quails and livers, keeping them warm.

Coat the croutons with a generous amount of goat's cheese. Place 4 on each serving plate. Place 4 quail egg halves and 4 cherry

ELLIMATTA, VICTORIA
*A warm salad of roast quail and pan fried duck livers with goat's cheese croutons*

*A*UTUMN

tomato halves around the edge of each plate.

Divide the salad mix into six and place loosely in a pile in the centre of each plate. Sprinkle the pine nuts over the salad.

Place the oil in a container and add the vinegar very gradually, beating between each addition until smooth. Stir in the egg yolk and mustard. Add the garlic and salt and pepper to taste.

Cut the quails into four pieces—two legs and two breasts—and place opposite each other on the salad. Cut the livers in half lengthways and place in between the quail pieces. Drizzle the garlic dressing over the salad. Serve immediately. Serves 6.

## STEAMED SEAFOOD WITH BRAISED FENNEL AND GREEN PEA BUTTER

### ELLIMATTA GUEST HOUSE AND RESTAURANT

*400 grams ocean trout, skinned and boned*
*400 grams white fish, skinned and boned*
*12 oysters*
*12 medium green prawns, shelled and cleaned*
*12 sardines*
*12 scallops*
*12 mussels*
*salt and pepper, to taste*
*1 kilogram fresh peas*
*150 grams butter (at room temperature)*
*Fish Sauce*

YOU CAN use whatever seafood is at the market, but keep colour in mind for your presentation.

Cut the ocean trout and white fish into 12 thin slices. Grease a steamer and line with foil or buttered paper if the fish is likely to fall through the steamer holes. Place a selection of seafood on the steamer trays, allowing two of everything per portion. Cook, rotating to allow for even cooking approximately every 2–3 minutes.

Pod the peas and cook in a saucepan of boiling water until they are very tender (young peas give a better colour). Purée in a food processor, then pass through a sieve or a mouille.

Place the butter into a mixer and cream. Combine with the pea purée. Once you have obtained an even colour, place on greaseproof paper to form a log shape, well in from the edges. Roll up to form a cylinder and twist the ends to make it firm. Place in the refrigerator to harden.

Place the fish sauce in a saucepan and bring to a boil. Cut the pea butter into thin slices and whisk it slowly into the sauce, being careful not to let the sauce boil. Make sure each slice of pea butter is incorporated before adding more. Once all of the butter has been added, season to taste with salt and pepper. Keep warm.

Place the fennel in the centre of a large, warmed plate in a pile. Place the seafood on top of the fennel, putting the same type of seafood on opposite sides of the plate. Pour the sauce around the base of the seafood. Serve immediately. Serves 6.

## FISH SAUCE

*1 litre fish stock*
*1 litre thickened cream*
*3 fennel bulbs*
*100 grams butter*

PLACE THE fish stock in a saucepan, bring to the boil, lower the heat and simmer until it reduces by three-quarters. Add the thickened cream and simmer further until the mixture has reduced to 500 ml. Remove from the heat and set aside.

Cut the stems off the fennel bulbs, cut into quarters and remove the core. Slice into fine strips and rinse.

Slowly sweat the fennel with the butter in a large saucepan over low heat. Add the fish sauce, increase the heat and bring to the boil. Cover, reduce the heat to low and cook, stirring occasionally, for 20 minutes or until the fennel is soft but not mushy. Remove from the heat and set aside.

## GLAZED HARCOURT APPLES WITH CINNAMON ICE-CREAM
### ELLIMATTA GUEST HOUSE AND RESTAURANT

*800 grams puff pastry*
*egg wash*
*icing sugar*
*300 ml double cream*
*Cinnamon Ice-cream*

*BUTTER CARAMEL SYRUP:*
*100 grams butter*
*200 grams brown sugar*
*6 medium Granny Smith apples, peeled and balled with a melon baller*

MAKE A template of an apple out of a 13 cm diameter plastic lid. Roll out the pastry and cut six apple shapes using the template. Place on a greased baking tray and brush the tops with an egg wash. Place in the refrigerator to rest for 1 hour. Bake in a 220°C oven for 10–15 minutes or until golden brown.

Place the butter and brown sugar in a saucepan and stir constantly over low heat until the sugar dissolves, making sure the mixture doesn't burn. Add the apple balls and stir through the syrup until they become soft (not stewed) and glazed.

Cut the hot pastry apples in half horizontally. Place the base on a large plate and fill with the apples and syrup. Cover with the pastry top then dust with icing sugar. Place one quenelle (ball) of double cream on the plate and accompany with one quenelle of the cinnamon ice-cream. Serve immediately. Serves 6.

**ANABEL'S OF SCOTTSDALE**
Northeastern Tasmania

•

*Golden nugget scallops*

*Tournedos of Tasmanian beef fillet*

*Chocolate and black cherry roulade served with home-made vanilla ice-cream*

## CINNAMON ICE-CREAM

½ cup castor sugar
1 cup full cream milk
8 egg yolks
1 cup thickened cream
1½–2 teaspoons ground cinnamon

Place the castor sugar and milk in a bowl and stir thoroughly. Place the egg yolks and cream in a bowl and mix well. Add to the milk mixture with the cinnamon and stir thoroughly. Churn in an ice-cream machine.

## GOLDEN NUGGET SCALLOPS
### ANABEL'S OF SCOTTSDALE

4 golden nugget pumpkins
4 teaspoons soft butter
2 teaspoons fresh minced ginger
1 kg butternut pumpkin, peeled, de-seeded and roughly chopped
1 teaspoon tomato paste
1 small onion, chopped
salt and pepper
16 Tasmanian scallops
100 grams King Island brie, cut into 4 wedges
100 grams lean bacon, julienne

SLICE THE tops from the golden nuggets to form lids. Remove all seeds and pith from the inside. Rub the insides first with butter and then ginger and replace the lids. Bake uncovered on a baking sheet in a 175°C oven until they are soft inside. Keep warm or set aside to cool and reheat when needed.

Place butternut pumpkin, tomato paste and chopped onion in a saucepan. Cover with water, season with salt and pepper and quickly bring to a boil. Reduce heat and simmer gently until very soft. Pour into a food processor and purée. Adjust the seasoning and reheat in a clean saucepan.

Wash the scallops and place in the simmering purée. Simmer for 5 minutes, stirring gently from time to time. Fill each golden nugget with scallops and a little purée, place a wedge of brie on each and top with bacon julienne. Glaze under a hot grill.

Place some pumpkin purée on each plate and present the golden nuggets on top with their lids arranged so they are half open. Serves 4.

ELLIMATTA GUEST HOUSE AND RESTAURANT, VICTORIA
*Glazed Harcourt apples with cinnamon ice-cream, page 141*

*A*UTUMN

# TOURNEDOS OF TASMANIAN BEEF FILLET

### ANABEL'S OF SCOTTSDALE

*1 litre good beef stock*
*175 grams brown shallots, chopped*
*225 grams carrots, finely chopped*
*175 grams onions, finely chopped*
*175 grams celery, finely chopped*
*½ teaspoon dried mixed herbs*
*1 teaspoon peppercorns*
*300 ml Pipers Brook Pinot Noir*
*75 ml ruby port*
*400 grams red currants*
*2 teaspoons red currant jelly*
*1 tablespoon green spring onion rings*
*1 teaspoon arrowroot*
*salt and pepper*
*1 teaspoon butter*
*8 x 125 grams tournados*

Over a medium heat, reduce the stock by one third, skimming constantly. Add the shallots, carrots, onions, celery, herbs, peppercorns, wine and port and simmer over a low heat, skimming carefully and reducing slowly by a further third.

Strain the sauce through muslin into a clean saucepan. Adjust the salt and pepper to taste.

Add the red currants, red currant jelly and onion rings. Simmer over a low heat. Mix the arrowroot in a little water and add drop by drop, stirring constantly until the sauce begins to thicken slightly.

Melt the butter in a heavy skillet over a high heat and quickly sauté the tournedos, turning once and cooking to medium rare. Allow to stand in a warm place.

Reheat sauce and pour onto serving plates with two tournedos placed on top. Serves 4.

# CHOCOLATE AND BLACK CHERRY ROULADE SERVED WITH HOME-MADE VANILLA ICE-CREAM

### ANABEL'S OF SCOTTSDALE

*1 tablespoon soft butter*
*225 grams cooking chocolate, chopped*
*2 tablespoons strong coffee*
*½ tablespoon vanilla essence*
*6 large eggs, separated*
*pinch salt*
*½ cup sugar*
*3 cups cream, whipped*
*1 kg black cherries, pitted, or 800 gram can black cherries, pitted*
*parchment paper*
*whipped cream, to serve*
*Vanilla Ice-cream*
*chocolate, grated*

Preheat oven to 175°C. Cut some parchment paper to fit a baking tray approximately 30 cm x 45 cm x 1 cm deep. Grease the tray with butter and line with parchment paper.

Place the chocolate, coffee and vanilla essence in a metal bowl and place over a pot of simmering water to melt the chocolate. Allow to cool slightly and then mix in the egg yolks.

Whip the egg whites and salt together until soft peaks have formed. Continue to whip, gradually sprinkling in all the sugar, until stiff peaks appear, about 4 minutes. Fold the egg white mixture thoroughly into the chocolate mixture and spread evenly on the baking tray.

Bake for about 20 minutes or until the cake is firm and has evenly risen. Turn out the cake onto a piece of parchment paper and carefully remove the lining paper from the bottom of the cake. Cover the cake with a moist tea towel and set aside for 4 hours. Re-moisten the towel occasionally.

Fold the cherries into the whipped cream and spread over the cake. Roll up the roulade using the parchment paper to help. To serve cut the roulade into 2 to 3 cm slices. Pipe a little whipped cream on each plate and lean a slice of roulade against it. Spoon on the Vanilla Ice-cream and sprinkle with grated chocolate.

## VANILLA ICE-CREAM

*1 whole vanilla pod*
*300 ml thick King Island cream*
*450 ml milk*
*sugar syrup (300 ml water, 200 grams sugar boiled until thickish)*
*9 egg yolks*

Split the vanilla pod and scrape out the seeds. Add the pod and seeds to the cream and milk and bring to a boil. Leave to infuse for 30 minutes.

Bring the sugar syrup to the boil. Place the egg yolks in a mixer and with the machine running add the sugar syrup to the yolks. Mix together until the mixture is fluffy. Combine the egg mixture with the cream and milk in a large bowl and allow to cool. Remove the vanilla pod.

Freeze in an ice-cream machine.

### SILK'S BRASSERIE
Blue Mountains,
New South Wales

•

*Ragout of wild Blue
Mountains mushrooms in
puff pastry*

•

*Braised oxtail with grapes
and mashed potato*

•

*Poached stone fruit from the
Orange district with
syllabub*

# RAGOUT OF WILD BLUE MOUNTAINS MUSHROOMS IN PUFF PASTRY

### SILK'S BRASSERIE

*500 grams flour*
*75 grams butter*
*15 grams salt*
*250 ml very cold water*
*500 grams butter, extra*
*1 onion, finely chopped*
*oil*
*200 grams pine cepes, chopped*
*200 grams blood, button, oyster or Swiss mushrooms (or a combination), chopped*
*2 cloves garlic, chopped*
*¼ cup parsley, chopped*
*150 ml madeira*
*200 ml chicken stock*
*salt, pepper and nutmeg, to taste*

PLACE THE flour, butter and salt in a mixer and mix until the butter is well incorporated. Add the water. Mix until just combined don't overwork the pastry. Cover with clingwrap and rest in the refrigerator for 30 minutes.

Roll out the extra butter with a rolling pin under some plastic wrap, foil or baking parchment, working it until it is reasonably soft. The texture of the pastry and the butter should be exactly the same.

Roll the pastry out to a 60 cm x 30 cm rectangle on a floured board. Place the butter in the middle, fold up in three like an envelope and roll out again to the same size. Rest for 20 minutes then repeat, folding the pastry up into three. As you fold up and roll, shake away any excess flour. Roll a third and fourth time, resting the pastry for 20 minutes between each roll. Rest in the refrigerator for 30 minutes, then roll a fifth and sixth time.

This pastry freezes very well. You can also use ready-made, frozen puff pastry for this dish.

Roll the pastry out to 2.5 mm thickness. Place on a cold baking dish and cut into either triangular or rectangular shapes. Rest for 30 minutes. Brush the pastry with an egg wash and bake in a 200°C oven for 15–18 minutes or until well browned and very light to the touch. It should be well puffed and look very appetising. This step can be done in advance and the pastry reheated on a low heat.

Place the onion in a saucepan and sauté in a little oil. Add the cepes and mushrooms and cook over medium heat until soft. Sprinkle with the garlic and parsley. Add the madeira, chicken stock, season to taste and cook until heated through.

Cut the warm pastry shapes in half horizontally. Place the base on a serving plate, spoon some of the mushrooms over and surround with the sauce. Sprinkle some parsley over and place the other pastry half on top. Garnish with parsley leaves or one or two asparagus spears, when in season. Serves 4.

SILK'S BRASSERIE, NEW SOUTH WALES
*Braised oxtail with grapes served on mashed potato, page 148*

Autumn

# BRAISED OXTAIL WITH GRAPES AND MASHED POTATO

### SILK'S BRASSERIE

1.5–2 kg oxtails
200 grams pork speck, rind removed
2 large onions, chopped
4 large carrots, diced

bouquet garni (2 bay leaves, parsley, thyme and 2 crushed cloves of garlic, tied in a bunch or in muslin)
salt, pepper and allspice, to taste
1 kg white sultana grapes
Mashed Potato

At least two oxtails, or about 1.5–2 kg of oxtail for 4 people, but it's the sort of dish you can make for lots of people so allow about 350 grams per person.

Steep the oxtails in cold water for a minimum of two hours so that the blood soaks out. Chop into 5 cm lengths.

Cut the pork speck into little cubes. Place the speck at the bottom of a heavy, heat-proof pot with the onions and carrots on top. Cook on low heat for 10 minutes, or until the fat from the speck is running. Add the pieces of oxtail and put the bouquet garni in the centre. Season the meat well. Cover the pot and cook, covered, over low heat for 20 minutes.

Pick the grapes off the stems and crush lightly, then add to the pot. Cover the meat and grapes with some greaseproof paper and replace the lid. Cook in a 130–150°C oven for about 3½ hours. (If this dish is cooked in the stove, it tends to stick.)

Check after 3 hours. If the oxtail is cooked, remove the pieces from the sauce and set aside. Put the remaining mixture through a vegetable mill or a food processor (be sure to check that there are no little bits of oxtail bone left) and purée. Pour back over the oxtail and adjust the seasoning if necessary.

If this dish is prepared a day or two in advance and the sauce left to cool off, you can remove any fat. To serve, reheat very slowly. Sprinkle with a little bit of finely chopped garlic and parsley and mix in some fresh grapes to give a nice freshness to the dish. Serves 4.

## MASHED POTATO

1 kg potatoes                    250 grams unsalted butter

Peel the potatoes and boil, steam or microwave until tender. Put through a vegetable mill or mash with the butter. Add milk if necessary for a creamy consistency. The mashed potato can be prepared in advance and reheated very successfully in a microwave oven. Whisk well just before serving.

# POACHED STONE FRUIT FROM THE ORANGE DISTRICT WITH SYLLABUB

### SILK'S BRASSERIE

1 litre white wine
250 grams sugar
2 bay leaves
1 tablespoon black peppercorns
vanilla essence, to taste
2 pears
4 apricots
4 peaches
4 figs
4 plums

*Syllabub:*
250 ml cream
25 ml good-quality cognac
50 ml good-quality sherry
80 grams sugar
juice of 2 lemons
zest of 1 lemon

COMBINE the white wine, sugar, bay leaves, peppercorns and vanilla essence together in a saucepan. Peel and quarter the pears and poach in the syrup. Stone the remaining fruit and poach lightly in the syrup until cooked.

This fruit can all be poached a few hours ahead of time, then served at room temperature. The dish will taste better if the fruit has not been stored in the refrigerator. A variety of dried fruit can be cooked in the poaching liquid (especially in winter when there is not a great deal of fresh fruit available) and served hot.

Divide the fruit and syrup into four and spoon into bowls. Serve with the syllabub on the side. Serves 4.

# SMOKED SALMON TIMBALE

### PROSPECT HOUSE

8–10 small sabagoes, cooked
1 clove garlic, minced
lemon juice
salt and pepper
4 eggs
½ cup flour
2 tablespoons paprika
½ cup Tasmaid thickened cream
12 slices smoked salmon

BLEND THE potatoes, garlic, lemon, salt and pepper, eggs, flour, paprika and cream together. Place in greased dariole moulds. Cook at 180°C for about 40 minutes.

Serve on seeded mustard flavoured mayonnaise with mescalin and cherry tomatoes and thinly sliced paprika toast. Wrap slices of smoked salmon around the timbales.

---

**PROSPECT HOUSE**
Richmond, Southeast Coast, Tasmania

•

*Smoked Salmon Timbale*

•

*Tasmanian venison with marjoram and thyme oven-baked served with crisp parsnip chips and a red currant stock sauce*

•

*Fruit crumble of apples and pears poached in brandy ginger and cloves*

# TASMANIAN VENISON WITH MARJORAM AND THYME OVEN BAKED SERVED WITH CRISP PARSNIP CHIPS AND A RED CURRANT STOCK SAUCE

### PROSPECT HOUSE

*Prime cut of venison, either backstrap or eye fillet*
*fresh marjoram*
*fresh thyme*
*1 kg venison bones*
*1 stalk celery*
*1 leek*
*1 onion*
*1 clove garlic*
*375 ml red wine*
*red currants*
*parsnips*
*olive oil*

Cut the venison into servings. Coat in fresh marjoram and thyme and leave in the refrigerator for 5 days if possible.

Place venison bones in a large stock pot. Add chopped celery, leek, onion and garlic. Fill the pot with water. Bring to the boil and simmer for 8 hours. Place in the refrigerator until the fat sets on top. Scrape off the fat and add the red wine. Bring to the boil and reduce until the sauce thickens. Add some red currants. The stock can be frozen and used as required.

Peel the parsnips and slice thinly. Deep fry in olive oil until they are golden brown. Keep hot.

Seal the venison in a hot frypan on both sides. Place in a hot oven for 3 to 5 minutes. Do not cook past rare or the meat will be dry and tough. Place the hot parsnip chips on plates, slice the venison and fan it beside the parsnip chips. Pour over the stock sauce and garnish.

# FRUIT CRUMBLE OF APPLES AND PEARS POACHED IN BRANDY GINGER AND CLOVES

### PROSPECT HOUSE

*200 grams butter*
*2 cups coconut*
*1¼ cups brown sugar*
*2 cups muesli*
*mixed spice*
*500 grams apples*
*500 grams pears*
*brandy*
*cloves*
*lemon juice*

Blend the butter, coconut, brown sugar, muesli and mixed spices together. Slice the apples and the pears into thin small slices and poach in brandy, cloves and lemon juice until tender. Place the fruit mix into small ramekins and place the muesli mix on top. Bake in a hot oven until brown and serve with vanilla ice-cream.

---

PROSPECT HOUSE, TASMANIA
*Tasmanian venison with marjoram and thyme oven-baked served with crisp parsnip chips and a red currant stock sauce*

*A*UTUMN

**PEREGIAN PARK HOMESTEAD RESTAURANT**
Sunshine Coast, Queensland

•

*Fresh fig and rocket salad with shaved parmesan, balsamic vinegar, virgin olive oil and toasted pine nuts*

•

*Tempura prawns, avocado and spiced tomato sauce with coriander*

•

*Beef tenderloin with red wine shallot sauce, sautéed mushrooms, roasted garlic and crispy leeks*

•

*Glazed pears with honey ice-cream, caramel sauce and glass biscuits*

# FRESH FIG AND ROCKET SALAD WITH SHAVED PARMESAN, BALSAMIC VINEGAR, VIRGIN OLIVE OIL AND TOASTED PINE NUTS

### PEREGIAN PARK HOMESTEAD RESTAURANT

9 large fresh figs
200 grams rocket
60 grams fresh Parmesan cheese, shaved
30 ml balsamic vinegar
90 ml virgin olive oil
50 grams pine nuts, toasted
freshly cracked black pepper

Slice the figs into rounds and toss gently with the rocket and Parmesan cheese. Pile on to serving plates, drizzle with the balsamic vinegar and virgin olive oil, and scatter over the toasted pine nuts and pepper. Serves 6.

# TEMPURA PRAWNS, AVOCADO AND SPICED TOMATO SAUCE WITH CORIANDER

### PEREGIAN PARK HOMESTEAD RESTAURANT

24 large green prawns
1 sheet nori seaweed (optional)
1½ avocadoes
15 ml lime juice
3 teaspoons Spanish onion, very finely diced
vegetable oil
plain flour
3 kaffir lime leaves, cut into fine threads
Spiced Tomato Sauce
Tempura Batter

Remove the heads from the prawns and peel the shell off the tails, leaving the end of the tails on. Devein each prawn and make a few shallow cuts on the underside to straighten the tails out. Cut 1.5 cm wide strips of nori and wrap around the prawns just below the tail shell.

Cut the avocadoes into 1 cm dice and sprinkle with the lime juice and onion. Make a bed of the avocado and onion in the centre of serving plates and pour the Spiced Tomato Sauce around the outside edge.

Pour vegetable oil into a large saucepan to a depth of 7.5 cm and heat to 180°C. Dip each prawn in flour and then in the tempura batter up to the edge of the nori (don't coat the seaweed or the tail). Slide into the hot oil a few at a time and cook until crisp. Drain on absorbent paper. Place the prawns on top of the avocado and sprinkle the kaffir lime leaves over the sauce. Serve immediately. Serves 6.

## SPICED TOMATO SAUCE

*40 ml olive oil*
*1 onion, sliced*
*3 cloves garlic, smashed*
*1 stalk of lemon grass, roughly chopped*
*1 bay leaf*
*1 lemon thyme sprig*
*2 kg very ripe tomatoes, halved*
*3 teaspoons sugar*
*100 ml dry white wine*
*1 large chilli, finely chopped*
*5 cloves garlic, extra*
*2 tablespoons green ginger, finely chopped*
*1½ tablespoons lemon grass, finely chopped*
*1½ tablespoons brown sugar*
*50 ml fish sauce*
*2 tablespoons sweet chilli sauce*
*90 ml lemon juice*
*juice and grated zest of 1 lime*
*150 ml peanut oil*
*1½ tablespoons sesame oil*

Heat the olive oil in a saucepan and sauté the onion and garlic until soft. Arrange in the bottom of a baking dish with the herbs. Place the tomato halves on top, cut side down. Combine the sugar and wine and pour over the tomatoes. Cover with foil and bake at 180°C for 1 hour or until the tomatoes have turned to pulp. Remove the herbs, blend in a food processor and sieve. Measure out 300 ml of the tomato purée and combine with the remaining ingredients.

## TEMPURA BATTER

*1 egg yolk*
*250 ml iced water*
*1 cup Japanese tempura flour*

Make the batter just prior to using. Combine the egg yolk and iced water, then quickly fold in the flour. There should still be a few lumps of flour in the mixture, overworking it will make the batter tough. Keep the mix over a bowl of ice.

# BEEF TENDERLOIN WITH RED WINE SHALLOT SAUCE, SAUTÉED MUSHROOMS, ROASTED GARLIC AND CRISPY LEEKS

### PEREGIAN PARK HOMESTEAD RESTAURANT

*1 teaspoon peanut oil*
*6 x 200 gram beef tenderloins*
*vegetable oil*
*2 leeks, white part cut into 3 cm julienne*
*18 whole garlic cloves, extra, peeled*
*olive oil*
*2 tablespoons butter*
*2 shallots, white part only, sliced*
*300 grams field mushrooms, sliced*
*1 teaspoon thyme leaves*
*salt and pepper, to taste*
*12 shallots, extra, cleaned and thick ends cut into 1½ cm lengths*
*Red Wine Shallot Sauce*

Heat a frying pan over high heat and add the peanut oil, then seal the tenderloins on all sides. Transfer to an oven-proof tray in an upright position and bake at 230°C for 8 minutes (for medium rare, longer if you like them well done). Remove to a warm place and rest for at least 10 minutes.

Heat the vegetable oil in a wok to 180°C and fry the leeks until golden. Drain on absorbent paper and set aside in a warm, dry place. Brush the garlic cloves with olive oil, wrap in foil and bake at 180°C for 10–15 minutes.

Heat a frying pan and melt 1 tablespoon of the butter in it, then add 1 clove of garlic, chopped, and the 2 shallots and cook until softened. Add the mushrooms and sauté over low heat until the mushrooms start to release their juices. Add the thyme leaves and salt and pepper and keep warm.

Place the garlic in the baking dish with the tenderloins and replace in the oven to heat through. Bring a pan of salted water to the boil and blanch the extra shallots, then transfer to a saucepan with the remaining butter and toss.

Ladle a mirror of warm Red Wine Shallot Sauce onto each serving plate. Place the mushrooms in the centre and top with the beef tenderloin. Scatter the shallot lengths and roasted garlic around the edge of the sauce. Top each tenderloin with a pile of crispy leeks. Serves 6.

---

PROSPECT HOUSE,
TASMANIA
*Fruit crumble of apples and pears poached in brandy ginger and cloves, page 150*

$\mathcal{A}$UTUMN

## RED WINE SHALLOT SAUCE

*2 kg meaty beef bones, finely cut*
*2 kg veal shanks*
*1 kg very ripe tomatoes*
*2 large onions*
*2 carrots*
*2 stalks celery*
*½ bunch parsley, stems included*
*1 teaspoon black peppercorns*
*oil*
*3 shallots*
*4 cloves garlic*
*350 ml red wine*
*1 bay leaf*
*1 sprig of thyme*
*½ teaspoon black peppercorns, extra*
*200 grams mushrooms*

Preheat the oven to 200°C. Roast the beef bones and veal shanks in a baking dish until brown then remove to a stockpot, draining off any fat. Place the tomatoes, onions, carrots and celery in the baking dish and roast until soft, then add to the stockpot. Deglaze the baking dish with water and add to the pot. Cover with water, bring to the boil and simmer over low heat for about 5 hours, adding the parsley and peppercorns halfway through. Skim any scum from the top as it appears. Remove from the heat, strain, then pass through muslin. Replace the mixture in the pot and simmer until reduced by half.

Brush a clean saucepan with oil and sauté the shallots and garlic. Add the red wine, bay leaf, thyme, extra peppercorns and mushrooms. Simmer over low heat until reduced by half. Add the strained mixture to the red wine mixture and simmer over low heat until reduced to a rich-flavoured sauce. Strain through a fine sieve, pressing down to extract all the vegetable juices. Return to the pan to reheat and skim off any impurities.

## GLAZED PEARS WITH HONEY ICE-CREAM, CARAMEL SAUCE AND GLASS BISCUITS

PEREGIAN PARK HOMESTEAD RESTAURANT

*200 ml orange juice, strained*
*400 grams sugar*
*500 ml water*
*250 ml white wine*
*6 medium William pears*
*Caramel Sauce*
*300 ml cream*
*Glass Biscuits*
*Honey Ice-cream*
*fresh lime leaves*

THIS DISH, with the exception of the biscuits, can be prepared the day before. Place the lorange juice, sugar, water and white wine in a saucepan large enough to hold the pears and bring to a simmer. Peel the pears and make a small slit just above their centres. Insert an apple corer up to the slit and remove the core. Submerge the pears in the liquid and cook until just tender. Remove from the heat and store in the refrigerator in the liquid. Return to room temperature just before serving.

Drain the pears. Gently warm the Caramel Sauce until smooth and glossy. Spoon 50 ml of the cream onto each plate, place a pear in the centre and drizzle Caramel Sauce over the pears so it mingles with the cream. Break off large chards of glass biscuit and rest up against the pears. Add a scoop of Honey Ice-cream set on a lime leaf. Serves 6.

## CARAMEL SAUCE

*250 grams castor sugar*
*150 ml hot water*
*60 ml cream*
*3 tablespoons Armagnac or brandy*

Place the castor sugar in a heavy-based saucepan and cook over low heat until warmed through and the sugar starts to dissolve. Gradually stir the melting sugar to the centre of the saucepan until it is a deep caramel colour. Remove from the heat immediately. Carefully add the water and cream, replace on the heat and stir until smooth. Stir in the Armagnac. Remove from the heat and store in the refrigerator (it will keep for several days).

## GLASS BISCUITS

*45 grams unsalted butter*
*45 grams glucose syrup*
*45 grams plain flour, sifted*
*90 grams castor sugar*
*2 tablespoons macadamia nuts, roasted and very finely chopped*

The biscuits are best made on the day of use. Place the butter and glucose syrup in a saucepan and melt over very low heat. Remove from the stove and combine with the flour and castor sugar. Refrigerate until cold.

Place 2 teaspoons of the dough at a time between two sheets of baking paper and roll until very thin. Remove the top sheet of paper and bake at 180°C for 5 minutes or until golden. Remove from the oven, replace the top sheet of baking paper and roll again until thin. Peel off the top sheet, sprinkle with the nuts and return to the oven for 2 minutes or just long enough for the nuts to stick. Store between sheets of greaseproof paper in an airtight container.

## HONEY ICE-CREAM

*3 whole eggs*
*1 egg yolk*
*600 ml cream*
*150 ml rainforest honey or any light, fragrant honey*

Beat the eggs and egg yolk together in a bowl, then fold in the cream and honey. Churn in an ice-cream machine.

**VUE GRAND HOTEL**
Bellarine Peninsula,
Victoria

•

*Myriad of fresh snails on jus of Scotchmans Hill Pinot Noir*

•

*Veal medallions with lemon butter and deep-fried celery leaves*

•

*Caramelised vanilla and Guajana chocolate chiboust with pistachio coulis*

# MYRIAD OF FRESH SNAILS ON JUS OF SCOTCHMANS HILL PINOT NOIR
## VUE GRAND HOTEL

*200 grams shallots, chopped*
*500 grams fresh snails*
*50 grams parsley, chopped*
*2 teaspoons pure olive oil*
*150 grams carrots, chopped*
*250 grams tomato concasse*
*300 grams mushrooms, chopped*
*olive oil, extra*
*500 ml Scotchmans Hill Pinot Noir*
*125 ml veal stock*
*500 grams large shell pasta*
*chervil, to garnish*

Sauté 100 grams of the shallots and the snails and parsley in the oil. Remove the snails and discard the mixture. Make a farce by sautéing the remaining shallots with the carrots, tomato concasse, mushrooms and olive oil. Reduce the heat and cook for 2 hours.

Make a sauce by placing the wine and veal stock in a saucepan and simmering until dark brown and thickened.

Blanch the pasta.

Place a snail and 1 teaspoon of farce into each pasta shell. Place on a baking tray and cook in a moderate oven for 5 minutes.

Place three filled shells on an entrée-size plate and cover with the sauce. Garnish with chervil. Serves 8.

# VEAL MEDALLIONS WITH LEMON BUTTER AND DEEP-FRIED CELERY LEAVES
## VUE GRAND HOTEL

*olive oil (three lots are needed)*
*150 grams shallots, chopped*
*500 ml chicken stock*
*375 ml chardonnay*
*6 lemons, juice only*
*250 ml cream*
*250 grams chives, chopped*
*1.5 kilograms veal fillet*
*100 grams plain flour*
*4 eggs, lightly beaten*
*200 grams breadcrumbs*
*60 grams celery leaves*
*500 grams taglioni, cooked*
*500 grams polenta, cooked*

Heat a little olive oil in a frying pan and sauté the shallots. Add the stock and simmer until the sauce reduces. Add the chardonnay, lemon juice, cream and chives.

Finely slice the veal and dust with the flour. Dip in the eggs and coat with the breadcrumbs. Pan fry in oil until golden brown. Remove from the heat and keep warm.

Heat some olive oil to 250°C and drop the celery leaves in. Remove after a couple of seconds. Place two dessertspoons of the sauce on a plate. Sit the veal slices on top and serve with the taglioni and polenta. Garnish with the celery leaves. Serves 8.

---

VUE GRAND HOTEL,
VICTORIA
*Myriad of fresh snails on jus of Scotchmans Hill Pinot Noir*

*Autumn*

**PADTHAWAY ESTATE**
Padthaway,
South Australia

•

*Asian inspired pumpkin soup*

•

*Fresh local yabbies served on crisp salad*

•

*Panfried kangaroo fillet flamed with brandy served with black peppercorn sauce*

•

*Individual apple crumble with fresh cream*

# CARAMELISED VANILLA AND GUAJANA CHOCOLATE CHIBOUST WITH PISTACHIO COULIS

## VUE GRAND HOTEL

*12 eggs, separated*
*150 grams sugar*
*250 grams plain flour*
*1 litre milk*
*2 vanilla sticks*
*7 gelatine leaves*
*180 grams honey*
*3 egg whites, extra*
*250 grams guajana chocolate, melted*
*60 grams sugar, extra*
*6 eggs, extra*
*500 ml milk, extra*
*40 grams fresh pistachios, shelled*
*icing sugar*

MIX TOGETHER the egg yolks, sugar and flour. Place the milk and vanilla sticks in a saucepan, bring to the boil then remove from the heat. Combine with the egg yolk mixture and the gelatine leaves then set aside.

Bake the honey in a small baking dish at 150°C until it caramelizes. Beat all of the egg whites until stiff peaks form. Add the honey, then fold the egg yolk and the egg white mixtures together. Place into a piping bag and pipe half of the mixture into 1 cup capacity moulds. Cover with the melted chocolate, then top with the remaining mixture.

Combine the extra sugar and extra eggs. Place the extra milk in a saucepan and bring to the boil. Add the sugar mixture to the milk, remove from the heat and cool over ice.

When cool, place the mixture in a food processor with the pistachios. Blend until the mixture turns a light green in colour.

Place the moulds in the freezer until frozen. Remove the chiboust from the moulds and dust with icing sugar. Place under a salamander or griller and caramelise. Serve on a plate surrounded with the pistachio sauce. Serves 8.

# ASIAN INSPIRED PUMPKIN SOUP

## PADTHAWAY ESTATE

*1 tablespoon oil*
*½ stalk lemon grass*
*1 teaspoon fresh chilli*
*2 cm piece fresh ginger, chopped*
*1 small clove garlic, chopped*
*1 medium onion, chopped*
*1 teaspoon ground coriander*
*½ teaspoon ground cumin*
*dash turmeric*
*salt and pepper*
*1 celery stalk, chopped*
*1 tomato, chopped*
*750 grams pumpkin, chopped*
*400 ml coconut milk*
*chicken stock*
*fresh coriander leaves*

IN A LARGE saucepan heat the oil with the lemon grass, chilli, ginger, garlic, onion, coriander, cumin, salt, pepper, turmeric, celery and tomato. Brown over a medium heat until the onion is soft. Add the pumpkin and cover with fresh chicken stock. Cook for half an hour or until the pumpkin is soft. Allow to cool, then blend and strain. Finally add the coconut milk. When serving garnish with fresh coriander leaves. Serves 6.

## FRESH LOCAL YABBIES SERVED ON CRISP SALAD

### PADTHAWAY ESTATE

*48 fresh live yabbies*
*mixed salad leaves*
*dressing of your choice*

COOK THE yabbies in a pot of boiling water. Peel and clean them. Leave six whole yabbies for a garnish. Can be served with a seafood dressing or a vinaigrette.

## PANFRIED KANGAROO FILLET FLAMED WITH BRANDY SERVED WITH BLACK PEPPERCORN SAUCE

### PADTHAWAY ESTATE

*1 kg kangaroo fillet*
*pepper and salt*
*1 teaspoon oil*
*2 tablespoon brandy*
*1 cup beef stock*
*2 cups thickened cream*
*black pepper, freshly ground*

TRIM THE kangaroo fillet and season with pepper and salt. Leave to rest for 4 hours if possible.

Heat the oil in a large frying pan. Sear the kangaroo fillet on both sides. Add the brandy and flame. Remove and place in an ovenproof dish in an oven at 170°C while making the sauce.

Add the fresh beef stock to the frying pan and heat. Add the thickened cream, lots of freshly ground black pepper and salt. Reduce the sauce over the heat until it thickens. Serves 6.

## INDIVIDUAL APPLE CRUMBLE

### PADTHAWAY ESTATE

*6 large apples*
*brown sugar to taste*
*¼ cup water*
*¾ cup self raising flour, sifted*
*½ teaspoon ground cinnamon*
*80 grams butter*
*½ cup brown sugar, firmly packed*
*2 tablespoons flaked almonds*

PEEL AND thinly slice the apples. Place in a microwave dish with the sugar and water. Cover with plastic wrap and microwave on high

## TALGAI HOMESTEAD
### Darling Downs, Queensland

*Pumpkin bread*

*Petite fillet of sesame beef over potato rosti with wild honey demi-jus*

*Spatchcock marinated in chilli, lime and ginger over Asian greens with lemon myrtle beurre blanc*

*Terrine of lime semi-freddo*

---

until apples appear soft. Or place in a saucepan and simmer until the apples appear soft. Allow to cool. Divide the apples between 6 individual 150 ml soufflé dishes.

Combine the sifted flour and cinnamon in a bowl. Rub in the butter, then add the sugar and the flaked almonds. Mix well.

Generously place the prepared crumble mixture over the apples in the soufflé dishes. Place the dishes on an oven tray and cook at 180°C until the crumble is golden brown, approximately 20 minutes. Allow to stand for five minutes before serving. Serves 6.

## PUMPKIN BREAD
### TALGAI HOMESTEAD

*3 cups self-raising flour*
*¼ cup olive oil*
*½ teaspoon salt*
*2 tablespoons gluten flour*
*30 grams fresh yeast*
*500 grams pumpkin, boiled and drained (still warm)*
*1 egg, lightly beaten*

COMBINE flour, olive oil, salt, gluten flour and yeast in a mixing bowl. Mix on a low speed until combined. Add the pumpkin with the mixer running, one piece at a time until the mixture is of an even consistency. This recipe should not require any water as all the moisture is derived from the pumpkin flesh. Allow the mixture to rise until doubled in size, knock down and lightly knead. Divide the dough into 8 equal portions and shape into rolls, brush with lightly beaten egg. Let the dough rise until doubled in size and bake for 20 minutes in an oven preheated to 220°C. Double serving for 4.

## PETITE FILLET OF SESAME BEEF OVER POTATO ROSTI WITH WILD HONEY DEMI-JUS
### TALGAI HOMESTEAD

*1 beef butt fillet, 1.5 kg*
*1 cup brown sugar*
*2 teaspoons crushed garlic*
*3 tablespoons olive oil*
*3 tablespoons sesame oil*
*1 cup pear juice*
*3 tablespoons soy sauce*
*1 egg*
*½ cup milk*
*1½ cups bread crumbs*
*½ cup sesame seeds, lightly toasted*
*1 cup plain flour*
*1 cup beef stock*
*2 tablespoons wild Australian honey*
*Potato Rosti*
*shallots*
*capsicum curls*

TRIM THE beef of all fat and sinew, slice into medallions about 1.5 cm thick. Mix the brown sugar, garlic, olive oil, sesame oil, pear

---

VUE GRAND HOTEL, VICTORIA

*Caramelised vanilla and Guajana chocolate chiboust with pistachio coulis, page 160*

$\mathcal{A}$UTUMN

163

juice and soy sauce to form a marinade. Place the beef in the mixture and leave to marinate overnight.

Drain the beef and pat it dry with a paper towel. In a bowl mix the egg and milk. Place the bread crumbs and sesame seeds in a bowl. Coat the beef in plain flour, dip in the egg mix then in the crumb and seed mix. Coat all the beef. Refrigerate until needed.

Heat some olive oil in a frying pan until very hot, cook the beef quickly and only until the coating mix is golden brown. Keep warm until needed. In the same pan place half the remaining marinade, along with the beef stock and honey. Reduce by half to make a demi jus. Place Potato Rosti on plates, top with the beef fillet and spoon over some demi jus. Garnish with shallots and capsicum curls. Serves 4.

## POTATO ROSTI

*3 large potatoes*
*1 egg*
*½ cup plain flour*
*1 teaspoon crushed garlic*
*8 basil leaves, chopped*
*salt and pepper*
*olive oil for frying*

Finely grate the potatoes and place in a clean tea towel. Bring the corners of the tea towel up and wring out the potato, draining as much liquid as possible. Place the potato in a bowl and add the egg, flour, crushed garlic, basil, salt and pepper. Mix well by hand. Heat some oil in a fry pan over a moderate heat. Spoon the mixture into the oil, one serving spoon at a time and flatten with a spatula. Cook each side until golden. Place on absorbent paper and keep warm in the oven.

## SPATCHCOCK MARINATED IN CHILLI, LIME AND GINGER OVER ASIAN GREENS WITH LEMON MYRTLE BEURRE BLANC

### TALGAI HOMESTEAD

*4 spatchcocks*
*2 limes, juiced*
*1 teaspoon ginger, crushed*
*½ cup sweet chilli sauce*
*1 cup sweet sherry*
*½ cup castor sugar*
*½ cup olive oil*
*½ cup rice wine vinegar*
*½ teaspoon mustard oil*
*2 cups chicken stock*
*1 bunch bok choy*
*½ wom bok*
*1 bunch Chinese spinach*
*½ bottle champagne*
*8 lemon myrtle leaves*
*150 grams butter*
*2 tablespoons castor sugar*
*4 round sheets rice paper*

FILLET THE spatchcock, removing the breast bone, leaving 4 portions from each bird. Mix the lime juice, crushed ginger, chilli sauce, sherry, castor sugar and olive oil together and marinate the spatchcocks in this for at least 2 hours.

Lightly grease a griddle pan with olive oil and heat well. Drain the spatchcocks and cook the pieces on each side until lightly browned. Place in an oven proof dish and continue cooking in a moderate oven until the juices run clear.

Meanwhile, make a poaching mixture of rice wine vinegar, mustard oil and chicken stock. Quarter the bok choy. Poach in this liquid until the leaves have wilted. Cut the Chinese spinach into 10 cm lengths and poach. Shred the wom bok and lightly poach also.

In a frying pan place the champagne and lemon myrtle leaves, and reduce by half. Remove the leaves and add the butter, sugar and ½ a cup of the spatchcock marinade (strained). Return the beurre blanc to the heat until it bubbles.

To assemble the dish, fry the rice paper until it is fully expanded, place the bok choy on plates followed by the Chinese spinach and shredded wom bok. Cover with the rice paper, then arrange the spatchcock pieces on top of the rice paper. Pour over the beurre blanc and serve with steamed vegetables. Serves 4.

## TERRINE OF LIME SEMI-FREDDO
### TALGAI HOMESTEAD

*150 grams cream cheese*
*½ cup castor sugar*
*2 eggs*
*300 grams cream*
*300 grams milk*
*1 teaspoon vanilla essence*
*150 grams glace cherries*
*½ cup pistachio nuts, chopped*
*3 limes, juice and rind*
*200 grams nougat, chopped*
*50 grams apricots, diced*
*Marinated Strawberries*
*double cream*

MIX THE cream cheese, sugar and eggs together until smooth, gradually add the cream, milk and vanilla. Place the ice-cream mixture into an ice-cream churn, with the machine running add all the cherries, pistachios, lime, nougat and apricots. Line a loaf tin with plastic film. When the mixture is ready spoon it into the loaf tin and freeze until needed.

Remove the terrine from the freezer five minutes before serving. Cut into 1½ cm thick slices and place one on each plate. Garnish with Marinated Strawberries and double cream. Serves 8.

## MARINATED STRAWBERRIES

*1 punnet fresh strawberries*
*½ cup castor sugar*
*2 tablespoons raspberry vinegar*
*1 nip Cointreau*

HULL THE strawberries and cut them in half. Mix with all the other ingredients and leave overnight.

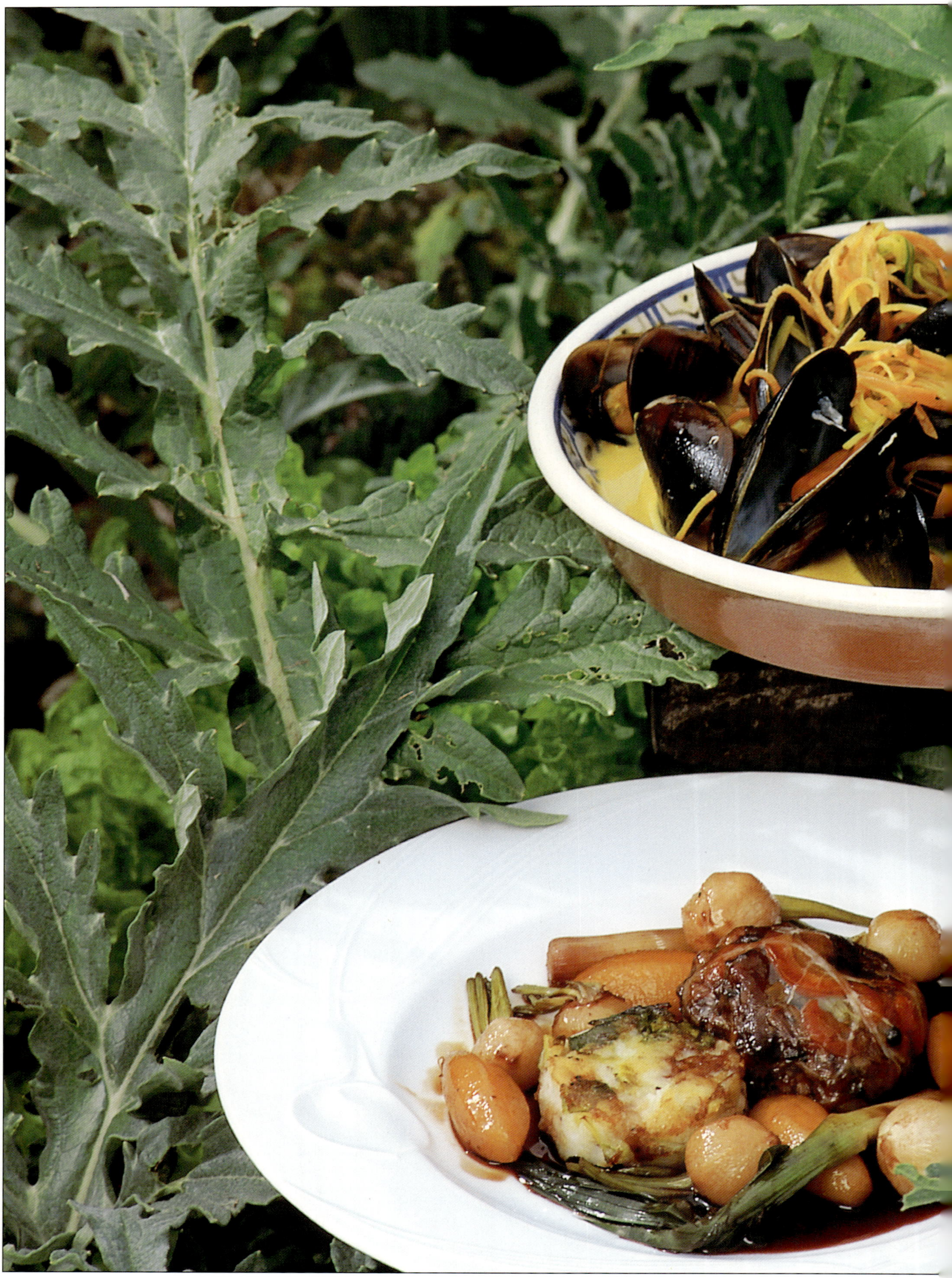

# Winter

## TAYLOR'S COUNTRY HOUSE
### Byron Bay, New South Wales

•

*Crisp risotto cake with a sauté of exotic mushrooms, roast peppers and shaved parmesan and rocket salad*

•

*Slow-braised lamb shank, roast root vegetables, lentils and pesto*

•

*Winter fruit tart with clotted cream*

# CRISP RISOTTO CAKE WITH A SAUTÉ OF EXOTIC MUSHROOMS, ROAST PEPPERS AND SHAVED PARMESAN AND ROCKET SALAD

### TAYLOR'S COUNTRY HOUSE

*2 large red capsicum*
*oil*
*Risotto Cakes*
*300 grams large firm white champignons, thickly sliced*
*150 grams oyster mushrooms*
*150 grams fresh shiitake mushrooms, sliced*
*2 cloves garlic, finely sliced*
*100 ml extra virgin olive oil, approximately*
*balsamic vinegar*
*salt and fresh ground pepper*
*100 grams Parmesan cheese, thinly shaved*
*1 bunch fresh small rocket leaves*

Cut the capsicums in half, brush with oil, place under a hot grill until the skin is well blistered and darkened. Place in a lidded plastic container. Peel when cooled and cut into strips.

Heat a non-stick pan or flat top grill, cook the Risotto Cakes until golden and crisp on both sides. Remove the rings carefully and keep the cakes warm.

Heat a pan until very hot, add a little oil and the sliced white mushrooms, sauté until golden. Add the shiitake and oyster mushrooms and garlic and cook. Add the capsicum strips and keep warm.

In a bowl, whisk some virgin olive oil and balsamic vinegar together with the seasoning. Lightly dress the rocket leaves.

Place a small thatch of rocket leaves in the centre of the plate. Using a palette knife, place a risotto cake on top of the rocket leaves. Pile the mushrooms on top of the risotto. Drape slices of shaved parmesan over the mushrooms and spoon any extra dressing around the cake.

## RISOTTO CAKES

*50 ml olive oil*
*2 brown onions, finely sliced*
*500 grams Aborio rice*
*large pinch good quality saffron threads*
*1 litre chicken stock, hot*
*100 grams peas, freshly shelled*
*50 grams Parmesan cheese, freshly grated*
*1 tablespoon unsalted butter*
*salt and freshly ground black pepper*
*1 bunch fresh coriander, leaves finely shredded*

Heat the olive oil and sweat the onion (cook without colouring). Add the rice and the saffron threads, cook for a further minute. Add the chicken stock to the rice and onion mix, one ladle at a time, stirring constantly. When the rice has absorbed the stock, add more stock until the rice is tender but still firm in the centre and the mixture is creamy. Add the peas, parmesan, butter, seasoning and coriander, stirring to combine well.

Lightly oil 8 metal rings 7 cm in diameter and 2 cm deep. Spoon in the rice mix and smooth over the tops, chill in a refrigerator until required (can be prepared the day before).

## SLOW-BRAISED LAMB SHANK, ROAST ROOT VEGETABLES, LENTILS AND PESTO
### TAYLOR'S COUNTRY HOUSE

*8 Frenched lamb shanks (ask your butcher to prepare them)*
*500 ml olive oil*
*3 brown onions, sliced*
*4 garlic cloves, peeled and sliced*
*2 carrots, peeled and sliced*
*half a celery including leaves, chopped*
*4 bay leaves*
*12 peppercorns*
*500 ml red wine*
*3 tablespoons tomato paste*
*500 ml water*
*150 grams brown lentils, soaked in water*
*Garnish*
*1 medium swede, cut into small dice (10 mm)*
*3 medium carrots, cut into small dice (10 mm)*
*3 medium parsnips, cut into small dice (10 mm)*
*3 medium onions, cut into small dice (10 mm)*
*½ bunch parsley, finely chopped*
*Pesto*

Heat the oil in a heavy based frying pan, season the shanks and sauté to seal and brown. Transfer to a baking dish. In the same pan sauté the onions and garlic, then add to the shanks. Add the carrots, celery, bay leaves and peppercorns. Pour the red wine into the frying pan, deglaze and add tomato paste. Pour over the shanks.

Barely cover the shanks with water, seal the top of the baking dish with aluminium foil. Braise in the oven for approximately 3 hours at 160°C until the shanks are very tender.

Blanch the garnish vegetables (except for the onions) in boiling water until tender, refresh, set aside until the shanks are cooked.

When the shanks are cooked remove from the baking dish and strain the cooking liquid (stock) into a clean pot. Allow this to settle and ladle off any fat.

Add the drained lentils to the stock. Place over a moderate heat to reduce the liquid and to cook the lentils. Meanwhile heat some olive oil in a pan and oven-roast the vegetable garnish. When the lentils are cooked, put the shanks back into the stock. Warm through at the last minute and add chopped parsley and the roast vegetables. Check the seasoning.

Serve the shanks standing upright in deep bowls, ladle over plenty of the lentils and vegetables and stock. Serve with the Pesto. This goes perfectly with mashed desiree potatoes.

## PESTO

*150 grams pumpkin seeds*  
*1 bunch basil*  
*200 ml olive oil*  
*30 grams fresh parmesan, grated*  
*2 garlic cloves*  
*pinch salt and pepper*

Place the pumpkin seeds on an oven slide and place in a moderate oven at 180°C until the seeds begin to 'pop'. Allow to cool and place in a blender with the other pesto ingredients. Process until well combined, add more olive oil if necessary.

## WINTER FRUIT TART WITH CLOTTED CREAM

### TAYLOR'S COUNTRY HOUSE

*250 ml honey*  
*300 ml water*  
*200 ml orange juice*  
*1 vanilla bean*  
*3 cinnamon sticks*  
*100 ml rosewater*  
*1 kg mixed dried fruit (including apples, prunes, figs, pears, peaches and apricots)*  
*Sweet Short Pastry*  
*200 grams sieved apricot jam*

PREPARE THIS at least the day before. Combine the honey, water, orange juice, vanilla bean and cinnamon stick in a pot and bring to the boil. Boil for several minutes. Remove from the heat and add the rosewater. Pour over the dried fruits and cover. Set aside to allow the fruits to swell and the flavours to develop.

Use the pastry to line a 26 cm spring form or loose based tart tin, prick the base lightly with a fork. Place the pastry in the freezer and chill for 30 minutes. Bake for 10 minutes at 200°C or until the bottom is cooked. Use the remaining pastry to be cut into strips for a lattice.

Drain the fruit. Chop it coarsely leaving some fruit whole, and fill the tart case, pushing down carefully with a wooden spoon so as much fruit as possible fits in. Smooth over the top. Brush the pastry strips with egg wash and place pastry lattice over the fruit.

Bake at 180°C for approximately 15 minutes until golden brown. Glaze with sieved apricot jam which has been boiled with a little water. Brush on while the jam mixture is still bubbling. Serve with your favourite clotted or double cream.

## SWEET PASTRY

*250 grams unsalted butter, cubed and chilled*  
*500 grams plain flour*  
*135 grams icing sugar*  
*pinch baking powder*  
*2 eggs*

Place the butter, flour, icing sugar and baking powder into a food processor. Pulse until the mixture resembles fine breadcrumbs.

COTSWOLD HOUSE RESTAURANT, VICTORIA  
*Pig's ear salad, page 172*

*Winter*

171

## COTSWOLD HOUSE RESTAURANT
### Dandenongs, Victoria

- *Pig's ear salad*
- *Kilmore kid*
- *Warm liquid centre banana bread pudding with caramel and chocolate sauces*

Add eggs one at a time, process lightly and tip out onto a bench. Quickly knead the mixture until it comes together. Roll into a sausage shape, place in a freezer bag and chill for at least 20 minutes.

# PIG'S EAR SALAD
### COTSWOLD HOUSE

*500 grams pig's ears*
*1 loaf of brioche, crumbed*
*mescalin lettuce leaves*
*1 jar Mount Emu Creek sheep's milk yoghurt*
*Orange Butter Sauce*

BOIL THE pigs ears for 35 minutes, in enough water to cover well. Remove from the water and allow to cool until just warm. Slice the flesh from the cartilage, trying to remove it in one piece.

Lay a sheet of plastic wrap down on a board. Spread the cleaned pig's ear on the plastic wrap making a 10 cm x 10 cm square and spoon the chicken mousse into the centre. Using the plastic wrap to help, roll the ear around the mousse to form a sausage. Roll the sides of the plastic wrap so as to totally enclose the sausage. Wrap the sausage in one more sheet of plastic wrap and place it in a baking dish of water. Poach in the oven for 45 minutes at 190°C.

Remove from the plastic and allow to rest for 1 hour.

Crumb the poached ears in the brioche crumbs and bake in the oven for 20 minutes at 200°C.

Slice the sausage into 1 cm thick slices and serve with mescalin lettuce leaves, yoghurt and Orange Butter Sauce.

## ORANGE BUTTER SAUCE

*1 litre orange juice*
*500 grams butter*

Bring the orange juice to the boil and reduce the juice by two thirds. Reduce the heat to simmer and whip in the butter. Do not allow the sauce to boil or the butter will separate and the sauce will break down. Keep warm.

## CHICKEN FARCE

*5 chicken breasts*
*3 eggs*
*500 ml cream*
*1 teaspoon coriander*

Purée the chicken in a food processor until smooth, then add the eggs, cream and herbs. Mix again until it is the consistency of a soft mousse.

# KILMORE KID
## COTSWOLD HOUSE

hind quarter of 1 kid, boned and cubed
1 tablespoon vegetable oil
6 cloves garlic, chopped
1 onion, chopped
500 ml veal jus
200 ml red wine
200 ml port
500 ml water
3 tablespoons fresh rosemary, chopped
1 teaspoon Tabasco sauce
5 tablespoons tomato paste
salt and pepper, to taste

Heat the oil in a heavy bottomed pan and sauté the kid in the oil. Add the garlic and onion and sauté until the onion is transparent and the meat is a golden colour. Add the veal jus, red wine and port. Bring to the boil then turn down to simmer. Add the water, rosemary, Tabasco and tomato paste while simmering. Continue to simmer for 1½ hours at 190°C. Add salt and pepper to taste and serve with braised vegetables.

## VEAL JUS

4 tablespoons shallots, peeled and chopped
2 teaspoons garlic, peeled and chopped
2 teaspoons butter
½ cup red wine
3 cups veal stock
1 teaspoon tarragon

Sweat the shallots and garlic in butter until thoroughly softened. Deglaze with the red wine and reduce to a glaze. Add the veal stock and reduce by half, skimming away any fat or impurities. Strain and continue to reduce to the desired consistency. Steep the tarragon in the reduction for 30 seconds then strain. Makes 500 ml.

## VEAL STOCK

1 kg veal bones
⅓ cup carrots, peeled and chopped
⅓ cup onions, peeled and chopped
2 tablespoons bacon, chopped
⅓ cup celery, chopped
2 cloves garlic, minced
200 ml red wine

Brown the veal bones, carrots and onion in the oven, then bake for 2 hours at 190°C. Remove from the oven and place the veal bones, bacon, garlic and all the vegetables in a large stock pot and cover with water. Bring to the boil, then reduce heat and simmer for 8 hours. Deglaze with red wine. Remove from the stove, strain and allow to cool. Skim to remove the fat.

# WARM LIQUID CENTRE BANANA BREAD PUDDING WITH CARAMEL AND CHOCOLATE SAUCES

## COTSWOLD HOUSE

*160 grams butter, softened*
*100 grams brown sugar*
*120 grams castor sugar*
*2 eggs*
*1¼ cups of ripe bananas, mashed*
*320 grams plain flour*
*1 teaspoon baking powder*
*Chocolate Anglaise*
*Ganache*
*Caramel sauce*
*Chocolate sauce*

Cream the butter and sugars very well, beat in the eggs and mix in the bananas. Sift in the flour and baking powder and mix well. Spoon the mixture into a greased and floured loaf tin and bake at 180°C for approximately 45 minutes or until cooked. Turn out onto a rack to cool. When cool, slice and dice into 1 cm cubes. Place the banana bread cubes into a bowl. Pour the Chocolate Anglaise over the banana bread. Cover with plastic wrap and set aside for 30 minutes.

Using dariole moulds or oven proof coffee cups, grease well and place a circle of greaseproof paper in the bottom. Spoon the soaked banana bread and chocolate anglaise into the moulds until they are about one third full. Place a hazelnut size ball of ganache into the centre and spoon in more of the bread mixture to fill the moulds.

Place the moulds onto an oven tray and bake at 180°C for approximately 20 minutes or until the mixture is slightly raised and slightly firm to touch. Allow to cool then refrigerate.

When they are cold turn out and remove the paper. Serve hot with the Caramel and Chocolate Sauces.

## CHOCOLATE ANGLAISE

*12 egg yolks*
*200 grams sugar*
*700 ml milk*
*300 ml cream*
*1 cup chocolate buttons*

Mix together the egg yolks and half the sugar in a bowl. Place the milk, cream and the other half of the sugar into a pot and bring to the boil. When it is boiling add the chocolate and whisk until the chocolate melts. Bring back to the boil, pour it over the eggs and mix well. Strain.

## GANACHE

*1 cup mixed fruit*
*30 ml brandy*
*½ cup cream*
*1½ cups chocolate buttons*

Soak the fruit in the brandy, cover with plastic wrap and warm for 30 seconds in a microwave. Place the cream in a pot and bring to

*Tynwald, Tasmania*
*Steamed game pudding, page 177*

*Winter*

**TYNWALD**
New Norfolk,
Southern Tasmania

•

*Carrot and oatmeal soup*

•

*Char-grilled ox tongue with beetroot and crème fraîche salad*

•

*Steamed game pudding*

•

*Apple crepe gateau with butterscotch sauce*

---

the boil. Pour the chocolate buttons into the cream and stir well until all of the chocolate has melted. Add the mascerated fruit and mix well. Set aside to cool.

## CARAMEL SAUCE

*1 cup castor sugar*  *600 ml cream*
*¼ cup water*

Combine the sugar and water in a pot, stir until the sugar has dissolved and bring to the boil. Keep boiling until the sugar begins to brown (approximately 175°C). Do not allow it to burn. Remove from the heat and carefully whisk in the cold cream. Use extreme care and stir well. If the sugar sticks to the whisk return the sauce to the heat and heat gently, whisking to combine.

Remove from the heat and cool. If it is too thick reheat it and add more cream. If it is too thin reheat it and simmer to reduce the liquid.

## CHOCOLATE SAUCE

*300 ml port*  *1 tablespoon cocoa*
*250 grams chocolate buttons*

Bring the port to the boil, add the chocolate and cocoa, stir until the chocolate has melted and the cocoa is well combined. Remove from the heat, strain and cool.

## CARROT AND OATMEAL SOUP
### TYNWALD

*2 large onions, chopped*  *1 tablespoon sugar*
*1 clove garlic, crushed*  *salt and pepper*
*50 grams butter*  *1½ litres vegetable or chicken*
*500 grams carrot, grated*  *stock*
*70 grams oatmeal (or rolled oats)*  *2 bay leaves*

SAUTÉ together the onion and garlic in butter. Add the grated carrot, oatmeal, sugar, seasonings and stock. Simmer until the carrots are soft and the oatmeal thickens.

# CHAR-GRILLED OX TONGUE WITH BEETROOT AND CRÈME FRAÎCHE SALAD

## TYNWALD

*1 pickled ox tongue*
*½ onion*
*½ carrot*
*½ stalk of celery*
*1 clove garlic*
*1 beetroot per person*
*1 tablespoon crème fraîche per person*
*1 lettuce cup per person*
*dill to garnish*

Dice the onion, carrot, celery and garlic. Place this mixture in a saucepan with the ox tongue and cover with cold water. Bring to the boil, reduce the heat and simmer, covered, for 2½ hours. Remove from the stove and cool in the liquid. Remove the skin and press into a bowl.

Boil the beetroot until cooked. Peel the beetroot while still warm, then dice. Set aside to cool. Slice the ox tongue into 1 cm thick slices, allowing 2 or 3 slices per person. Grill the ox tongue slices and arrange on each plate. Add the crème fraîche to the diced beetroot and spoon into a lettuce cup. Serve with the ox tongue, garnished with dill.

# STEAMED GAME PUDDING

## TYNWALD

*3 onions, diced*
*1 kg game meat, diced*
*1 bay leaf*
*500 ml stock*
*salt and pepper*
*2 tablespoons tomato paste*
*2 tablespoons roux*
*250 ml red wine*
*250 grams suet, grated*
*500 grams self raising flour*
*salt and pepper*
*water*
*mashed potatoes*

Sauté the onion. Add the meat, bay leaf, stock, salt and pepper, tomato paste, roux and wine. Simmer until the meat is tender.

To make the suet pastry, mix the grated suet with the flour, salt and pepper. Add enough water to bind it into a dough. Set aside to rest.

Roll out the suet pastry for individual pots or one large pudding basin. Line the base and sides of the containers. Fill with the meat mixture, moisten the edges and top with more pastry. Cover with greaseproof paper and pleat around the edges to seal. Repeat with aluminium foil. Steam for 45 minutes, turn out, and serve with mashed potatoes. Serves 4.

## APPLE CREPE GATEAU WITH BUTTERSCOTCH SAUCE

### TYNWALD

1.3 litres milk/water (approximately ¾ milk)
230 grams plain flour
4 eggs
½ teaspoon salt
4 tablespoons melted butter
20 golden delicious apples
250 grams unsalted butter
½ cup cognac
1 cup sultanas, softened in ½ cup rum
½ cup cinnamon, freshly ground
½ castor sugar
Butterscotch Sauce

To make the crepes, whisk together the milk and water, plain flour, eggs, salt and melted butter and set aside to rest for 30 minutes. Using a crepe pan make 10 or 12 crepes of about 23 cm in diameter.

Peel, core and finely slice the apples. Retain the cores to make a syrup. Fry the sliced apples in butter over a high heat until slightly soft. Add the cognac and continue frying for a minute or two then set aside.

Line the base of a 23 cm cake tin with silicon paper and lightly grease the sides of the tin. Place one pancake on the base of the tin. Cover with sliced apple then sprinkle with some of the sultanas, cinnamon and sugar. Repeat until the tin is filled to the top, finishing with a crepe just above the rim of the tin. Make a syrup by boiling the apple cores with a little sugar to taste. Strain and pour ½ a cup of syrup over the cake.

Cover the cake with foil and bake at 160°C for 40 minutes. Remove the foil and place a plate on top of the cake with a weight on it. Leave overnight in the refrigerator. To turn the cake out, run a knife around the inside of the tin. Cut into wedges and serve warm with warm Butterscotch Sauce. Serves 10.

### BUTTERSCOTCH SAUCE

500 ml cream
250 grams soft brown sugar
3 tablespoons black treacle
230 grams butter
2 teaspoons vanilla essence

Combine all the ingredients in a saucepan and bring to the boil. Simmer for a few minutes before using.

---

ADAMS OF NORTH RIDING RESTAURANT, VICTORIA
*Thick onion soup with a bone marrow soufflé, page 180*

*Winter*

# Fine Food from Country Australia

**ADAMS OF NORTH RIDING RESTAURANT**
St Andrews, Victoria

• 

*Thick onion soup with a bone marrow soufflé*

•

*Pot-roasted squab with a truffle pie and port wine and balsamic jus*

•

*Baked chocolate pudding with a bitter chocolate sauce and sour cream mousse*

## THICK ONION SOUP WITH A BONE MARROW SOUFFLÉ

### ADAMS OF NORTH RIDING RESTAURANT

8 large onions, sliced
6 cloves garlic
50 ml olive oil
200 ml white wine
100 ml brandy
2 litres strong beef stock
salt and pepper
10 pieces marrow bone, 6 cm long
1 tablespoon chopped parsley
3 egg whites
butter
flour
CHICKEN MOUSSE:
400 grams minced chicken
400 ml cream
1 egg white
salt, pepper and paprika

In a heavy-based pot, fry the sliced onions and garlic in oil until golden. Add the white wine and brandy, and reduce. Add the beef stock, bring to the boil and simmer for 15 minutes. Skim any scum off the top. Purée and pass through a sieve. Season to taste.

To make the chicken mousse, chill the chicken and cream in a freezer. Blend the chicken in a processor. Season with salt, pepper and paprika. Slowly add the cream. Whip the egg white until soft peaks form and fold into the chicken and cream mixture.

To make the bone marrow soufflés, push the bone marrow out of the bones and soak in water overnight. In a bowl, combine 200 grams of Chicken Mousse, the diced bone marrow and parsley. Whisk the egg whites to form stiff peaks and fold into the marrow mixture. Butter and flour the inside of the bones. Spoon the mixture into the bones and bake at 180°C for 10 minutes.

Serve the soup hot in a soup plate with the bone marrow soufflé in the middle. Serves 10.

## POT-ROASTED SQUAB WITH A TRUFFLE PIE AND PORT WINE AND BALSAMIC JUS

### ADAMS OF NORTH RIDING RESTAURANT

10 x 400 gram squabs
1 onion, leek and carrot
3 cloves garlic
100 ml vegetable oil
50 grams tomato paste
1 litre chicken stock
2 bay leaves
1 teaspoon black peppercorns
100 ml port
100 ml balsamic vinegar
30 grams fresh or preserved truffles
200 grams Chicken Mousse, see preceding recipe
500 grams Lard Short Pastry
½ bunch baby turnips
100 grams butter
500 grams assorted fresh mushrooms

Roast the squabs in an oven at 180°C for 10 minutes. Allow to rest for 10 minutes, then bone. Place the breasts on a tray and take the leg meat off the bone. Roast the bones at 200°C until brown.

Brown the onion, leek, carrot and garlic in a heavy pot in vegetable oil. Add the tomato paste, roasted bones, chicken stock, bay leaves and peppercorns. Simmer for 3 hours, skim and strain.

Reduce the port and balsamic in a saucepan to a glaze, then add the stock. Reduce to the correct consistency and strain.

For the pies, dice the truffles and fold through the Chicken Mousse. Line pie tins with the Lard Short Pastry and spoon in the mousse. Dice the squab meat and place on top of the mousse. Cover the pies with pastry and bake at 200°C for 15 minutes.

Cook the turnips in salted water with a knob of butter until soft. Fry the mushrooms in a hot pan and arrange on plates. Warm the squab breasts in the oven and place on the mushrooms. Place the turnips and pies on the plates. Pour on the sauce and serve. Serves 10.

## LARD SHORT PASTRY

*500 grams plain flour*
*125 grams butter*
*125 grams lard*
*pinch salt*
*100 ml water*

Sift the flour. Rub the butter and lard into the flour. Add the salt. Make a well in the flour and mix in the water. Knead quickly. Allow the pastry to rest for half an hour before using. Makes 1 kg.

## BAKED CHOCOLATE PUDDING WITH A BITTER CHOCOLATE SAUCE AND SOUR CREAM MOUSSE

### ADAMS OF NORTH RIDING RESTAURANT

*200 grams dark chocolate*
*120 grams butter*
*200 grams sugar*
*6 egg yolks*
*100 grams flour*
*6 egg whites*
*250 grams dark chocolate*
*500 ml cream*
*1 tablespoon coffee extract*

MELT 200 grams of chocolate with the butter, then reduce the temperature to 37°C. Beat the sugar and egg yolks together until they form a ribbon. Add the chocolate mixture to the egg mixture. Fold in the flour. Whisk the egg whites and fold into the pudding mixture. Spoon into greased and floured tins and bake at 200°C for 13 minutes.

To make a bitter chocolate sauce, melt 250 grams of dark chocolate together with the cream and coffee extract and pour over the hot pudding. Serve with Sour Cream Mousse. Serves 10.

## ROBERTS AT PEPPER TREE
Hunter Valley,
New South Wales

*A clear soup, with fine diced vegetables, pasta, borlotti beans, red kidney beans, and lastly finished with a pesto*

*Little parcel of salmon wrapped in a cabbage leaf, served with an essence of tomato and saffron*

*Osso bucco of veal with turnips, red onions, carrots and orange zest potato mash*

*Marinated strawberries with a Cointreau zabaglione*

## SOUR CREAM MOUSSE

5 leaves gelatine
120 grams castor sugar
juice of 3 oranges
300 grams sour cream
250 ml cream
4 egg whites
30 grams sugar

Soak the gelatine. Boil the sugar and orange juice together. Add the gelatine, then the sour cream. Whip the cream and fold it into the sour cream mixture. Whisk the egg whites and 30 grams of sugar together and fold into the mixture. Allow to set. Serves 10.

## A CLEAR SOUP, WITH FINE DICED VEGETABLES, PASTA, BORLOTTI BEANS, RED KIDNEY BEANS, AND LASTLY FINISHED WITH A PESTO

**ROBERTS AT PEPPER TREE**

3 chicken carcasses, chopped into pieces
1 onion, cut in half
1 chicken cube
1 carrot, cut in pieces
1 celery stick, cut in pieces
1 bay leaf
salt and pepper
4 egg whites and shells
1 medium carrot, diced
1 stick celery, diced
100 grams broccoli, stalks diced and flowers separated
100 grams borlotti beans, cooked
100 grams red kidney beans, cooked
100 grams bow tie pasta, cooked
12 dozen Chicken Wontons, to serve with the soup
100 grams pesto

To make the stock, boil the chicken carcasses, onion, chicken cube, carrot, celery, bay leaf, salt and pepper, egg whites and shells together for at least ½ an hour or until reduced by half. Strain through a cloth. Taste and adjust seasonings. When cool take the fat off the top with a spoon.

Add the diced carrot, celery, and the broccoli to the stock and cook gently. When the vegetables are nearly cooked add the beans, the pasta and the wontons. Serve with pesto. Serves 6.

## CHICKEN WONTONS

100 grams chicken, minced
fresh parsley, chopped
1 garlic clove, mashed
salt and pepper
wonton wrappers (available from Chinese stores)
water and corn flour, mixed

Mix together the chicken, parsley, garlic, salt and pepper. Place tiny portions of the mince in the centre of the wonton pastry. Seal with a mixture of water and corn flour.

---

ADAMS OF NORTH RIDING RESTAURANT, VICTORIA
*Baked chocolate pudding with a bitter chocolate sauce and sour cream mousse, page 181*

*W*INTER

# LITTLE PARCEL OF SALMON WRAPPED IN A CABBAGE LEAF, SERVED WITH AN ESSENCE OF TOMATO AND SAFFRON

### ROBERTS AT PEPPER TREE

*300 grams salmon, diced*
*1 egg*
*1 shallot, chopped*
*1 clove garlic, chopped*
*¼ red capsicum, chopped finely*
*salt and pepper*
*1 teaspoon pernod*
*1 branch chervil, chopped*
*some Chux cloths cut in halves*
*3 large cabbage leaves (green), cut in halves and blanched until softened*
*thin string*
*½ cup white wine*
*6 bay leaves*
*Tomato Essence*

MIX THE salmon, egg, shallot, garlic, capsicum, salt and pepper, pernod and chervil in a bowl.

Spread out on a bench the Chux cloths and place on top of this the cabbage leaves. Pick up the chux with one of the cabbage leaves in it and place it in the palm of your hand, and fill the centre of the cabbage leaf with some of the salmon mixture (about 50 grams).

Form the cabbage leaf around the salmon mixture in a tight ball using the chux cloth to hold it together. Tie the parcel with the string. Do all of the six parcels.

To cook, poach in a pot of hot boiling salted water, with ½ a cup of white wine and 6 bay leaves. Cook for 15 minutes maximum. Don't forget to remove the Chux and string. Serve in a pool of Tomato Essence. Serves 6.

## TOMATO ESSENCE

*3 soupspoons virgin olive oil*
*1 red onion, chopped*
*4 large ripe tomatoes, diced*
*salt and pepper*
*a few saffron threads*
*1 soupspoon water*

Heat the oil, add the chopped onion, and fry well to extract its flavour. Add the tomatoes, salt and pepper, saffron and the water. Simmer until half reduced and well softened. Sieve and serve.

# OSSO BUCCO OF VEAL WITH TURNIPS, RED ONIONS, CARROTS AND ORANGE ZEST POTATO MASH

### ROBERTS AT PEPPER TREE

*24 veal knuckles*
*1 cup flour*
*1 cup oil*
*400 grams speck, cut into thin strip*
*4 onions, diced*
*3 carrots, peeled and turned*
*1 kg small champignons*
*3 turnips, peeled and turned*
*salt and pepper*
*3 cloves garlic, peeled and chopped*
*1 small bunch thyme, chopped*
*2 cups dry white wine*
*2 oranges, juice and rind*
*1 litre veal stock*

LIGHTLY FLOUR the veal knuckles and fry in the oil in a big shallow pot until golden. Fry the speck and onion with the knuckles. After 10 minutes, add the carrots, champignons and turnips, turning all the time. Add the salt, pepper, garlic and thyme. When all are evenly done, add the white wine, stirring again. Heat the orange juice and veal stock and add. Season with salt and pepper to taste.

Cook over a gentle heat with a lid on for 1¼ hours, removing the lid and stirring now and then. Lastly add the orange rind. Serves 12.

# MARINATED STRAWBERRIES WITH A COINTREAU ZABAGLIONE

### ROBERTS AT PEPPER TREE

*3 punnets strawberries, hulled*
*3 lemons, squeezed*
*150 grams castor sugar*
*2 soupspoons cointreau*
*6 egg yolks*
*4 soupspoons cointreau, extra*
*80 grams castor sugar, extra*
*2 soupspoons milk*

MARINATE the strawberries in the lemon juice, castor sugar and cointreau. Chill for one hour. Whisk the egg yolks, extra cointreau, extra sugar and milk over a boiling pot of water. Do not allow the bowl to touch the water, whisk to fluff the mixture until it reaches a thicker consistency and is warm. Do not overdo it.

Place the fruit and its liquid into a coupé and pour over the hot zabaglione.

## NEWTOWN HOUSE RESTAURANT
### Margaret River Region, Western Australia

*Clover Cottage trout with English spinach and shallots and Rose Valley mozzarella with a thyme flavoured cream sauce*

*Confit of duckling with lentils and a fig and ginger cognac sauce*

*Quinces in syrup with prune and cognac ice-cream and shortcrust shards*

# CLOVER COTTAGE TROUT WITH ENGLISH SPINACH AND SHALLOTS AND ROSE VALLEY MOZZARELLA WITH A THYME FLAVOURED CREAM SAUCE

### NEWTOWN HOUSE RESTAURANT

*8 pieces puff pastry, 10 cm x 6 cm (either make your own for perfection or substitute commercial butter puff pastry)*
*8 golden shallots, peeled and thinly sliced*
*1 knob unsalted butter*
*1 bunch English spinach, washed at least twice and stalks removed*
*salt and cracked black pepper to taste*
*2 shallots, peeled, finely chopped*
*30 grams carrot, finely chopped*
*30 grams celery, finely chopped*
*1 knob butter*
*1 sprig thyme*
*100 ml white wine*
*300 ml cream*
*cornflour and water (to thicken sauce)*
*3 x 100 grams smoked 'Clover Cottage' trout fillets, sliced thinly off the skin*
*8 slices Rose Valley mozzarella*
*thyme, garnish*

PLACE THE pastry pieces on a baking tray in a hot oven at 220°C and bake until golden brown. Split the pastry pieces in half and place the bases back on the baking tray and set aside. Sauté the sliced shallots in butter until they are opaque, add the spinach and season with salt and pepper. Cook the spinach for 2 to 3 minutes until cooked, set aside to cool.

To make the sauce, first sauté the chopped shallots, carrots and celery in butter with the thyme. Cook for about 5 minutes. Do not brown. De-glaze the pan with the white wine, then add the cream and reduce for 2 to 3 minutes. Adjust the seasoning to taste. Pass through a sieve to remove the vegetables and thyme. Place back on the heat and add some of the cornflour and water mixture to achieve the desired consistency for a sauce.

Place a little of the thickened sauce on the pastry bases, then the spinach mixture, followed by the trout. Repeat this procedure and top with mozzarella. Reheat in the oven until hot through, place on plates, pour some sauce over and place the pastry cap on top. Garnish with fresh thyme. Serves 8.

## ROBERTS AT PEPPER TREE, NEW SOUTH WALES
*Little parcel of salmon wrapped in a cabbage leaf, served with an essence of tomato and saffron, page 184*

*W*INTER

# CONFIT OF DUCKLING WITH LENTILS AND A FIG AND GINGER COGNAC SAUCE

### NEWTOWN HOUSE RESTAURANT

*2 x 1.8 kg ducks*
*60 grams rock salt*
*2 teaspoons ground black pepper*
*2–3 sprigs tarragon*
*2–3 bay leaves, crumbled*
*1.5 kg lard or duck fat*
*1 onion, chopped*
*1 carrot, chopped*
*1 celery stalk, chopped*
*100 grams onion, chopped*
*100 grams carrot, chopped*
*100 grams celery, chopped*
*8 figs*
*1 tablespoon ginger, finely chopped*
*10 ml red wine vinegar*
*30 ml cognac*
*salt*
*cracked black pepper*
*cornflour*
*250 grams lentils*
*2 shallots, chopped*
*8 fresh tarragon sprigs*

Bone the duck, removing the thighs and breasts. Remove all excess fat except that covering the thighs and breasts. Collect the bones, including the wings, for stock. The fat can be rendered and added to the lard for the cooking process. Place the pieces of duck in a dish and sprinkle with the rock salt, cracked black pepper, tarragon and bay leaf, cover and leave for about 4 hours, depending on the depth of flavour you want. Turn the pieces occasionally.

When it is ready to cook, wipe the excess salt off the duck pieces and place the duck, skin down, in a heatproof casserole dish. Put in a pre-heated (150°C) oven for 15 to 20 minutes. Add enough duck fat or lard to cover the browned duck and cook in the oven for 2 hours or until the duck is very tender and has rendered all its fat.

To make a duck stock, take all the reserved bones and brown them in a hot oven. In a saucepan brown the onion, carrot and celery stalk in a little oil. When the bones are done add them to the vegetables and cover with cold water. Bring to a simmer and cook for 3 hours.

Strain the stock off the bones and vegetables then leave to rest. The fat left in the stock will rise to the surface as it cools. Skim this off and place the remaining liquid in a saucepan. Reduce the stock by half over a high heat.

To make the sauce, chop four of the figs. Cook the figs with the chopped vegetables and ginger in a little butter in a saucepan. Add the red wine vinegar and 500 ml of duck stock, reduce by half. Strain through a sieve and return the sauce to the heat. Add the cognac, adjust the seasoning and thicken to the desired consistency with cornflour.

Cook the lentils in water until cooked. Finish with the chopped shallots and a little duck stock. Place the lentils on the plates, top with well drained pieces of duck and coat with the sauce. Garnish with quarters of fresh figs and sprigs of tarragon. Serves 8.

# QUINCES IN SYRUP WITH PRUNE AND COGNAC ICE-CREAM AND SHORTCRUST SHARDS

### NEWTOWN HOUSE RESTAURANT

*4 large quinces (1 kg)*
*250 grams sugar*
*1 lemon, rind and juice*
*1 cinnamon stick*
*10 cloves*
*water, to cover*
*shortcrust pastry, for pastry shards*
*castor sugar*
*Prune and Cognac Ice-cream*
*cream, whipped*

Peel, core and slice the quinces thinly. Place them in a saucepan with the sugar, lemon and cinnamon and cloves. Cover with water, and simmer until the quinces are tender, approximately 1 hour. Remove the quinces from the pan and reduce the remaining liquid to a syrup. Strain, pour over the quinces and refrigerate.

Make your favourite shortcrust pastry and roll thinly. Cut the pastry into long triangles (approximately 16 cm long with a base of 2.5 cm). Place on a baking sheet, sprinkle with castor sugar and bake until golden brown.

Place one or two scoops of Prune and Cognac Ice-cream (or a square if you have a rectangular mould) on the serving plates, top with quinces in syrup. Add a little whipped cream and arrange three shortbread triangles in a tee-pee effect and dust with icing sugar. The ice-cream, pastry shards and quinces in syrup can all be prepared in advance.

## PRUNE AND COGNAC ICE-CREAM

*20 unpitted prunes*
*30 ml cognac*
*6 egg yolks*
*200 grams sugar*
*250 ml milk*
*½ vanilla bean cracked*
*350 ml cream*

Chop the prunes and steep in cognac for 1 hour. Combine the egg yolks with the sugar and whisk until a pale straw colour is achieved. Bring the milk to the boil with the vanilla bean. Set aside for a few minutes to allow the vanilla flavour to permeate. Strain and add to the yolk mixture. Whisk until well combined. Return to the saucepan and cook until the custard coats the back of the wooden spoon. Place in the refrigerator until well chilled. Whip the cream and add to the custard mixture. Fold in the prunes and the cognac. Put into a container and freeze. Stir occasionally as it freezes to ensure the prunes are evenly distributed.

**SILK'S BRASSERIE**
Blue Mountains, New South Wales

•

*Crepezes*

•

*Grain-fed fillet with Yorkshire pudding and onion gravy*

•

*Chocolate marquise with coffee sauce*

# CREPEZES

### SILK'S BRASSERIE

25 grams unsalted butter
100 grams flour
1 egg yolk
1 egg
250 ml milk
salt and pepper, to taste
500 ml cream
1 small onion, chopped
4 parsley stalks, chopped
1 teaspoon peppercorns
ham offcuts, diced
250 grams good-quality leg ham, finely sliced
250 grams gruyère cheese or similar
mixed cress lightly dressed with olive oil and balsamic vinegar, to garnish

PLACE THE butter in a saucepan and cook over medium heat until lightly browned. Combine with the flour, egg yolk and egg in a bowl. Add the milk and mix until smooth, then season and sieve. Allow to stand for at least 2 hours, then cook in large rounds with a little butter in a frying pan.

Place the cream in a saucepan and cook over medium heat until reduced by one-third. Add the onion, parsley stalks, peppercorns and ham offcuts and cook until heated through.

Butter the inside of six straight-sided, heat-proof cups or small bowls about 8 cm in diameter. Cut circles from the pancakes using a cutter with the same diameter as the cups. You need approximately 6 to 8 pancake rounds per cup. Place a pancake circle in the bottom of the cup, top with a slice of ham, a pancake, a round of cheese and another pancake, repeating the layers until the cup is nearly full. Place about 100 ml of the sauce on top of the layers.

Cook in a 180°C oven until brown and bubbling. Tip out onto a warm plate and garnish with the cress. Serves 6.

# GRAIN-FED FILLET WITH YORKSHIRE PUDDING AND ONION GRAVY

### SILK'S BRASSERIE

1.2 kg beef fillet, sirloin or rib eye (180–200 grams per serve)
pepper, to taste
oil
12 button onions
6 tablespoons flour
6 eggs
90 ml milk
pinch baking powder
salt and pepper, to taste
lard
2 onions, finely chopped
1 tablespoon flour, extra
750 ml beef stock
thyme, chopped

SEASON THE beef with pepper, then place in a heat-proof baking dish with the oil and brown all over. Roast in a 220°C oven for 20

*SILK'S BRASSERIE,*
*NEW SOUTH WALES*
*Crepezes*

*W*inter

minutes. During the cooking time, add the button onions to the dish to brown. Remove from the oven and set aside to rest.

Place the flour, eggs, milk, baking powder and salt and pepper in a bowl and beat for 2 minutes. Strain into Yorkshire pudding dishes with hot lard. Bake at 200°C for 10 minutes or until browned, puffed and crisp.

Place the chopped onions, extra flour, beef stock and button onions in a saucepan and cook over medium heat until the onions are tender. Season to taste, then sieve. Place the beef fillets on a serving plate and garnish with the button onions and thyme. Serve with roast vegetables and green beans. Serves 6.

## CHOCOLATE MARQUISE WITH COFFEE SAUCE

### SILK'S BRASSERIE

*Finger Biscuits:*
5 eggs, separated
150 grams sugar
125 grams flour
100 grams icing sugar
*Chocolate Marquise:*
145 grams chocolate

7 egg yolks
250 grams sugar
300 grams butter, softened
165 grams good-quality cocoa
500 ml cream
Coffee Sauce

Beat the egg yolks with 125 grams of the sugar, then fold in the flour. Whip the egg whites, then add the remaining 25 grams of sugar. Fold the two egg mixtures together.

Place in a piping bag with a 2 cm plain nozzle and pipe out biscuits about 8 cm long onto a baking tray covered with baking parchment. Bake at 180°C for 18 minutes. Remove from the oven and sprinkle liberally with icing sugar. This makes about 40 biscuits. Keep for about 1 week in a well-sealed container.

To make the Chocolate Marquise, melt the chocolate. Beat the egg yolks with the sugar and add the chocolate. Mix the butter and cocoa together and add to the egg mixture. Whip the cream and fold into the egg mixture.

Line a mould with the biscuits, pour in some of the chocolate marquise and top with biscuits. Allow to firm for 3 hours before serving. To serve, unmould and serve with the Coffee Sauce.

### COFFEE SAUCE

250 ml milk
1 heaped tablespoon ground coffee

3 egg yolks
75 grams sugar

Place the milk and coffee in a saucepan and heat over medium heat. Beat the egg yolks and sugar together and add to the milk mixture. Heat until it reaches 80°C, then sieve and set aside to cool.

## MUSHROOM MENAGE
### SKILLOGALEE

20 grams butter
6 button mushrooms, halved
2 swiss brown mushrooms, cut in thick slices
4 tablespoons spring onions, chopped
2 tablespoons parsley, finely chopped
250 ml cream
2 shiitake mushrooms, halved
2 pieces black fungus
2 small bunches enoki
2 oyster mushrooms
2 large croutons
parsley, chopped

Melt the butter in a frying pan. Fry the button mushrooms with the swiss brown mushrooms. Add the spring onions and parsley and pour in the cream. Boil to thicken, add the shiitake and black fungus then the enoki and oyster mushrooms and cook a little more. Put two croutons on two warm plates and arrange the mushrooms on top, pouring the sauce over the top. Sprinkle with a little chopped parsley and serve. Serves 2.

## KANGAROO AND SKILLOGALEE SHIRAZ PIE
### SKILLOGALEE

1 kg kangaroo fillet
seasoned flour
6 tablespoons olive oil
2 onions, peeled and chopped
2 carrots, diced
12 peppercorns
2 cups Skillogalee Shiraz
1 cup port
bouquet garni made from thyme, bay leaves, parsley and celery leaves
salt and pepper
200 grams mushrooms, sliced
puff pastry sheets
1 egg yolk, beaten with a little milk

Cube the kangaroo fillet and toss in the seasoned flour. Heat 4 tablespoons of olive oil in a cast iron casserole and fry the meat in batches. Remove to a bowl. Add the other 2 tablespoons of oil and fry the onion until transparent. Put the meat back in the casserole and add the carrot, peppercorns, Shiraz and port. Put in the bouquet garni and season with salt and pepper.

Cook in a moderate oven for 1½ hours or until the meat is tender; 15 minutes before cooking is finished add the mushrooms.

Divide the meat between 8 individual pie dishes. Cut pastry tops for the dishes and strips to go around the edge of each dish. Press the strip of pastry around the dish, brush with water and press on the pastry top. Slash the edges with a knife. Decorate the top with pastry scraps and paint with eggwash. Bake in a 200°C oven for 30 to 35 minutes until golden. Serve with vegetables.

---

SKILLOGALEE
Clare Valley,
South Australia

•

*Mushroom menage*

•

*Kangaroo and Skillogalee shiraz pie*

•

*Sticky toffee pudding with warm butterscotch sauce*

**SAN SOLERO BAY**
Cox Peninsula, Northern Teritory

•

*Mixed crustacean salad*

•

*Roasted kangaroo fillet with Illawarra plum and chilli sauce and wild mint polenta diamonds*

•

*Pear, date and ginger upside down pudding with walnut and butterscotch sauce*

## STICKY TOFFEE PUDDING WITH WARM BUTTERSCOTCH SAUCE

### SKILLOGALEE

175 grams soft brown sugar
100 grams soft butter
4 eggs, beaten
225 grams self raising flour
300 ml boiling water
225 grams sultanas
2 tablespoons strong coffee
1 teaspoon bicarbonate of soda
Butterscotch Sauce
cream
icing sugar

Line a 22.5 cm round loose bottomed cake tin on the base and sides with Gladbake. In a mixer, cream the sugar and butter until pale yellow. Add the eggs and the flour alternately. Pour the boiling water over the sultanas. Mix the coffee and the bicarbonate together and add to the sultanas. Using a wooden spoon, mix the sultanas and coffee liquid into the cake mixture. Pour the mixture into the lined cake tin and bake in a 180°C fan forced oven for 1 hour or until a skewer comes out clean.

Cut the warm sticky pudding into wedges and place in the centre of a white dinner plate. Pour Butterscotch Sauce on one side and cream on the other. They will run and meet in the middle. Dust with a little icing sugar on top of the pudding.

## BUTTERSCOTCH SAUCE

1 x 450 gram tin golden syrup
75 grams butter
100 grams soft brown sugar
150 ml cream
½ teaspoon vanilla essence

Put the golden syrup, butter and sugar in a pan and heat slowly until the butter has melted and the sugar dissolved. Cook for a few minutes, stirring. Remove from the heat and cool, add the cream and vanilla essence and whisk until smooth. Reheat when needed.

## MIXED CRUSTACEAN SALAD

### SAN SOLERO BAY

2 yabbies
6 tiger prawns
4 sea bugs
20 grams macadamia nuts, crushed
20 grams mango purée
30 ml olive oil
10–15 ml lime juice
seasoning
50 grams mescalin or rocket or cress
50 grams mixed julienne, for salad garnish
8 lemon or lime slices
8 whole macadamia nuts, roasted

Steam or boil all the seafood and then refresh. Cut the bugs and yabbies in half. Clean all the seafood appropriately. Mix the crushed macadamia nuts, mango purée, olive oil and lime juice

**SILK'S BRASSERIE, NEW SOUTH WALES**
*Chocolate marquise with coffee sauce, page 192*

*W*INTER

together for the dressing. Taste for seasoning. Place the washed and spun greens on the serving plates in mounds. Arrange the seafood on and around the greens. Either dollop dressing on the seafoods or place the dressing in a separate bowl. Garnish with heaped julienne. Finish with citrus slices and macadamia nuts placed around the edge of the plate.

# ROASTED KANGAROO FILLET WITH ILLAWARRA PLUM AND CHILLI SAUCE AND WILD MINT POLENTA DIAMONDS

## SAN SOLERO BAY

*200 grams kangaroo fillet*
*100 grams olive oil*
*3 sprigs wild thyme, chopped*
*10 grams cracked pepper*
*50 grams Illawarra plums*
*50 ml port*
*10 ml balsamic vinegar*
*100 ml game glaze*
*¼ teaspoon red chillies, finely chopped*
*2 teaspoons blue gum honey*
*pinch native ground mint*
*Wild Mint Polenta Diamonds*

MARINATE the kangaroo in oil, thyme and cracked pepper overnight. For the sauce, place the plums, port, balsamic vinegar, game glaze, red chillies, blue gum honey and native ground mint in a pan to blend and reduce. Seal the kangaroo in a hot pan and lightly season. Roast in a hot oven 200–220°C for approximately 8 minutes. Remove from the oven and rest in a warm place for 5 minutes before slicing for presentation. Spoon some of the sauce onto the serving plates and arrange the sliced kangaroo on top of the sauce. Garnish with Wild Mint Polenta Diamonds.

## WILD MINT POLENTA DIAMONDS

*20 grams fine polenta*
*50 grams chicken stock*
*pinch salt*
*pinch chopped wild mint*
*1 teaspoon butter*
*1 teaspoon parmesan cheese, grated*
*50 grams coconut milk*

MIX ALL the ingredients together. Bring to the boil while stirring all the time. Simmer gently for 10 minutes. Pour onto an oiled tray 2 cm deep. Smooth out and refrigerate overnight. Cut into diamonds and deep fry in oil until golden brown.

# PEAR, DATE AND GINGER UPSIDE DOWN PUDDING

### SAN SOLERO BAY

*60 grams butter*
*100 grams soft brown sugar*
*4 ripe pears, peeled, cored and cut in ½ lengthwise*
*6 dates, seeded*
*pecan nuts for garnish*
*125 grams flour*
*½ teaspoon bicarbonate of soda*
*pinch salt*
*2 teaspoons cinnamon*
*1 teaspoon ground ginger*
*¼ teaspoon nutmeg*
*pinch ground cloves*
*1 egg, beaten*
*125 grams soft brown sugar*
*90 grams black treacle*
*½ cup milk*
*60 grams butter, softened*
*Walnut and Butterscotch Sauce*

MELT THE butter in a saucepan, add the brown sugar and stir until dissolved. Pour this mixture into a 20 cm springform tin. Arrange the pears and dates around the edge of the tin, placing a pecan nut between them.

Sift together the flour, bicarbonate of soda, salt, cinnamon, ginger, nutmeg and cloves. Combine together the beaten egg, brown sugar, treacle, milk and softened butter and stir them into the flour mix. Beat well until the mix is smooth, then pour this over the pears and dates. Bake at 180°C for 40 to 45 minutes. Allow to cool slightly in the tin before removing. Serve with Walnut and Butterscotch Sauce.

## WALNUT AND BUTTERSCOTCH SAUCE

*200 grams brown sugar*
*½ cup cream*
*130 grams butter*
*½ teaspoon vanilla essence*
*100 grams walnut pieces*

Place all the ingredients except the walnuts in a saucepan and bring to the boil, simmer for 5 minutes. Drop the walnuts in the sauce before serving.

**LAKE HOUSE**
Central Victoria

*Brioche with a ragout of local wild mushrooms*

*Duckling cooked confit style with duck sausage over Asian style vegetables*

*La dolce vita*

# BRIOCHE WITH A RAGOUT OF LOCAL WILD MUSHROOMS

### LAKE HOUSE

*185 ml milk, lukewarm*
*1 envelope dry yeast or 15 grams fresh yeast*
*1 tablespoon sugar*
*100 grams unsalted butter, melted*
*1 teaspoon salt*
*2–2½ cups plain flour*
*2 eggs*
*eggwash, for glazing*
MUSHROOM SAUCE:
*butter and oil, for frying*
*500 grams shallots, peeled*
*500 grams large, flat field mushrooms, sliced*
*700 grams forest mushrooms (pine or boletus)*
*a handful of dried ceps or morels, soaked in 1 cup of warm water, drained and liquid reserved*
*3–4 sprigs fresh tarragon (or ¼ teaspoon dried)*
*salt and pepper*
*2 cloves garlic, optional*
*2 cups strong beef stock*

TO MAKE the brioche, combine the lukewarm milk with the yeast and sugar. Stir well. Leave aside until the top is foamy then stir in the melted butter and salt.

Add 1 cup of flour and beat until smooth. Add the two eggs and beat until combined. Add another cup of flour and beat until the dough is soft. The dough should be sticky but manageable. If necessary add a little more flour. Turn the dough out onto a floured surface and cover with a towel. Rest for 10 minutes.

Knead the dough until smooth and elastic, adding more flour if it is difficult to manage. Put the dough into a large buttered bowl, turning the dough to ensure the entire surface is well greased.

Cover and allow to rise in a warm place until doubled in size, about 45 minutes. Punch the dough down and knead until smooth. Roll into a log shape and cut into even sized pieces. From each piece remove about a fifth and roll these into small balls. Roll the larger pieces into balls also.

Place the larger balls into greased brioche tins and make a small indentation in the top. Attach a small ball to the top of each.

Place filled brioche tins on a tray, glaze with egg and allow to rise until doubled in volume. Preheat oven to 180°C. Bake until golden brown, about 25–30 minutes.

To make the mushroom sauce, heat a little oil in a large pan, adding a little butter. Fry the shallots until golden brown, reduce the temperature and continue to cook until the shallots have softened but are still whole. Remove them with a slotted spoon and set aside. Add all the mushrooms with a little more butter if necessary, cook for 10–12 minutes. Put the shallots back in the pan and add the tarragon, salt, pepper, garlic, stock and reserved soaking liquid from the dried mushrooms. Simmer for about 15 minutes. Strain out all the solid ingredients. Pour the liquid back

LAKE HOUSE, VICTORIA
*Brioche with a ragout of local wild mushrooms*

*W*INTER

in the pan and reduce by half or until the liquid is syrupy. Place the mushrooms and shallots back in the pan, stir and adjust the seasoning.

To serve slice the top off each brioche, hollow out the centre a little. Fill with hot mushrooms and a little liquid. Replace the top and spoon mushrooms and liquid around the brioche. Serves 8.

## DUCKLING COOKED CONFIT STYLE WITH DUCK SAUSAGE OVER ASIAN STYLE VEGETABLES

### LAKE HOUSE

3 ducklings
duck fat, additional, to make up 1 litre when rendered
coarse salt
3 garlic cloves
12 peppercorns
2 cloves
1 bay leaf
1 knob ginger, unpeeled, roughly chopped

*Duck sausage:*
500 grams pork mince, finely ground
½ cup fresh white breadcrumbs
½ teaspoon fresh ginger, finely chopped
⅓ cup dry sherry
⅓ teaspoon five spice powder
salt and pepper
1 egg, beaten

*Sauce:*
duck stock made from reserved bones
200 grams sugar
200 ml red wine vinegar
100 grams Chinese red dates

*To serve:*
18 baby bok choy leaves
1 red capsicum, julienned
12 abalone mushrooms
6 shiitake mushrooms, sliced thinly
1 small handful bean sprouts

To prepare the ducklings, chop off their necks. Keeping the skin intact, remove the neck bones and reserve these for stock. Keep the neck skins for later. Remove the back bone by chopping down on either side with a sharp heavy knife. Split birds along the breastbone and then into leg and breast pieces. Remove and reserve any fat. Reserve any bones for stock. Place duck fat pieces and additional duck fat with a little water into a pot over a gentle heat to render.

Rub the quartered duck pieces generously with coarse salt. Leave them in a bowl with the garlic, peppercorns, cloves, bay leaf and ginger for 24 hours, moving the pieces occasionally so that each is covered with salt. After 24 hours, wipe off the salt and dry the pieces with a towel.

Cook the duck pieces in the rendered duck fat, simmering slowly either on the stove or in the oven for about an hour until the duck is completely cooked through. Remove ducks from the fat. When cool, remove the breast bones and reserve for the stock. If you need to store the duck - strain the duck fat carefully, separating out any gravy. Store the duck in a crock in the refrigerator completely surrounded and sealed in duck fat.

To make a duck neck sausage, make a farce combining the pork mince, breadcrumbs, spices, sherry and seasonings. Bind with the egg and fill the 3 reserved duck neck skins loosely (the skins will shrink when cooked). Truss the ends with string. Roast the duck necks in duck fat, basting frequently for about 40 minutes in a medium oven.

To make the sauce, use a rich brown stock made from the reserved duck back bone and breast bones. Skim off any fat then reduce the stock to concentrate the flavours.

In a heavy based pan, cook the sugar to a clear, caramel colour. Remove from the heat and carefully add the vinegar, stirring to dissolve the caramel. Add 500 ml of rich brown stock, bring to the boil and reduce. Add the dates and continue to boil the sauce until it is syrupy. Adjust the flavour with more stock or vinegar as necessary.

To complete the dish, roast the duckling pieces at 200°C until heated through and crisp on the outside. Slice the duck neck sausage and pan fry until crisp and brown. Place the vegetables in a bowl, season well and moisten with a little duck sauce. Place the bowl in a steamer and cook until the vegetables are cooked but still crisp.

Mound the vegetables onto individual plates, top with a crisp leg and breast of duckling. Surround with sliced duck sausage. Pour over a little of the duck sauce with some dates.

## LA DOLCE VITA
### LAKE HOUSE

*4 large eggs*
*140 grams sugar*
*20 grams clarified butter*
*115 grams plain flour, sifted*
*250 ml fresh ricotta*
*3 tablespoons sugar*
*200 ml cream*
*finely chopped zest of 1 lemon*
*finely chopped zest of 1 orange*
*50 grams slivered almonds, toasted*
*2 tablespoons dark chocolate, finely chopped*
*2 tablespoons currants, soaked in 1 teaspoon Amaretto*
*150 ml Amaretto liqueur*
*250 ml sugar syrup*
TO SERVE:
*Granita*
*Vin Santo Jelly*
*200 grams mascarpone, whipped with a little sugar*
*cocoa powder, for dusting*
*crostolli or biscotti*
*chocolate, melted*

PREHEAT THE oven to 180°C. Coat the bottom and sides of a 20 cm springform pan with butter and dust with flour. Whisk the eggs in an electric mixer until fluffy. Continue to whisk and slowly add the sugar in a steady stream. Whisk until the sugar has dissolved. Pour the mixture into a large bowl over a pot of boiling water. With a balloon whisk, beat continuously until the mixture is just warm, about 1 minute. Remove from the heat and return the mixture to the electric mixer. Whisk until the mixture is completely cool and the batter has doubled in volume. It should form a ribbon when the beaters are lifted. Add the butter, stirring gently. Fold in the flour using the balloon whisk to aerate the mixture and incorporate the flour. Do not overmix or the batter will collapse. Pour the batter into the pan and smooth the surface. Bake until set in the middle about 18–20 minutes. Remove from the oven and cool before turning out.

Cream together the ricotta and sugar. Add the cream and whip to combine. Add the almonds, zest, chocolate and currants, stirring until evenly distributed. Slice the sponge through the middle horizontally. Combine the Amaretto and sugar syrup and brush all over the surface of the sponge. Smooth a layer of the ricotta over the bottom half of the sponge and replace the top half, brushing more of the sugar mixture over it. Refrigerate for at least 4 hours.

To serve, cut the cake into slices. Place a slice on each plate. Scoop some of the Granita into a chilled espresso glass and top with whipped mascarpone. Dust with cocoa powder. Warm the outside of each Vin Santo Jelly mould with a warm cloth. Unmould the jelly onto each plate. Serve with crostolli or biscotti. La Dolce Vita written in melted chocolate finishes this dessert.

## VIN SANTO JELLY

*300 ml Vin Santo (good quality ie. Antinori)*
*50 ml sugar syrup*
*3½ gelatine leaves*

Soak the gelatine leaves in cold water until softened. Combine the Vin Santo and sugar syrup. Heat gently. Add the softened gelatine leaves, stirring until completely dissolved. Pour the mixture into decorative 50–60 ml jelly moulds. Refrigerate until firm.

## GRANITA

*2½ cups good quality ground coffee*
*6 tablespoons sugar*
*1 litre boiling water*

Pour the water over the coffee and sugar. Cover and stand in a saucepan of boiling water. Leave to infuse for 20–30 minutes. Cool.

Strain through a filter, which will take several hours. Taste and adjust sweetness. Some sugar syrup can be added for sweetness but granita should have some bite. Pour the filtered coffee into a shallow tray and freeze until frozen to a granular but solid mush. Stir through the granita with a fork.

LAKE HOUSE, VICTORIA
*La dolce vita, page 201*

*W*INTER

## PICNICS AT FAIRHILL
### Sunshine Coast, Queensland

•

*Macadamia-coated lamb's brains on smoked eggplant with lemon aspen mayonnaise*

•

*Native spiced chicken sausages on Kumera mash with bush tomato relish*

•

*Frozen aniseed myrtle parfait served with hot Turkish doughnuts and lime syrup*

# MACADAMIA-COATED LAMB'S BRAINS ON SMOKED EGGPLANT WITH LEMON ASPEN MAYONNAISE

PICNICS AT FAIRHILL

6 lamb's brains
¼ lemon, sliced
1 sprig parsley
2 bay leaves
4 peppercorns
2 teaspoons vinegar
½ teaspoon salt
plain flour
3 eggs
1 cup milk
pinch salt, extra
1 cup macadamia nuts, crushed
½ cup Japanese or ordinary breadcrumbs
12 large eggplants (56 cm in diameter)
olive oil
sawdust, for smoking
2 tablespoons olive oil, extra
oil, for deep frying
200 grams Tsetsoi or English spinach
Lemon Aspen Mayonnaise
½ lemon, sliced, to garnish
sprig of parsley, to garnish

Soak the lamb's brains in heavily salted water overnight. Drain, place in a saucepan and cover with cold water. Add the lemon, parsley, bay leaves, peppercorns, vinegar and salt, place on the stove and gently bring to a simmer. Simmer for 3 minutes.

Remove from the heat and cool in the cooking liquid. When cool, remove the cortex and any fatty bits. Pat dry and leave to set in the refrigerator for 12 hours.

Roll the brains in the flour, shaking off any excess. Lightly beat together the eggs, milk and salt without frothing. Coat the brains in the egg mixture, then roll in the macadamias and breadcrumbs. The brains can be stored in the refrigerator until ready to cook.

Remove the ends of the eggplants and slice into 2 cm thick rings (each person will receive one slice). Score each slice halfway through with a sharp knife, then turn 45° and score again (to make crosses). Brush twice with olive oil on both sides, then rest for 10 minutes to allow the eggplant slices to absorb the oil.

Spread ½ to ¾ cm of sawdust (good gourmet-style butchers or trout fishing shops can supply this) in an old aluminium baking tray. Place a cake rack over the sawdust, ensuring there is at least a 2 cm clearance.

Evenly space the eggplant slices on the rack, cover loosely with foil and stab with about 10 holes. If you have a good exhaust system, place the baking dish on a medium heat on the stove top, otherwise use an outside barbecue. Allow the smoke to penetrate the eggplant for 10–15 minutes.

Heat the extra olive oil in a frying pan large enough to hold the eggplant in a single layer. Cook until golden brown. In another pan deep fry the lamb's brains in oil until golden brown. Remove the eggplant once it is cooked and toss in the spinach to sear quickly. Divide the spinach evenly between the serving plates. Top with the eggplant and lamb's brains and serve with Lemon Aspen Mayonnaise. Garnish with the lemon slices and parsley. Serves 4.

## LEMON ASPEN MAYONNAISE

*1 egg*
*1 egg yolk*
*1 tablespoon lemon juice*
*5 lemon Aspen fruit (or*
  *2 teaspoons lemon zest)*
*1 teaspoon dijon mustard*
*½ teaspoon salt*
*1 cup oil*

Blend all of the ingredients except the oil in a food processor, then rest for 3 minutes. Slowly add the oil while the motor is running. Strain before using.

## NATIVE SPICED CHICKEN SAUSAGES ON KUMERA MASH WITH BUSH TOMATO RELISH AND SEARED WARRIGAL GREENS

PICNICS AT FAIRHILL

*1 kg chicken, minced*
*300 grams pork fat, minced*
*1 tablespoon salt*
*½ teaspoon dried native mint*
*¼ teaspoon ground Dorigo pepper*
*4 lemon myrtle leaves, finely*
  *chopped*
*sausage skins*
*kumera or sweet potato, peeled*
  *and diced (80 grams per*
  *serving)*
*butter*
*salt and pepper, to taste*
*few drops lemon juice*

MIX THE minced chicken, pork fat, salt, mint, pepper and lemon myrtle well in a mixer for 10 minutes. Force into the sausage skins, then rest overnight to allow the flavours to blend. If a sausage filler and skins are unavailable, the sausages can be rolled in plastic wrap (tie the ends tightly) and then poached, unwrapped and briefly grilled or pan fried to add colour.

Boil the kumera in lightly salted water until tender. Drain well. Add the butter and cream the potatoes with a spoon, not a food processor. Add the salt, pepper and lemon juice. Keep warm until needed. Pan fry the sausages and serve with the kumera mash and Bush Tomato Relish. Makes 12 to 15 sausages.

## BUSH TOMATO RELISH

1.5 kg Roma tomatoes, peeled
500 grams onions, peeled and sliced
¼ cup salt
1½ cups brown vinegar
2 cups brown sugar
1 tablespoon curry powder
2 teaspoons mustard
¾ cup cornflour
¾ cup brown vinegar, extra
½ teaspoon ground ginger
½ teaspoon cinnamon
1 tablespoon native mint
½ tablespoon dried ground bush tomatoes

Cover the tomatoes, onions and salt with water and stand overnight. Drain.

Combine with the vinegar and brown sugar in a heavy saucepan, bring to the boil, then reduce the heat and simmer for 10 minutes.

Make a smooth paste with the curry powder, mustard, cornflour and extra vinegar. Gradually stir this mixture into the saucepan and simmer for a further 40–45 minutes.

Add the ginger, cinnamon, mint and bush tomatoes. Remove from the heat immediately, otherwise the relish will turn bitter. Pack into clean, sterilised jars. Makes 6 cups.

## FROZEN ANISEED MYRTLE PARFAIT
### PICNICS AT FAIRHILL

6 egg yolks
1½ cups icing sugar
⅛ cup aniseed myrtle leaves, finely chopped (the fresh, reddish purple shoots are best)
4 egg whites
¾ cup castor sugar
3 cups double cream
2 tablespoons Ouzo or Sambucca

Make a sabayon by gently heating the egg yolks, icing sugar and aniseed myrtle leaves in the top of a double saucepan, beating constantly until thick. Cool slightly.

Whip the egg whites and castor sugar until soft peaks form. Whip the double cream until soft peaks form.

Fold the sabayon, egg white mixture, cream and Ouzo together very gently. Pour into a loaf tin lined with greaseproof paper and freeze overnight.

Remove from the tin and slice with a warm knife. Serve with Hot Turkish Doughnuts and Lime Syrup. Serves 12.

*ARCOONA, TASMANIA*
*Chunky vegetable soup with lentils and venison salami, page 208*

*W*INTER

207

## ARCOONA
### Deloraine, Northern Tasmania

•

*Chunky vegetable soup with lentils and venison salami*

•

*Trio of birds poached in Notley Gorge Cabernet Merlot with bintje potatoes and glazed onion*

•

*Heart-warming chocolate and hazelnut torte with poached pears and old-fashioned custard*

## HOT TURKISH DOUGHNUTS (LOUKMA)

½ teaspoon dry yeast
1 teaspoon sugar
50 ml warm water
1 cup plain flour
¾ teaspoon salt
150 ml milk
100 ml warm water (approximately), extra
oil, for deep frying
castor sugar mixed with a little cinnamon

Mix together the yeast, sugar and water until frothy.

Combine the yeast mixture with the flour, salt, milk and extra water until it makes a smooth batter. Set aside in a warm place for 1 hour to prove (rise) and thicken. Stir again.

Heat the oil in a deep fryer or wok until it reaches 170–180°C. Drop teaspoonfuls of the mixture into the oil, rolling them to ensure even cooking.

When golden, remove from the pan and sprinkle with castor sugar and cinnamon. Serves 6 to 8.

## LIME SYRUP

zest of 8 limes
200 grams sugar
300 ml water
juice of 3 limes

Combine the zest, sugar and water in a stainless steel saucepan, bring to the boil and cook for 30 minutes. Strain.

Add the lime juice and chill in the refrigerator. Makes 1½ cups.

## CHUNKY VEGETABLE SOUP WITH LENTILS AND VENISON SALAMI

### ARCOONA

2 onions
3 carrots
½ bunch celery
100 grams broccoli
100 grams cauliflower
3 medium-sized Tasmanian Kenebec potatoes
200 grams pumpkin
2 tablespoons olive oil
500 grams venison salami or smoked venison sausage
1 teaspoon juniper berries
bouquet garni
1 litre beef stock
250 ml red wine
200 grams red lentils
salt and pepper, to taste
200 grams Heidi barrel cheese, grated
parsley, chopped, to garnish

Chop all of the vegetables into similar sized pieces.

Place the olive oil in a large saucepan and brown the onions. Add the carrots and celery and cook until softened, approximately 5 minutes. Add all of the other vegetables and fry for 5 minutes.

Add the venison salami, juniper berries, bouquet garni, stock and red wine and simmer for 2 hours, stirring occasionally. Add the lentils 30 minutes before the cooking is complete. Season.

Serve in large bowls with the cheese and garnish with the parsley. This dish goes very well with a hot crusty sourdough that has been warmed in the oven and buttered with Northern Tasmanian butter.

## TRIO OF BIRDS POACHED IN NOTLEY GORGE CABERNET MERLOT WITH BINTJE POTATOES AND GLAZED ONION

ARCOONA

*olive oil*
*3 quails, halved*
*6 duck breasts*
*3 spatchcocks, halved*
*1 bunch shallots*
*1 carrot*
*2 sticks celery*
*200 ml chicken or duck stock*
*200 ml Notley Gorge Cabernet Merlot*
*2 tablespoons tomato paste*
*1 bay leaf*
*1 large bunch each of fresh sage, thyme and tarragon (reserve some for garnish)*
*freshly ground black, white and green pepper, to taste*
*12 small bintje potatoes*
*salt*
*250 grams unsalted butter, cut into lumps*
*1 bunch each of rosemary and thyme, chopped together*
*2 tablespoons butter*
*12 small pickling onions*

Place the oil in a frying pan and sear the quails, duck breasts and spatchcocks.

Chop the shallots, carrot and celery and place in a large saucepan. Combine the stock, wine, tomato paste, bay leaf, herbs and seasoning and add to the pan. Add the duck breasts and spatchcocks and poach for 1 hour, or until tender. Add the quail in the last 15 minutes. Remove the birds from the stock and reserve in a warm oven. Strain the poaching liquid and reserve (this liquid is called jus lie).

Place the potatoes in a saucepan with a little salt and enough water to cover. Bring to the boil, then reduce the heat and simmer for approximately 30 minutes, or until tender. Drain and pat dry. Add the butter and sprinkle over the rosemary and thyme.

Melt 2 tablespoons of butter in a heavy saucepan and gently sauté the onions for approximately 20 minutes, or until caramelised.

Place a duck breast, half a spatchcock and half a quail on a large plate and accompany with 3 bintje potatoes and 2 glazed onions. Drizzle over the jus lie. Garnish with sprigs of rosemary, thyme and tarragon.

# HEART-WARMING CHOCOLATE AND HAZELNUT TORTE WITH POACHED PEARS AND OLD-FASHIONED CUSTARD

### ARCOONA

*9 eggs, separated*
*6 tablespoons sugar*
*2 tablespoons sugar, extra*
*240 grams hazelnuts, roasted and ground*
*2 tablespoons plain flour, sifted*
*2 tablespoons fresh breadcrumbs*
*200 grams dark chocolate*
*2 tablespoons light corn syrup*
*60 grams unsalted butter*
*125 grams roasted hazelnuts, chopped*
*6 Beurre Bosc pears*
*100 ml water*
*100 ml sweet white wine*
*2 tablespoons sugar*
*Old-fashioned Custard*
*whole roasted hazelnuts, to garnish*

Grease two 20 cm sponge tins and line with greased, greaseproof paper. Whisk the egg whites with the sugar until stiff peaks form.

Cream the egg yolks with the extra sugar until thick and creamy. Fold in the hazelnuts, flour and breadcrumbs. Lightly fold into the egg white mixture. Divide the mixture between the sponge tins and bake at 170°C for 40 minutes.

Combine the dark chocolate, corn syrup and unsalted butter in the top of a double saucepan and cook, stirring, over a low heat until glossy and pourable. Remove from the heat and cool.

Remove the sponges from the oven and cool on a cake rack. Sandwich the two cakes together with the chocolate glaze, then cover the top and sides with the glaze. Sprinkle the chopped hazelnuts over.

Peel and core the pears. Place in a saucepan with the water, wine and sugar. Poach for approximately 20 minutes, or until softened. Drain.

Place slices of warm torte and a pear on a plate and serve with the custard drizzled around. Garnish with the whole hazelnuts.

## OLD-FASHIONED CUSTARD

*3 egg yolks*
*400 ml milk*
*100 ml cream*
*⅓ cup sugar*
*vanilla essence, to taste*

Whisk the egg yolks in a bowl. Place the milk, cream and sugar in a saucepan and warm over a gentle heat. Add the egg yolks and stir constantly until thickened. Do not allow to boil. Remove from the heat and add the vanilla essence.

LAKE HOUSE, VICTORIA
*Duckling cooked confit style with duck sausage over Asian style vegetables, page 200*

*W*INTER

**WARRENMANG VINEYARD RESORT**
Pyrenees, Central Victoria

•

*Goat's cheese terrine*

•

*Saddle of Pyrenees Hare*

•

*Blue cheesecake with port jelly*

•

*Poached Avoca quinces with vanilla anglaise and brioche*

## GOAT'S CHEESE TERRINE
### WARRENMANG VINEYARD RESORT

*4–5 kg potatoes*
*1.5 kg Milawa goat's cheese*
*1 bunch coriander*
*8 red capsicums, roasted and skinned then finely chopped*
*100 grams plain flour*
*¼ bunch spinach*
*lettuce leaves*
*300 ml honey*
*300 grams mustard*
*300 ml chicken stock*
*salt and pepper, to taste*

Make a large rostis with the potatoes. Place the goat's cheese, coriander and capsicum together in a bowl and beat until it forms a smooth paste.

Layer the rosti with the goat's cheese mixture in a terrine mould, then set in the refrigerator. When set, demould the terrine and cut into 1–2 cm thick slices. Place on a plate covered with the flour, so one side of each slice gets coated. Fry the goat's cheese in a little olive oil, flour side down, until golden brown.

Braise the spinach then place in the centre of a serving plate with a variety of lettuce leaves surrounding it. Place the cheese slices on top of the spinach. Combine the honey, mustard, chicken stock and seasonings in a bowl and mix well. Garnish with the dressing. Serves 15.

## SADDLE OF PYRENEES HARE
### WARRENMANG VINEYARD RESORT

*1 large whole hare*
*100 grams wild rice*
*salt, to taste*
*oil*
*300 ml cream*
*1 bunch spinach, washed*
*salt and pepper, to taste*
*Hare Stock*
*50 grams butter*
*60 grams butter, extra*

Cut the hare to the second rib at the front and remove the hind legs, leaving the saddle. Remove all layers of skin from the hare, leaving just the meat on the bone.

Soak the rice in enough water to cover for about 1 hour. Change the water, add salt to taste and bring to the boil over high heat. Reduce the heat and simmer until the rice opens. Strain and refresh.

Season the hare with salt. Cover the base of a heavy saucepan with oil and heat over high heat until the oil is smoking. Seal the hare on both sides, then place in a 250°C oven and cook for approximately 8 minutes, or until it is cooked rare. Remove from the oven and place on a cooling rack to rest.

While the hare is resting, place the cream in a saucepan and cook over a medium heat until reduced slightly. Add the spinach and cook until reduced further and the spinach is soft. Season.

Place the Hare Stock in a saucepan and bring to the boil. Cook until it reduces and becomes quite thick. When thick, whisk in 50 grams of the butter. Remove from the heat and keep warm.

Put the wild rice in a saucepan with the extra butter and cook, stirring constantly, over low heat until fluffy.

Bone the fillet off the saddle and slice thinly. Place the spinach with a little cream on a serving plate, then place the sliced hare on top. Heat in the oven until very hot, about 1 minute. Remove from the oven and spoon the wild rice over the hare. Finish by spooning over enough of the stock to cover the hare, plus a little to run into the cream. Serves 2.

## HARE STOCK

*hare legs*
*1 carrot, chopped*
*1 onion, chopped*
*100 ml red wine*
*6 cloves garlic*
*water*
*100 ml dry sherry*

Place the leg meat in a frying pan with half of the carrot and half of the onion and roast until brown. When brown, place in a medium-sized saucepan.

Heat the juices left in the frying pan over a high heat and deglaze with the red wine. Add to the pot with the hare legs and sauté over high heat until the bones have broken up slightly.

Add the garlic and cover with water. Bring to the boil and simmer for at least 6 hours, continuously skimming the fat. When cooked, strain through a fine sieve and reduce the stock by one-third.

Sweat off the remaining carrot and onion, then add the sherry and cook over a medium heat until reduced to an almost caramel texture. Add the stock and reduce by half or until the sherry has a quite pronounced flavour. Strain and set aside.

## BLUE CHEESECAKE WITH PORT JELLY
### WARRENMANG VINEYARD RESORT

*1 kg King Island blue brie*
*400 ml thickened cream*
*750 ml Warrenmang Vintage Port*
*8 pre-softened gelatine sheets*

Leave the brie at room temperature for a couple of hours to soften. Place in a mixer with a hook attachment and beat slowly until creamy. Add the cream and continue beating until very light in texture.

Line a 30 cm springform tin with greaseproof paper. Pour in the brie mixture, smooth the top until it is even, then place in the refrigerator to set.

Place the port in a saucepan and cook over a medium heat until reduced by two-thirds. Add the gelatine sheets and refrigerate until it almost sets.

Once the cheese has set, remove from the springform tin. Place an even layer of jelly on the top, then put back into the refrigerator to set completely.

To serve, remove from the refrigerator and leave until it reaches room temperature. Cut into thin wedges. 20 serves per cake.

## POACHED AVOCA QUINCES WITH VANILLA ANGLAISE AND BRIOCHE

### WARRENMANG VINEYARD RESORT

*80 grams sugar*
*250 ml milk*
*250 ml cream*
*6 egg yolks*
*1 vanilla bean, split*
*400 ml white wine*
*juice of 3 lemons*
*250 grams sugar*
*300 ml port*
*4 quinces, peeled and sliced*
*Brioche*

To make the vanilla anglaise, cream the egg yolks and sugar together. Place the milk, cream and vanilla bean in a saucepan and bring to the boil.

Add to the egg mixture, put back in the saucepan and cook until it coats the back of a spoon. Set aside to cool.

Place the wine, lemon juice, sugar and port in a saucepan and bring to the boil. Put the quinces in the saucepan, reduce the heat and poach until the quinces are cooked.

Place a quince on each serving plate and spoon the vanilla anglaise around. Serve with Brioche. Serves 4.

### BRIOCHE

*40 grams fresh yeast*
*100 ml warm water*
*1 kg plain flour*
*20 grams salt*
*100 grams sugar*
*500 grams eggs*
*500 grams butter*

Mix the yeast with the water and a handful of flour, then let prove (rise) for 20 minutes. Slowly stir in the salt, sugar and remaining flour, then gradually add the eggs and beat until smooth.

Chop the butter into small pieces and add slowly, beating until incorporated. Prove until double in size, then knock back.

Form into 80 gram balls and place into small fluted moulds. Prove until doubled in size. Bake in a 220°C oven for 20 minutes. Makes about 40.

DARLEYS RESTAURANT,
LILIANFELS,
NEW SOUTH WALES
*Wild mushroom soup with horseradish cream, page 216*

*W*INTER

**DARLEYS RESTAURANT, LILIANFELS**

Blue Mountains, New South Wales

•

*Wild mushroom soup with horseradish cream*

•

*Slow-braised pork cheeks with traditional stock pot vegetables and lardons of smoked bacon*

•

*Steamed puddings with vanilla bean custard and marmalade treacle sauce*

## WILD MUSHROOM SOUP WITH HORSERADISH CREAM

### DARLEYS RESTAURANT, LILIANFELS

*500 grams saffron milkcap mushrooms*
*75 grams onions, chopped*
*75 grams leeks, chopped*
*75 grams celery, chopped*
*½ clove garlic, chopped*
*200 grams unsalted butter*
*1.5 litres chicken stock*
*300 grams potatoes, peeled and roughly chopped*
*2 tablespoons freshly grated horseradish*
*4 tablespoons sour cream*
*freshly ground black pepper, to taste*
*150 grams cepes (slippery Jack mushrooms), sliced*
*butter, extra*
*1 tablespoon parsley, chopped*
*salt and white pepper*

SLICE THE saffron milkcap mushrooms. Place the onions, leeks, celery, half the garlic and the butter in a saucepan and sweat over a low heat until soft. Add the mushrooms to the pan and cook for 5–6 minutes. Add the chicken stock and potatoes, increase the heat and bring to the boil. Simmer for 45 minutes. Place the mixture in a food processor and purée (the mixture will be quite thick).

Combine the horseradish, sour cream and pepper. Quickly fry the cepes with the rest of the garlic in a little butter. Add the parsley, toss together and drain off the butter using a fine sieve.

To serve, season the soup to taste with salt and freshly ground white pepper and pour into deep bowls. Sprinkly some of the cepes over and add a little horseradish cream to the middle. Serves 4 to 6.

## SLOW-BRAISED PORK CHEEKS WITH TRADITIONAL STOCK POT VEGETABLES AND LARDONS OF SMOKED BACON

### DARLEYS RESTAURANT, LILIANFELS

*2 pig's heads, cut in half through the snout*
*300 grams smoked speck or belly bacon*
*vegetable oil*
*1 kg carrots, cut into large dice*
*1 kg onions, cut into large dice*
*1 kg leeks, cut into large dice*
*500 grams celery, cut in large dice*
*½ head of garlic, crushed*
*½ bunch marjoram, chopped*
*½ bunch oregano, roughly chopped*
*6 bay leaves*
*375 ml red wine*
*400 grams tomato paste*
*8 baby carrots*
*8 baby onions*
*4 baby leeks*
*2 small celery hearts*
*250 grams wild mushrooms (cepes)*
*salt and pepper, to taste*

PLACE THE pig's heads in a large stockpot, cover with cold water and bring to the boil. Reduce the heat and simmer for 5 minutes, then remove the pig's heads. Discard the water.

Cut the rind from the speck and place in a very large saucepan or large braising pan with the oil, diced vegetables, garlic, marjoram, oregano and bay leaves. Fry over low heat until lightly coloured. Increase the heat, add the red wine and tomato paste, and bring to the boil. Cook for 5 minutes.

Add the pig's heads to the saucepan and cover with plenty of cold water. Bring to the boil, reduce the heat to low and cook, covered, for about 10 hours, making sure the heads are always covered with water. Alternatively, cook in the oven in a covered casserole dish at 190°C for 10 hours. At the end of the cooking time the meat should be falling off the bone. Remove the heads from the liquid and set aside to cool.

Strain the liquid through a sieve into a clean saucepan and return to the stove. Bring to the boil and cook until the liquid has reduced a little.

Cut the speck into small dice. Place in a saucepan, cover with cold water and bring to the boil. Drain and set aside.

When the pig's heads have cooled enough to handle, gently remove the cheeks from the bone, cleaning the meat of any fatty tissue. There should be some dark meat and some white meat.

Peel and clean the baby vegetables and celery hearts and put them in a saucepan with the reduced stock. Cook over a medium heat, then remove the vegetables and set aside. Continue to cook the liquid to reduce it to a rich, thick and shiny sauce. Season.

Place the cooked meat in a casserole dish with the vegetables and enough sauce to cover and bake in a 200°C oven for 1 hour. Just before serving, sauté the diced speck in a little oil with the wild mushrooms. Drain the mixture of any excess oil and sprinkle on top of the pork. Serve with boiled or mashed potato. Serves 4.

## STEAMED PUDDINGS WITH VANILLA BEAN CUSTARD AND MARMALADE TREACLE SAUCE

### DARLEYS RESTAURANT, LILIANFELS

*250 grams butter*
*250 grams castor sugar*
*5 eggs*
*375 grams plain flour*
*25 grams baking powder*
*150 ml cold milk*
*Marmalade Treacle Sauce*
*Vanilla Bean Custard*

USING AN electric whisk, blend the butter and castor sugar together then gradually add the eggs. Sieve the flour and baking powder together and fold into the butter mixture. Stir in the cold milk.

Lightly butter six individual moulds and place a spoonful of sauce in the bottom of each mould. Fill the moulds with the mixture and steam for 50 minutes. Leave the puddings to cool in the moulds for about 10 minutes, then turn out onto a plate and cover with plastic wrap until ready to serve.

Spoon a generous amount of Marmalade Treacle Sauce on top of each pudding and warm in a microwave oven for 2 minutes on medium. Serve with a spoonful of Vanilla Bean Custard on the side. Serves 6.

## VANILLA BEAN CUSTARD

*1 leaf gelatine*
*water*
*8 egg yolks*
*80 grams sugar*
*400 ml thickened cream*
*1 vanilla pod*

Soak the gelatine in cold water. Beat the egg yolks and sugar together. Place the cream and vanilla pod in a saucepan, bring to the boil then strain onto the egg yolks and sugar.

Return the mixture to the stove and heat over low heat for about 5 minutes or until the custard coats the back of a spoon. Do not let the custard boil. Pass the custard through a sieve into a clean bowl, add the soaked gelatine leaf and stir until dissolved. Place in the refrigerator to set.

## MARMALADE TREACLE SAUCE

*12 large oranges*
*750 grams castor sugar (approximately)*

Peel the rind from the oranges using a potato peeler and cut into fine strips. Place the rind in a saucepan and cover with cold water. Bring to the boil, remove from the heat and strain.

Segment the oranges into a previously weighed bowl, then squeeze all the juice from the pulp into the same bowl. Add the blanched rind, then weigh the bowl again. Calculate the weight of the orange segments, juice and rind, then add the same amount of sugar (this will vary immensely depending on the size of the oranges and how much juice they contain).

Place the combined orange pulp mixture and sugar in a saucepan and simmer gently, stirring occasionally, over low heat for about 4 hours or until the mixture is dark, thick and treacly.

DARLEYS RESTAURANT,
LILIANFELS,
NEW SOUTH WALES
*Slow-braised pork cheeks with traditional stock pot vegetables and lardons of smoked bacon, page 216*

*W*INTER

**BAWLEY POINT GUEST HOUSE**
South Coast, New South Wales

•

*Corn and prawn fritters*

•

*Greek lamb and lettuce stew*

•

*Steamed persimmon and raisin pudding*

## CORN AND PRAWN FRITTERS
**BAWLEY POINT GUEST HOUSE**

*450 gram tin sweet corn kernels*
*500 grams green prawns, finely chopped*
*5 shallot stalks, thinly sliced*
*2 eggs*
*2 tablespoons plain flour*
*1 tablespoon ground coriander*
*salt and pepper, to taste*
*coriander leaves and sweet chilli sauce, to garnish*

Drain the corn and process in a food processor for 5 seconds. Place in a bowl with all of the other ingredients and mix well.

Cook in hot oil in a large frying pan, turning once, until golden brown. Drain on kitchen paper and serve garnished with coriander and sweet chilli sauce.

## GREEK LAMB AND LETTUCE STEW
**BAWLEY POINT GUEST HOUSE**

*1 large onion, peeled and chopped*
*2 tablespoons butter*
*1 kg lamb, cubed*
*1 cup hot water*
*salt and pepper, to taste*
*4 heads of lettuce, chopped*
*2 tablespoons parsley, chopped*
*1 tablespoon cornflour*
*3 eggs, separated*
*juice of 1 lemon*
*1 teaspoon chopped dill, to garnish*

Gently fry the onion in butter until transparent. Increase the heat, add the lamb and stir until sealed but not browned. Reduce the heat, add the water and salt and pepper and simmer gently for 1¼ hours, or until tender.

Add the lettuce and parsley and simmer for a further 5 minutes. Drain, reserving 1½ cups of the stock from the pan (if necessary, add water to make up the quantity). Set the lamb aside.

In a separate saucepan bring the stock to the boil. Stir in the cornflour and boil for 1 minute. Set aside.

Beat the egg whites until stiff peaks form. Add the yolks and beat until light and fluffy. Add the lemon juice. While beating, gradually pour in the thickened stock.

Return the sauce to a saucepan and cook gently only until the egg is cooked, being careful not to let the sauce boil.

Pour the sauce over the lamb and lettuce and stir through. Sprinkle with the dill and serve with mashed potato.

## STEAMED PERSIMMON AND RAISIN PUDDING

### BAWLEY POINT GUEST HOUSE

*1½ cups raisins*
*brandy*
*180 grams butter*
*1½ cups sugar*
*3 eggs*
*1½ teaspoons lemon juice*
*vanilla essence*
*1½ teaspoons cinnamon*
*1½ cups plain flour*
*5–6 persimmons, pulp only*
*3 teaspoons bicarbonate of soda*

SOAK THE raisins in brandy for a few hours.

Cream the butter and sugar, then add the eggs, lemon juice, vanilla essence, cinnamon, flour, persimmon pulp and bicarbonate of soda. Fold in the raisins. Transfer to a 3½ litre pudding bowl and boil for 3 hours. Serve with a brandy flavoured custard.

## FRESH PASTA WITH KERVELLA GOAT'S CHEESE AND WINTER GREENS

### LAMONT'S WINERY AND RESTAURANT

*2 bunches English spinach*
*1 cup fresh peas*
*fresh pasta (enough for 6 serves)*
*olive oil*
*4 cloves garlic, chopped*
*salt and pepper, to taste*
*3 fresh Kervella goat's cheese, roughly chopped*
*½ cup mixed herbs, chopped*
*pepper, extra to taste*

WASH THE spinach and spin dry. Chop roughly. Shell the peas and cook in boiling water for 5 minutes. Drain. Cook the pasta according to directions and drain. Keep warm.

Place the olive oil, garlic, salt and pepper and goat's cheese into a large pan and heat over medium heat. After 1 minute, add the peas, spinach and herbs and toss for a further 2 minutes.

Combine with the pasta. Divide the mixture into 6 pasta bowls and top with a sprinkling of pepper. Serves 6.

---

**LAMONT'S WINERY AND RESTAURANT**
Swan Valley,
Western Australia

•

*Fresh pasta with Kervella goat's cheese and winter greens*

•

*Beef fillet with roast vegetables and crispy onions*

•

*Rhubarb and orange roly poly*

## BEEF FILLET WITH ROAST VEGETABLES AND CRISPY ONIONS

**LAMONT'S WINERY AND RESTAURANT**

*2 tablespoons oil*
*½ butternut pumpkin, cubed*
*4 large cooked potatoes, roughly diced*
*sea salt and pepper, to taste*
*rosemary sprigs, to taste*
*2 red onions, cut into 8 pieces*
*1 large zucchini, cubed*
*3 red capsicums, roughly chopped*
*2 onions*
*oil, for frying*
*beef stock*
*6 pieces of good-quality beef fillet (around 180–200 grams each)*

Preheat the oven to 180°C. Put the oil on a large oven tray and warm in the oven. Place the pumpkin and potato on the tray and sprinkle with sea salt, pepper and rosemary. Place in the oven to cook, after 20 minutes, add the red onions, zucchini and capsicums and cook for a further 20 minutes.

Peel and halve the onions and shave finely. Pat dry to remove any moisture. Heat the oil over a high heat in a saucepan or deep fryer. Immerse the onions and cook until golden and crisp. Drain on kitchen paper and leave to cool.

Bring the beef stock to the boil in a saucepan, lower the heat and simmer until reduced by half and has a thick sauce consistency.

Cook the beef to your preference, rare, medium-rare or well done. Place one piece of beef on each serving plate. Arrange the vegetables on the plate and pour the stock sauce over the meat. Top with the crispy onions. Serves 6.

## RHUBARB AND ORANGE ROLY POLY

**LAMONT'S WINERY AND RESTAURANT**

*2 cups orange juice*
*1 cup sugar*
*180 grams butter*
*2¾ cups plain flour, sifted*
*4½ teaspoons baking powder*
*½ teaspoon salt*
*1 cup milk*
*2 cups rhubarb, cut in 1 cm pieces*
*1 cup orange chunks, skin and pith removed*
*⅓ cup castor sugar*
*½ teaspoon ground cinnamon*
*1 tablespoon butter, extra*

Combine the orange juice and sugar together in a pouring jug.

Rub the butter into the sifted flour, baking powder and salt. Add the milk to form a dough. Roll the dough on a board and spread the rhubarb and orange pieces evenly over the dough. Top with the castor sugar, cinnamon and dobs of extra butter.

Roll into a Swiss roll and cut into 3 cm thick rounds. Lay out on a greased baking tray, making sure all the edges are touching. Drizzle the orange juice over the top and bake at 200°C for 30–40 minutes.

---

ELLIMATTA GUEST HOUSE AND RESTAURANT, VICTORIA
*Gateau of Ellimatta smoked salmon, page 224*

*Winter*

**ELLIMATTA GUEST HOUSE AND RESTAURANT**
Central Victoria

•

*Gateau of Ellimatta smoked salmon*

•

*Breast of Kyneton pheasant*

•

*Date and ginger pudding*

Spoon out evenly onto six serving plates and serve with a scoop of vanilla ice-cream. Serves 6.

# GATEAU OF ELLIMATTA SMOKED SALMON

ELLIMATTA GUEST HOUSE AND RESTAURANT

*350 grams smoked salmon*
*Horseradish Cream*
*Russian caviar*
*2 hard-boiled egg yolks, sieved*
*150 ml thickened cream*
*1–2 tablespoons strained lemon juice*
*salt and pepper, to taste*
*1 continental cucumber, peeled, deseeded and finely sliced*
*3 teaspoons dill, finely chopped*
*salt and pepper*
*100 grams salad mix, washed*

Cut the salmon into 5 mm squares using a sharp knife, cutting small pieces at a time so as not to mash the salmon. Mix the salmon squares with just enough Horseradish Cream to bind it together.

Pack the salmon down into a 5 cm round scone cutter until it is level with the top. Gently push out of the cutter and onto a large plate. Smear the top with some more Horseradish Cream. Repeat until all of the mixture has been used.

Place a dot of Russian caviar in the centre of each round and sprinkle some of the sieved egg yolks around the base.

Place the cream in a bowl and whip to a soft but firm consistency. Add half the lemon juice and salt and pepper to taste. Check for flavour and add more lemon juice if needed.

Mix the cucumber, dill, salt and pepper and enough of the lemon cream to bind. Place at a 45° angle from the gateau, then place the salad at a 45° angle from the gateau in the opposite direction. Serves 6.

# HORSERADISH CREAM

*150 ml thickened cream*
*1–2 tablespoons grated horseradish purée*
*salt and pepper, to taste*

Place the cream in a bowl and whip to a soft but firm consistency. Add half of the horseradish purée and salt and pepper to taste. Check for flavour and add more horseradish if needed; the flavour should be mild, not hot.

# BREAST OF KYNETON PHEASANT

### ELLIMATTA GUEST HOUSE AND RESTAURANT

*3 x 1 kg whole pheasants*
*Pheasant Mousse*
*ghee or vegetable oil*
*salt and pepper, to taste*
*1 kg puff pastry*
*1 egg yolk*
*1 teaspoon milk*
*50 ml brandy*
*400 ml game jus, made from pheasant shanks*

BONE THE pheasants and cut the legs at the knee joints. Retain the thighs for the mousse and the shanks for the game jus. Remove the wing bones to the first joint and use these parts also for the game jus. Remove the meat from the wing bone nearest to the breast, leaving the breast meat intact. Leave the skin on the breasts.

Insert a sharp boning knife into the breasts near where the bone joins the flesh and push towards the front of the breasts, making sure not to push the knife through the surface. Bring the knife back under the surface along the edge to where the knife was originally inserted. Repeat on the opposite side of the breasts. Fill the cavities with Pheasant Mousse. Seal the hole with a toothpick pushed through the flesh. If the breasts have been punctured and the mousse comes through, patch the holes with toothpicks.

Place the breasts in a frying pan with a little ghee and seal over high heat. Season to taste with salt and pepper. Remove from the pan and place on kitchen paper. Chill for at least 1 hour. Once they are cold, remove all toothpicks.

Preheat the oven to 180°C. Roll out the puff pastry. Place the pheasant breasts skin side down on the pastry and cut around the breasts, making sure there is enough pastry to wrap them. Brush the edges of the pastry with the combined egg yolk and milk and bring the edges together, making sure that the bones are exposed. Turn the pastry parcels over so that the joins are hidden underneath, place on a greased baking tray and brush with the egg wash. Refrigerate for a while to rest the pastry. Cook for 20–25 minutes, rotating for an even colour.

Place the brandy in a saucepan and simmer over medium heat until it reduces by half. Add the game jus, increase the heat and bring to the boil, being careful that the brandy doesn't ignite.

Place the pheasant breasts on serving plates and serve with the brandy sauce and a selection of green vegetables.

## PHEASANT MOUSSE

*1 egg white*
*1 cup cream*

Remove the skin and bones from the thighs. Cut the meat into squares and place in a food processor and purée. Scrape down the sides of the food processor with a rubber spatula and purée again.

Add the egg white and process until combined. Place in a bowl and chill in the refrigerator for 30 minutes.

Remove from the refrigerator and place the bowl into a larger bowl that has a small amount of cold water and ice in it. Gradually add the cream with a wooden spoon, making sure that it has all combined before adding any more. Once the cream has all been added, pass the mousse through a mouille and chill. If you want an even finer mousse, you can pass it through a hair sieve. Once it is cold, add salt and pepper to taste and place in a piping bag with a plain tube attachment.

## DATE AND GINGER PUDDING
### ELLIMATTA GUEST HOUSE AND RESTAURANT

*190 grams chopped dates*
*225 ml water*
*¼ teaspoon ground cinnamon*
*¼ teaspoon vanilla essence*
*½ teaspoon baking powder*
*75 grams butter*
*160 grams sugar*
*2 eggs*
*140 grams plain flour*
*¾ teaspoon baking powder, extra*
*icing sugar*

Place the dates, water, cinnamon and vanilla in a saucepan. Bring to the boil over high heat, then add the baking powder. Remove from the heat and stand to one side.

Cream the butter and sugar together in a bowl. Stir in the eggs, one at a time. Add the flour and the baking powder, then combine with the date mixture.

Place in a 75 mm greased dariole mould, filling only three-quarters of the mould. Bake at 180°C for 20–30 minutes. Remove from the oven and rest for 5 minutes. Remove from the mould and level the tops with a sharp knife.

Place 3–4 teaspoons of Caramel Sauce on the centre of a large plate and spread out towards the edges. Place the puddings in the centre of the plate and dust with icing sugar. Serves 6.

## CARAMEL SAUCE

*250 grams castor sugar*
*500 ml cream*

Place the sugar in a heavy-based saucepan and stir over medium heat until the sugar has dissolved and the mixture is a caramel colour. At the same time, place the cream into another saucepan and bring to the boil. Once the sugar has caramelised, place the saucepan into the sink and very gradually add the cream. Be careful, because the mixture is very hot and will bubble up when the cream is first added.

ELLIMATTA GUEST HOUSE AND RESTAURANT, VICTORIA
*Date and ginger pudding*

*Winter*

**THE VALLEY COUNTRY HOME**
Tilba Tilba, Southern Coast, New South Wales

•

*Seafood chowder*

•

*Corn-fed squab breasts with its jus and buttermilk polenta, red cabbage and apple*

•

*Hot chocolate soufflé with blood orange and Grand Marnier ice-cream*

Return the cream and caramel mixture to the stove and bring back to the boil over a low heat. Dissolve any lumps of caramel. Pour the caramel through a chinois and allow to cool.

## SEAFOOD CHOWDER
### THE VALLEY COUNTRY HOME

*100 grams butter*
*2 medium brown onions, finely chopped*
*2 medium carrots, finely chopped*
*2 sticks celery, finely chopped*
*1 clove garlic, bruised*
*100 grams flour*
*2 litres fish stock*
*salt, to taste*
*pinch ground white pepper*
*500 ml milk*
*375 ml dry white wine*
*150 ml cream*
*1 kg fish fillets and/or seafood (John Dory, blue eye, oysters, hermit crab)*
*1 tablespoon parsley, finely chopped*
*1 tablespoon chives, finely chopped*

HEAT THE butter in a saucepan over high heat but do not brown. Add the onions, carrots, celery and garlic and sauté, stirring until the onions are clear. Add the flour and continue to stir for 3 minutes, or until cooked. Pour in the fish stock and beat the mixture with a whisk. Continue to stir until the soup is simmering, add the salt and pepper and simmer for 15 minutes. Ten minutes before serving, add the milk and simmer for 5 minutes.

Place the white wine and cream in a saucepan and bring to the boil. Add any fish or seafood that needs a little longer to cook (such as blue eye and crab). Turn off the heat and add the John Dory and oysters. Using a slotted spoon, place the just cooked seafood into the bottom of soup bowls, tip any liquid back into the saucepan with the fish stock mixture, stir, and serve a ladleful over each bowl of fish. Garnish with parsley and chives. Serves 8–10.

## CORN-FED SQUAB BREAST WITH ITS JUS AND BUTTERMILK POLENTA, RED CABBAGE AND APPLE
### THE VALLEY COUNTRY HOME

*squab (350 grams per serving)*
*1 clove garlic, chopped*
*6 shallots, chopped*
*2 medium carrots, roughly chopped*
*2 sticks celery, roughly chopped*
*3 sprigs thyme*
*2 bay leaves*
*250 ml dry red wine*
*salt and pepper, to taste*
*50 grams clarified butter*
*2 tablespoons balsamic vinegar*
*Buttermilk Polenta*
*Red Cabbage and Apple*

REMOVE THE legs and breasts from the squab. Skin the breasts. Chop the carcasse and legs in halves and put in a baking dish with the garlic, shallots, carrots and celery. Bake in a 250°C oven until brown, turning the bones and vegetables every 5 minutes.

Tip the contents of the baking dish into a pot and cover with water. Bring to a steady boil, add the thyme and bay leaves and simmer for 2–3 hours, remove any scum that comes to the surface.

While the stock is cooking, pulverise the bones and vegetables, extracting as much flavour as possible. Strain into a smaller pot and add the red wine. Cook over a medium heat until reduced by half and season. This is the jus. To add a little more richness to the colour of the jus, caramelise 2 tablespoons of sugar with enough water to cover and add to the jus before seasoning.

Place the clarified butter in a saucepan and melt over low heat. Slowly increase the heat, being careful not to brown the butter. As soon as it's sizzling hot, lay the squab breasts in the pan with the fillet side facing up. Cook gently for 2 minutes, turn and cook for another 2 to 3 minutes. Remove from the heat and let sit with a pan over the breasts for 10 minutes. Remove the breasts from the pan, add the balsamic vinegar and bring to the boil. Add to the jus.

To serve, pour the jus onto the plates, lay some Buttermilk Polenta on top and place the squab breasts on the polenta. Serve with Red Cabbage and Apple.

## BUTTERMILK POLENTA

*5 litres buttermilk, or 2.5 litres milk with 2.5 litres yoghurt*
*½ litre water*
*1 teaspoon salt*
*2 cups golden cornmeal*

Place the buttermilk, water and salt in a saucepan and cook over high heat until on the point of boiling. Reduce the heat to a simmer, then take a handful of cornmeal and pour it slowly into the pot, stirring continuously with a wooden spoon. Continue adding the cornmeal in a very thin stream (so as not to develop lumps) until it is all added.

Simmer, stirring, for 20 minutes or until the polenta pulls away from the sides of the pot. Wet a chopping board or clean bench and pour the polenta straight out onto it. Using wet hands, shape the polenta before it sets. Serve hot with melted butter.

## RED CABBAGE AND APPLE

*½ red cabbage*
*½ teaspoon salt*
*½ teaspoon pepper*
*2 tablespoons cider vinegar*
*2 tablespoons duck fat or butter*
*2 queen apples, sliced with skin on*
*⅓ cinnamon stick*
*3 cloves*
*1 tablespoon brown sugar*

Shred the cabbage and work the salt, pepper and cider vinegar through with your fingers.

Place the duck fat in a saucepan and melt over medium heat. Add the cabbage and simmer, stirring occasionally, for about 15 minutes or until nearly cooked.

Add the apples, cinnamon stick, cloves and brown sugar, stir, then transfer to a pottery casserole dish with a lid. Bake, covered, in a 180°C oven for 1 hour.

# HOT CHOCOLATE SOUFFLÉ WITH BLOOD ORANGE AND GRAND MARNIER ICE-CREAM

### THE VALLEY COUNTRY HOME

*1 cup best cooking chocolate*
*5 egg yolks*
*8 egg whites*
*butter*
*sugar*
*icing sugar*
*Blood Orange Grand Marnier Ice-cream*

MELT THE chocolate over a double boiler. Let cool for a few minutes, then stir in the egg yolks one at a time. Beat the egg whites until stiff peaks form, then fold through the chocolate mixture.

Wipe soufflé dishes with the butter, tip the sugar in and then shake it out. Gently spoon in the chocolate mixture and bake in a 180°C oven for 15–20 minutes.

Remove from the oven, dust with icing sugar and serve, plunging a scoop of ice-cold ice-cream into the soufflé at the table.

## BLOOD ORANGE AND GRAND MARNIER ICE-CREAM

*2 blood oranges*
*1 egg*
*125 grams castor sugar*
*300 ml cream*
*300 ml milk*
*50 ml Grand Marnier*

Juice the oranges and grate the rind of one of them.

Beat the egg and sugar together until thick and creamy. Add the orange juice and rind and continue beating. Add the cream and milk, blend well together, then add the Grand Marnier. Pour into an ice-cream maker, churn and freeze.

VUE GRAND HOTEL, VICTORIA
*Soupière of fruit of the sea with vegetables julienne, page 232*

*W*INTER

**VUE GRAND HOTEL**
Bellarine Peninsula,
Victoria

•

*Duck ravioli and black truffle in a wild mushroom fumet*

•

*Soupière of fruit of the sea with vegetables julienne*

•

*Chocolate lover's fantasy on banana coulis*

## DUCK RAVIOLI AND BLACK TRUFFLE IN A WILD MUSHROOM FUMET

### VUE GRAND HOTEL

*250 grams duck breast*
*250 grams free-range chicken*
*24 lasagne sheets*
*1 egg, for eggwash*
*4 morrels*
*150 grams dried mushrooms*
*500 ml bouillon*
*50 grams chanterelle*
*250 grams shiitake mushrooms*
*150 grams abalone mushrooms*
*250 grams leek, julienned*
*250 grams carrot, julienned*
*black truffles, to garnish*

CHOP THE duck breast and chicken into small cubes and place into a bowl with the egg. Put in the freezer for 15 minutes.

Blanch the lasagne sheets in boiling water then set aside to cool. Place a portion of the duck and chicken mixture on the lasagne sheets and seal with eggwash to form ravioli (there will be three ravioli per person).

Place the morrels and dried mushrooms in a saucepan with the bouillon, bring to the boil and cook until tender. This is the fumet.

Sauté the chanterelle and shiitake and abalone mushrooms in a frying pan. Add the morrel fumet, bring to a simmer and cook until reduced. Blanch the leek and carrot in boiling water, and blanch the ravioli in boiling water.

Arrange the leek and carrot on serving plates. Place three ravioli on top, then spoon over the fumet. Garnish with a black truffle. Serves 8.

## SOUPIÈRE OF FRUIT OF THE SEA WITH VEGETABLES JULIENNE

### VUE GRAND HOTEL

*250 grams carrots*
*250 grams celery*
*250 grams leek*
*500 ml crayfish fumet*
*500 ml fish fumet*
*500 ml tomato sauce*
*500 ml cream*
*16 oysters*
*16 prawns*
*38 scallops*
*400 grams fish*
*500 grams puff pastry*

CUT THE carrots, celery and leek into juliennes and blanch in boiling water.

Place the crayfish fumet, fish fumet, tomato sauce and cream in a saucepan, bring to the boil, reduce the heat and simmer until reduced by one quarter.

Sauté each seafood separately in a frying pan and add to the sauce, gently folding through each time.

Divide the mixture into eight and place into individual baking dishes. Place the julienned vegetables on top.

Cut the puff pastry to fit the dishes, with a 1 cm overhang, then place on top of each dish to form a lid. Cook at 200°C for 15 minutes or until a light golden brown.

Serve with a separate plate of seasonal vegetables. Serves 8.

# CHOCOLATE LOVER'S FANTASY ON BANANA COULIS

### VUE GRAND HOTEL

*175 grams unsalted butter*
*250 grams couverture chocolate*
*5 egg yolks*
*75 grams plain flour*
*100 grams sugar*
*4 egg whites*
*500 ml milk*
*3 bananas*
*1 teaspoon cinnamon*
*1 vanilla stick*
*100 grams sugar*

THIS RECIPE must be prepared two days in advance. Melt the butter and chocolate together in a saucepan. Whisk the egg yolks, flour and sugar together in a bowl, and combine with the chocolate.

Beat the egg whites until stiff peaks form, then fold into the chocolate mixture. Rest in the refrigerator for two days.

Brush eight brioche moulds with butter and sugar. Fill with the chocolate mixture, then bake in the oven at 180°C for 12 minutes.

Place the milk, bananas, cinnamon, vanilla and sugar in a saucepan, bring to the boil then blend until it is a creamy sauce.

Remove the baked mousses from the moulds. Spoon the sauce onto serving plates and place the mousse on top. Serves 8.

# BROCCOLI TIMBALE WITH CHAMPAGNE AND CHIVE SAUCE

### THORN PARK COUNTRY HOUSE

*500–600 grams broccoli*
*150–200 grams cream cheese*
*4 eggs*
*nutmeg*
*chives, chopped*
*salt and pepper, to taste*
*Champagne Chive Sauce*

CUT THE broccoli into small pieces and wash well. Steam for a few minutes or until just tender, then set aside to cool. Place in a food processor with the cream cheese and blend until smooth. Add the eggs, nutmeg, chives and salt and pepper.

Butter individual moulds and pour some of the mixture in. Place into a water bath or bain marie and cook in a 175°C oven for 30 minutes or until firm. Leave for a few minutes, then invert onto a serving plate and serve with the Champagne Chive Sauce. Serves 8.

---

**THORN PARK COUNTRY HOUSE**
Clare Valley,
South Australia

•

*Broccoli timbale with champagne and chive sauce*

•

*Tagine of kid with prunes and pickled lemons*

•

*Cheese custards with red capsicum purée*

•

*Apricot bread and butter pudding*

## CHAMPAGNE CHIVE SAUCE

*125 ml white wine*
*zest of 1 lemon*
*500 ml cream*
*ground pepper, to taste*
*salt, to taste*
*2 tablespoons chives, chopped*
*250 ml champagne*

Place the white wine and lemon zest in a saucepan and reduce over a low heat. When most of the liquid has evaporated, add the cream and reduce by at least half. Watch this stage carefully as the cream will boil over. Add the pepper and salt and chives. The sauce may be prepared to this stage a few hours ahead.

Just before serving, return the cream to the boil and then pour over the champagne (the sauce will froth up and lighten). Serve immediately.

## TAGINE OF KID WITH PRUNES AND PICKLED LEMONS

### THORN PARK COUNTRY HOUSE

*¼ cup olive oil*
*1½–2 kg kid, trimmed and cut into 4 cm cubes*
*4–5 medium onions, sliced*
*1 teaspoon turmeric*
*½ teaspoon cinnamon*
*pinch saffron threads*
*1–2 chillies, chopped*
*1 tablespoon ginger, chopped*
*3–4 bay leaves*
*parsley stalks*
*4–5 cups rich chicken stock*
*4 potatoes, thickly sliced*
*2–3 turnips, cut into quarters or smaller*
*8 carrots, cut into 5 cm slices, or 16 baby carrots*
*18–24 prunes, pitted*
*Moroccan-style Preserved Lemon slices*
*salt and pepper, to taste*
*Couscous*
*Harissa Sauce*
*parsley or coriander, chopped, to garnish*

Heat the olive oil in a saucepan over high heat. Sauté the kid in the oil until browned on all sides. Remove the kid and set aside.

Add the onions to the pan and sauté for 2–3 minutes. Mix in the spices and cook over medium heat for a few minutes to release the flavours. Return the meat to the pan and pour over the stock. Return the mixture to the boil, reduce and simmer for 45 minutes.

Add the potatoes, turnips and carrots and cook for a further 30 minutes. The meat should be tender and well flavoured. Add the prunes and lemon slices, using the peel only as the flesh can be salty and sour. Season with the salt and pepper.

Place a mound of Couscous onto warm serving plates and spoon over some of the meat, making sure that you divide the vegetables equally between the plates. Ladle over some Harissa Sauce or serve it separately in a sauce boat. Garnish with the parsley or coriander.

*Thorn Park Country House, South Australia*
*Tagine of kid with prunes and pickled lemons*

*W*INTER

## COUSCOUS

water or stock (or half-and-half)  
1 box instant couscous  
butter or oil  
salt and pepper, to taste

Bring the water or stock to the boil, pour in the couscous and stir well. Remove from the heat and cover. Leave for 5–10 minutes, then stir in the butter, salt and pepper. Reheat in a microwave.

## HARISSA SAUCE

1 tablespoon harissa or hot chilli paste  
125 ml meat stock  
juice and zest of 1 lemon  
1 tablespoon olive oil  
1–2 tablespoons coriander, chopped

Place the harissa and stock in a saucepan and mix well. Bring to the boil and cook for 2–3 minutes. Add the remaining ingredients and cook until heated through.

## MOROCCAN-STYLE PRESERVED LEMONS

12–14 lemons  
salt  
whole peppercorns  
4–5 whole garlic cloves, peeled  
6 bay leaves  
2 cinnamon quills  
paprika  
vegetable or nut oil

Cut the lemons in half lengthwise and then cut into quarters or thirds. Sprinkle well with salt and leave to drain for 24 hours in a plastic or stainless steel colander. Wipe off any obvious salt and pack the lemons into large clean sterilised jars, mixing in the spices and sprinkling each layer with paprika. Cover the lemons with oil and seal. Leave for at least 3 to 4 weeks before using. The lemons will darken with age but they should keep for some time. Remove the flesh before eating.

## CHEESE CUSTARDS WITH RED CAPSICUM PURÉE

### THORN PARK COUNTRY HOUSE

*Red Capsicum Sauce:*  
3–4 red capsicums, charred and seeded  
1 tablespoon tomato paste  
zest and juice of 1 lemon  
2 tablespoons olive oil  
salt and ground pepper, to taste  
150 grams soft blue cheese  
250 grams cream cheese  
3–4 eggs  
25 grams unsalted butter, melted  
100 grams sour cream  
ground pepper, cayenne pepper and salt, to taste

To make the sauce, chop the capsicums and place into a food processor with the tomato paste, lemon zest and juice and olive oil.

Purée until smooth and no lumps remain (sieve if necessary). Add the salt and pepper.

Bring the cheeses to room temperature, then blend in a food processor until smooth. Add the eggs, butter and sour cream and blend well. Season to taste, adding salt only if needed.

Butter eight ½ cup capacity moulds and pour the mixture in. Cook in a bain-marie at 165°C for 20–30 minutes or until set. Let stand for 10–15 minutes. Up-end onto entrée plates and spoon a little of the warm sauce around.

This dish can be served as a cheese course with home-made cheese straws and cheese biscuits. Serves 8 as an entreé.

## APRICOT BREAD AND BUTTER PUDDING
### THORN PARK COUNTRY HOUSE

½ cup dried apricots, shredded
60 ml dark rum
5 eggs
½ cup castor sugar
vanilla extract
pinch cinnamon
pinch ground cloves
zest of 2 oranges and 1 lemon, finely chopped
750 ml cream
250 ml milk
1 apricot fruit loaf
1 cup soft brown sugar
dessicated coconut (optional)
crème anglaise
rich cream

SOAK THE apricots in the rum for a few minutes. Place the eggs, castor sugar, vanilla extract, spices and citrus zest together in a bowl and beat well. Beat in the cream and milk. Fold in the rum and apricots.

Slice the fruit loaf and place in a single layer in a buttered baking dish. Sprinkle over some of the brown sugar, then ladle over some of the custard mixture. Cover with more fruit loaf, sugar and custard. Continue layering until all of the fruit loaf and custard have been used. Sprinkle over some coconut if desired and bake at 160–170°C for 25–35 minutes or until set and golden in colour. Serve with crème anglaise and rich cream.

## FLUTES OF BROOKLAND VALLEY
Margaret River Region, Western Australia

•

*Vegetable Pistou with duck confit*

•

*Jerusalem artichoke and trout ravioli with sage, lemon and brown butter*

•

*Braised Margaret River venison shanks with soft polenta and creamed fennel and leeks*

•

*Chocolate soufflé with mascarpone gelato*

# VEGETABLE PISTOU WITH DUCK CONFIT

### FLUTES OF BROOKLAND VALLEY

*1 small onion, peeled and diced*
*100 grams carrots, sliced*
*100 grams celeriac, peeled and cut into 2 cm square slices*
*100 grams leek, sliced*
*4 sprigs thyme*
*30 ml olive oil*
*salt and pepper, to taste*
*2 litres vegetable stock*
*100 grams haricot beans, cooked*
*100 grams flageolet beans, cooked*
*100 grams pumpkin, flesh cut into 1 cm cubes*
*100 grams kohlrabi, peeled, cut into 8 and finely sliced*
*100 grams zucchini, trimmed and cut into thin rounds*
*100 grams cabbage, finely shredded*
*2 tablespoons parsley, finely chopped*
*Duck Confit*

Sweat the onion, carrots, celeriac, leek and thyme together in the olive oil for a few minutes. Season lightly. Stir in half of the stock and the haricot and flageolet beans and bring to the boil. Add the pumpkin and kohlrabi and cook for 5 minutes before adding the zucchini and cabbage and the remaining stock. Simmer for 15 to 20 minutes or until the vegetables are tender but still retain a little texture. Serve with the Duck Confit and garnish with the parsley.

## DUCK CONFIT

*55 grams salt*
*4 duck legs*
*4 sprigs thyme*
*2 bay leaves*
*1 teaspoon black pepper*
*1.5 kg duck fat*

Scatter the salt in a layer in a large metal tray. Rub the thyme, bay leaves and pepper into the duck legs and place on top of the salt. Scatter the salt and refrigerate overnight. Pat the duck pieces dry.

    Melt the duck fat in a large pot. Immerse the duck legs, bring to the boil and immediately lower to a simmer. Cook for 2½ hours. The meat will start to come away from the lower point of the drumstick when it is cooked. Remove from the heat and cool. Transfer the duck pieces to a plate and chill the duck fat, eventually freezing it for use at a later date. Shred the duck meat.

---

ADAMS OF NORTH RIDING RESTAURANT, VICTORIA
*Pot-roasted squab with a truffle pie and port wine and balsamic jus, page 180*

*W*INTER

239

# JERUSALEM ARTICHOKE AND TROUT RAVIOLI WITH SAGE, LEMON AND BROWN BUTTER

## FLUTES OF BROOKLAND VALLEY

240 grams strong plain flour
1 pinch salt
3 eggs
1 tablespoon olive oil
40 grams semolina
1 egg, extra
1 bunch English spinach, washed, blanched and chopped
1 large trout, filleted, boned, skinned and diced into 1 cm squares
200 grams Jerusalem artichokes, steamed, peeled and puréed
100 grams unsalted butter, finely diced
4 sage leaves, finely julienned
juice of 1 lemon
lemon wedges, sage sprigs and Parmesan cheese (optional)

Place the flour and salt in a food processor, turn the machine on and add the eggs one at a time until the mixture is cohesive but not tacky. Blend in the olive oil. Knead the mixture into a ball, wrap and chill for at least 1 hour.

Scatter the semolina over a work surface. Divide the dough in half, then roll both pieces thinly over the semolina to about the same size. Beat the extra egg and brush over one half of the pasta dough, then mark lightly with a round 8 cm cutter.

Combine the spinach, trout and artichokes in a bowl and spoon 1 heaped teaspoon of this filling onto each lightly etched circle. Lay the second piece of pasta dough on top and press lightly. Cut through both layers of dough around the mounds of filling, to make separate ravioli. Press the edges together well to seal. Cook the ravioli for about 4-5 minutes or until al dente in a large pan of boiling salted water. Place on a serving plate and keep warm.

Heat the butter in a saucepan, add the sage leaves and cook until the butter is bubbling and just slightly brown. Add the lemon juice and nap over the plated ravioli. Serve with lemon wedges, sage sprigs and Parmesan cheese.

# BRAISED MARGARET RIVER VENISON SHANKS WITH SOFT POLENTA AND CREAMED FENNEL AND LEEKS

### FLUTES OF BROOKLAND VALLEY

*2 kg venison shanks, cut into osso bucco steaks with bone*
*plain flour*
*clarified butter*
*1 red onion, roughly chopped*
*2 litres hot venison stock*
*¼ butternut pumpkin, roughly chopped*
*100 grams cooked borlotti beans or cannelloni beans, cooked*
*salt and pepper, to taste*
*½ leek, finely sliced*
*¼ fennel bulb, finely diced*
*salt and pepper, to taste*
*30 ml white wine*
*50 ml chicken stock*
*50 ml cream*
*Polenta*
*4 mint leaves, julienned*
*2 Roma tomatoes, peeled, seeded and diced*

COAT THE veal shanks in flour then seal over high heat in a frying pan with the butter. Remove the shanks from the pan, add the onion and cook for 2 minutes. Add a little more flour to soak up the fat, then slowly pour in the veal stock, stirring constantly. Bring to the boil then remove from the heat. Skim the fat from the top.

Place the veal shanks, pumpkin and beans in a baking dish and cover with the gravy. Season and cover, cook at 190°C for 2 hours.

Sweat the leek, fennel bulb and salt and pepper in a saucepan, then add the white wine, chicken stock and cream and cook over a medium heat until heated through.

Serve the shanks set on one side of a bowl with the Polenta on the other side. Top the Polenta with the sauce and garnish with the mint leaves and tomato.

## POLENTA

*500 ml chicken stock*
*250 grams coarse polenta*
*200 ml milk*
*salt and pepper, to taste*

Mix half of the chicken stock with the polenta to make a paste. Place the other half of the stock in a saucepan and bring to the boil. Whisk into the paste, then return to the saucepan with the milk and salt and pepper. Cook over medium heat for 10 minutes, stirring constantly.

## CHOCOLATE SOUFFLÉ WITH MASCARPONE GELATO
### FLUTES OF BROOKLAND VALLEY

90 grams chocolate
60 grams granulated sugar
3 tablespoons milk
2 egg yolks
3 egg whites
1½ tablespoons granulated sugar, extra
Mascarpone Gelato
confectioner's sugar

In a double boiler, melt the chocolate then add the sugar and milk and beat until well combined. Remove from the heat and allow the mixture to cool for 5 minutes. Add the egg yolks, beating constantly. Whip the egg whites until very stiff peaks form, adding the extra sugar halfway through. Fold the egg whites into the chocolate mixture.

Pour the mixture into a buttered and sugared soufflé mould and bake at 180°C for 20 minutes. Serve immediately with the Mascarpone Gelato and sprinkle with confectioner's sugar.

## MASCARPONE GELATO

190 ml milk
¾ cup cream
1 teaspoon vanilla essence
6 egg yolks
½ cup sugar
freshly grated nutmeg, to taste
1½ cups mascarpone

Heat the milk, cream and vanilla essence in a saucepan until just under boiling point. Beat the egg yolks and sugar in a bowl until the sugar is almost dissolved. Whisk half of the hot cream mixture into the yolk mixture, then pour all the yolk mixture back into the remaining hot cream, stirring constantly. Return the saucepan to a low heat and cook, stirring gently, until the mixture thickens slightly and coats the back of a spoon. Remove immediately from the heat and add the freshly grated nutmeg, remembering that the flavour will not be as intense when it is frozen.

Strain the mixture into a clean bowl and set aside to cool. Refrigerate until very cold, then stir in the mascarpone and freeze in an ice-cream machine. Transfer the gelato to a covered container and store in the freezer until required.

---

SUNNYBRAE COUNTRY RESTAURANT, VICTORIA
*Pot of Portarlington mussels and saffron,
Crepinette of boned oxtail and beef cheek with glazed turnips and swedes,
page 244*

WINTER

## SUNNYBRAE COUNTRY RESTAURANT
Southern Coast, Victoria

•

*Pot of Portarlington mussels and saffron*

•

*Crepinette of boned oxtail and beef cheek with glazed turnips and swedes*

•

*Hungarian chocolate walnut cake with Borsodo (spicy Zabaglione)*

# POT OF PORTARLINGTON MUSSELS AND SAFFRON

### SUNNYBRAE COUNTRY RESTAURANT

*2 kg of black cultivated mussels*
*2 leeks, finely julienned*
*2 cloves garlic, finely chopped*
*2 small carrots, finely julienned*
*1 stick celery, finely julienned*
*olive oil*
*150 ml good-quality riesling*
*150 ml Noilly Prat Vermouth*
*1 bay leaf*
*pinch fennel seeds*
*pepper, to taste*
*good pinch saffron powder or threads crushed in a mortar*
*2 drops Tabasco sauce or pinch of fresh chillies*

WASH AND debeard the mussels under cold running water. Set aside to drain in a colander. Sauté the vegetables in a pan with a little olive oil for 2 minutes. Add the remaining ingredients and cook for 1 minute. Add the mussels and cook, covered with a tight-fitting lid, over a high heat for 3 minutes or until the mussels have opened. Be careful not to overcook the mussels as they will toughen.

At Sunnybrae we serve this dish in the pot in which it was cooked, straight to the table or in a large serving bowl. Be sure to have a ladle and soup spoons as the remaining liquor is a highlight of the dish (the shells are often used as a spoon at the end).

# CREPINETTE OF BONED OXTAIL AND BEEF CHEEK WITH GLAZED TURNIPS AND SWEDES

### SUNNYBRAE COUNTRY RESTAURANT

*2 onions, finely chopped*
*2 leeks, finely chopped*
*2 carrots, finely chopped*
*2 sticks celery, finely chopped*
*2 oxtails*
*flour*
*1 kg beef cheek, well trimmed*
*salt and pepper, to taste*
*400 ml beef stock (optional but desirable) or water*
*200 grams crepinette, well washed*
*small piece smoked bacon*
*18 small turnips, peeled*
*3 small swedes, peeled and cut into quarters*
*6 slices smoked pork fat (optional)*
*4 cloves garlic, finely chopped*
*¼ hot chilli, chopped*
*150 ml good-quality red wine or water*

PLACE THE onions, leeks, carrots and celery in a heat-proof baking dish. Dust the oxtails with flour and brown over high heat, remove from the pan and brown the smoked pork fat with the garlic. Deglaze the pan with red wine. Place the oxtail in the baking dish with the vegetables, with the cheek in one piece on top in the baking dish. Season lightly and add the beef stock until it reaches halfway up the sides of the baking dish. Seal tightly with foil and bake for about 3½ hours or until the meat falls off the bone. Check after 2 hours to see that it has not cooked dry, and add more stock or water if necessary. Remove from the oven when cooked.

When cool enough to handle, remove the oxtail and cheek from the dish and strain the remaining liquid, but do not discard the vegetables or stock. Remove the meat from the bone of the oxtail and cheek and form into six even serves.

Combine the oxtail meat with the braised vegetables in the proportion of two-thirds meat and one-third vegetables and form into the shape of large meatballs. Taste and season with sea salt and freshly ground black pepper if desired. Cut the crepinette into 10 cm squares and layer the bacon, cheek and oxtail on it. Carefully wrap the mixture in the crepinette and place on a baking tray.

Remove the fat from the stock (this is easily done if it is placed in the freezer for 30 minutes—the fat will sit on top and solidify). Add the turnips and swedes to the baking dish with the stock and bake, uncovered, for about 15 minutes or until the turnips and swedes are cooked. The resulting sauce should be unctuous and delicious. Serve with mashed potato to soak up the juices. Serves 6.

## HUNGARIAN CHOCOLATE WALNUT CAKE WITH BORSODO (SPICY ZABAGLIONE)

### SUNNYBRAE COUNTRY RESTAURANT

*9 large eggs, separated*
*250 grams castor sugar*
*1 teaspoon finely ground or instant coffee*
*juice of ½ a lemon*
*1 heaped teaspoon grated lemon rind*
*300 grams walnuts, ground*
*4 tablespoons breadcrumbs*
*3 tablespoons Kirsch or rum*
*Chocolate Cream*
*walnuts, ground, extra*
*Borsodo*

COMBINE THE egg yolks, sugar, coffee, lemon juice and lemon rind in a bowl and beat well. Whip the egg whites until stiff peaks form, then fold in the walnuts and breadcrumbs. Fold the egg white mixture into the egg yolk mixture.

Pre-heat the oven to 200°C. Place the mixture in a greased cake tin and cook for 5 minutes. Lower the heat to 180°C and cook for 40 minutes or until the cake is cooked. Remove from the oven and cool on a rack. Moisten with the Kirsch.

Spread the Chocolate Cream over the cake, with a thick layer on top. Decorate with ground walnuts and serve with the Borsodo and strong coffee.

**DEAR FRIENDS GARDEN RESTAURANT**
Swan Valley, Western Australia

- Oyster and Guinness soup
- Beetroot ravioli
- Kangaroo and venison pie
- A date with a pudding

## CHOCOLATE CREAM

3 eggs
375 grams dark chocolate, chopped
250 grams butter
3 tablespoons Kirsch or rum

Beat the eggs well over a bowl of hot water, whisking until the mixture rises and thickens. Remove from the heat and add the chocolate, butter and Kirsch, mixing it into a smooth cream. Set aside to cool.

## BORSODO

3 egg yolks
20 grams castor sugar
tiny pinch cinnamon
tiny pinch nutmeg
tiny pinch black pepper
juice of ½ lemon
150 ml sweet Hungarian Tokai

Whisk the egg yolks and sugar in a bowl until white and the sugar has lost its graininess. Add the spices, lemon juice and Tokai. Whisk over lightly boiling water until a light, airy, creamy foam is formed. Serve immediately.

## OYSTER AND GUINNESS SOUP
### DEAR FRIENDS GARDEN RESTAURANT

30 grams butter, softened
40 grams plain flour
12 x 15 grams fresh mushrooms
12 fresh oysters, beards removed
75 grams butter, extra
900 ml veal stock
150 ml Guinness beer
120 ml cream

Mix the butter and flour into a smooth paste. Clean the mushrooms and carefully twist off the stalks without damaging the caps. Thinly spread the inside of the caps with the butter mixture. Insert an oyster into each mushroom cap and cover with the rest of the butter mixture. Refrigerate for 1 hour. Slice.

Heat the extra butter in a frying pan and lightly fry the mushroom slices. Pour in the veal stock and Guinness, heat until almost boiling then thicken with the cream. Serves 6.

---

SUNNYBRAE COUNTRY RESTAURANT, VICTORIA
*Hungarian chocolate walnut cake with Borsodo (spicy Zabaglione), page 245*

*Winter*

247

## BEETROOT RAVIOLI

### DEAR FRIENDS GARDEN RESTAURANT

*120 grams fetta cheese*
*blanched orange rind, to taste*
*salt and pepper, to taste*
*60 grams beetroot powder*
*225 ml water*
*450 grams flour*
*½ teaspoon salt*
*75 ml oil*
*eggwash*

*15 grams butter*
*30 grams green asparagus spears*
*60 grams smoked cheese, grated*
*2 egg yolks*
*pinch cayenne pepper*
*25 ml cream*
*250 ml béchamel sauce*
*salt and pepper, extra, to taste*
*smoked cheese, extra, grated*

PLACE THE fetta cheese, orange rind and salt and pepper in a bowl and stir well. Mix the beetroot powder and water together. Sift the flour and salt and combine with the beetroot mixture add the oil until it forms a pliable dough. Roll out into two very thin rectangles. Lay one sheet on a flat surface and, using a plain piping tube, pipe the fetta cheese mixture on it in rows 2 cm apart. Eggwash the edges of the pastry and lay the second rectangle on top. Cut between the fetta cheese rows with a ravioli cutter or small round cutter. Cook the ravioli for 15 minutes in boiling water, drain and toss in the butter.

Blanch the asparagus spears and cut into small dice. Combine with the smoked cheese, egg yolks, cayenne pepper and cream. Place the mixture in a saucepan with the béchamel sauce, season with the extra salt and pepper and cook over medium heat until reduced to a sauce consistency. Coat the ravioli with the sauce and sprinkle over the extra smoked cheese. Serves 4 to 6.

## KANGAROO AND VENISON PIE

### DEAR FRIENDS GARDEN RESTAURANT

*400 grams venison fillet, diced*
*400 grams kangaroo fillet, diced*
*100 grams mushrooms, halved*
*150 grams butter*
*30 grams plain flour*
*200 grams button onions, peeled*
*10 grams mixed herbs*
*50 ml red wine*
*300 ml demi-glace*

*15 grams parsley, chopped*
*salt and pepper, to taste*
*1 litre brown stock*
*puff pastry*
*eggwash*
*capsicum, chopped chives,*
*   chopped zucchini and fine*
*   beans, to garnish*

QUICKLY TOSS the venison, kangaroo and mushrooms in the butter. Drain, mix with the flour and cook for 2–3 minutes. Add the onions, mixed herbs, red wine, demi-glace, parsley and salt and pepper. Place in a round baking dish and cover with the stock. Top with puff pastry cut to fit and design a motif on top. Egg wash the top of the pastry and bake at 190°C for 1¾ hours. Serve garnished with the capsicum, chives, zucchini and beans. Serves 4.

# A DATE WITH A PUDDING
## DEAR FRIENDS GARDEN RESTAURANT

*170 grams dates, pitted and chopped*
*300 ml water*
*1 teaspoon bicarbonate of soda*
*60 grams butter*
*170 grams castor sugar*
*2 eggs*
*170 grams self-raising flour*
*1/2 teaspoon vanilla essence*
*200 grams brown sugar*
*125 ml thickened cream*
*130 grams butter, extra*
*½ teaspoon vanilla essence*
*King Isalnd cream*
*mint*
*orange julienne*

THOROUGHLY grease an 18 x 28 cm (or smaller) cake tin. Place the dates in a saucepan, pour the water over and bring to the boil. Remove from the heat, add the bicarbonate of soda and set aside.

Cream the butter and castor sugar together and add the eggs one at a time, beating well after each addition. Gently fold in the flour. Combine with the date mixture and vanilla essence, then pour into the prepared tin. Bake in the centre of a 160°C oven for 30–40 minutes or until cooked when tested with a skewer.

Place the brown sugar, cream and extra butter in a saucepan. Bring to the boil, add the vanilla essence, reduce the heat and simmer for 3 minutes.

Pour a little sauce over the warm pudding and return to the oven for 2–3 minutes so that the sauce soaks in and the top bubbles to a golden brown colour. Cut into squares and serve with King Island cream, mint and orange julienne. For a nice touch, feather the sauce with a pattern of chocolate sauce and vanilla anglaise. Serves 6 to 8.

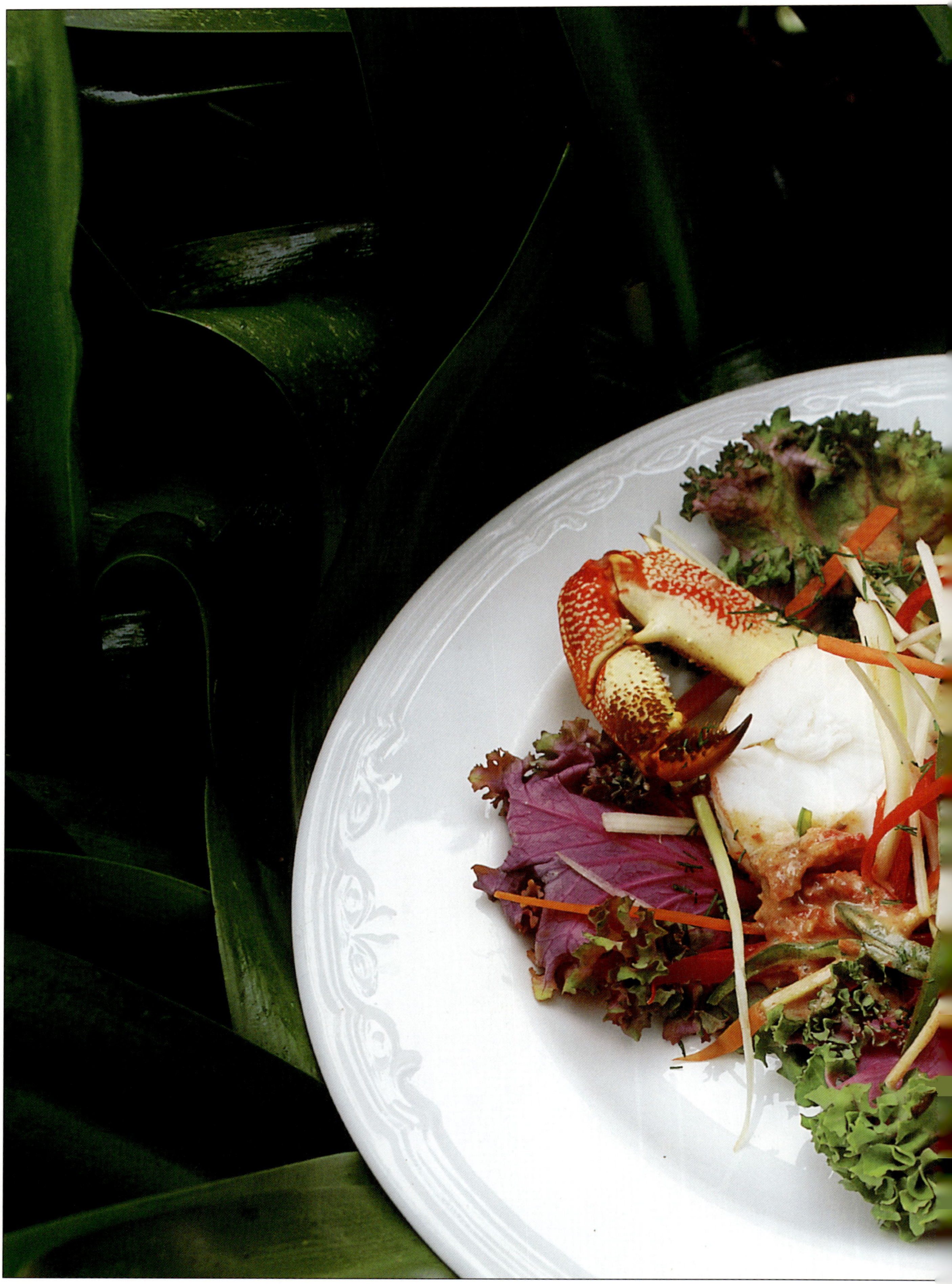

# Spring

**THE URAIDLA ARISTOLOGIST**
Adelaide Hills,
South Australia

•

*Artichokes Barigoule*

•

*Lamb chops with sorrel sauce*

•

*Raised gooseberry tart*

## ARTICHOKES BARIGOULE

### THE URAIDLA ARISTOLOGIST

*6 large artichokes*
*water*
*1 tablespoon lemon juice*
*1 lemon, halved*
*250 grams mushrooms*
*6 anchovy fillets*
*200 grams ham, chopped*
*pepper*
*200 ml olive oil*
*1 carrot, sliced*
*1 onion, sliced*
*6 cloves garlic, peeled*
*1 sprig thyme*
*1 bay leaf*
*400 ml dry white wine*

TO PREPARE the artichokes, cut off the stem, peel it thickly and leave in acidulated water (water and lemon juice). Snap off and discard the two outside rows of hard leaves. With kitchen scissors, snip off the pointed end of each leaf. Rub the artichoke with the cut half of the lemon and put in the bowl of acidulated water. Lift out the artichokes one at a time, and with a sharp teaspoon dig out the centre core of leaves and scrape free the tough fibrous material lining the heart. (young artichokes will not require this).

To prepare the stuffing, chop the mushrooms finely and chop the anchovy fillets to a paste. Combine with the chopped ham and mix well. Add pepper to taste. Stuff the hollowed out centre of the artichokes as well as behind the leaves with the stuffing.

Pour the olive oil into an enamelled baking dish. Lightly colour the carrot and onion in the hot oil. Place the stuffed artichokes and their stems into the baking dish, scatter around the whole garlic cloves, the thyme and bay leaf, and pour over the white wine to half-way up the sides of the artichokes.

Bring the liquid to simmering point, then adjust to simmer gently. After about 20 minutes, test to see if a fine skewer will pierce the artichokes easily right to the centre. When the artichokes are cooked, garnish with the onion and carrots from the braise.

## LAMB CHOPS WITH SORREL SAUCE

### THE URAIDLA ARISTOLOGIST

*12 lamb cutlets about*
  *800 grams each*
*120 grams sorrel*
*100 grams butter*
*100 ml dry white wine*
*100 ml veal stock (optional)*
*400 ml double cream*
*juice of ½ lemon*
*salt*
*freshly ground black pepper*
*fresh mint leaves*

IF YOU LIKE, trim the chops of all fat and connecting tissue. Scrape clean the ends of the bones with a small knife. Keep the cutlets in a cool place.

Remove the stalks of the sorrel and wash and drain the leaves. Shred the sorrel leaves into very fine strips. Set aside.

Heat 30 grams of butter in a pan. Put in the lamb cutlets and brown them on both sides; when they are pink in the middle or done to how you like them, transfer to a serving dish.

Pour off the fat from the pan, and set over a low heat. Put in 1 tablespoon of butter and the sorrel and sweat gently for a few minutes. Add the white wine, reduce it by half, then pour in the veal stock if you are using it, and the cream. Cook for 4 to 5 minutes, then stir in the remaining butter, a little at a time, and add a few drops of lemon juice. Season to taste. Pour the sauce over the lamb cutlets and snip the mint over the top.

# RAISED GOOSEBERRY TART
## THE URAIDLA ARISTOLOGIST

⅓ cup milk, plus milk for egg wash
1 envelope of instant yeast
2 cups plain flour, sifted
4 tablespoons castor sugar
9 tablespoons unsalted butter, cut into small bits
½ teaspoon salt
2 eggs plus one yolk for wash
1 kg gooseberries
2 tablespoons water
600 grams sugar
rich cream

GENTLY HEAT the milk until it feels just warm to the touch of the fingertip, then stir the dried yeast into it and leave to develop and dissolve. Assemble in a large mixing bowl the sifted flour, castor sugar, butter and salt. Work the ingredients together with the tips of the fingers, or mix these ingredients in the food processor. Add the eggs, lightly beaten, with water, plus the warm milk-yeast mixture. The dough should be kept between 20°C and 25°C. (At a warmer temperature, the butter would melt and ooze out of the dough.) Leave to rise for 3 hours, during which time it will double or triple in bulk, then stir down with a wooden spoon, roll into a ball, cover, and leave to refrigerate at least 4 hours, or preferably overnight.

When chilled, roll out the dough to fit a buttered 25 cm springform pan or flan ring, then leave it to rise another 2 hours, again at a temperature of 20°C to 25°C. Shortly before the end of the 2 hour rising time, preheat the oven to 200°C. Bake blind at 120°C (with aluminium foil and dried pulses). Remove foil and pulses after approximately 10 minutes. Lower the temperature to 110°C. Brush the sides with the egg yolk and milk wash and continue baking for approximately another 10 minutes or until pastry is lightly golden.

Wash, top and tail the gooseberries. Place in a poaching pan covered with water and add the sugar. Poach until tender and lift

**CHARDONNAY LODGE**
Coonawarra,
South Australia

•

*Scallop and Penola trout with fried ravioli and a tomato and capsicum coulis*

•

*Loin of Tatiana lamb with macadamia nut crust, roasted fennel and a rosemary jus*

•

*Freshly baked lemon tart with black tea sorbet*

out of the syrup with a slotted spoon. Reduce the syrup to a jelly consistency. Leave to cool. Place the gooseberries in the tart case and spoon the partially set jelly over them. Serve with lots of rich cream.

# SCALLOP AND PENOLA TROUT WITH FRIED RAVIOLI AND A TOMATO AND CAPSICUM COULIS

### CHARDONNAY LODGE

*1 boned Penola trout fillet (skin on) per portion, cut into 3 diamonds*
*3 scallops per portion*
*sea salt*
*freshly ground pepper*
*1 lime*
*olive oil*
*Tomato and Capsicum Coulis*
*witlof*
*Ravioli*
*tomato, diced*
*chervil*

Season the trout and scallops with the sea salt and pepper, then grate the zest of the lime over the fish. In a large sauté pan heat the olive oil over a medium high heat, place the trout (skin down) and scallops in the pan and sauté until golden brown. Turn them over and finish cooking, squeeze the lime juice over the fish, remove from the pan and keep warm.

Spoon some coulis into the centre of a plate, surround with 3 witlof leaves and place a scallop on each leaf. Place a piece of Penola trout in between each scallop and balance a ravioli on top of the fish. Drizzle the plate with lime infused olive oil and garnish with diced tomato, picked chervil and freshly ground pepper.

## RAVIOLI

*190 grams plain flour*
*15 ml olive oil*
*1 egg*
*40 ml spring water*
*pinch of salt*
Ratatouille:
*40 ml olive oil*
*1 small red onion, finely chopped*
*1 small garlic clove, finely chopped*
*½ small eggplant, finely diced*
*½ red capsicum (flesh only), finely diced*
*1 small zucchini, finely diced*
*1 small tomato, peeled, seeded and finely diced*
*salt and pepper*

Combine the flour, olive oil, egg, water and salt in a food processor and process until the ingredients resemble coarse breadcrumbs. Remove from the bowl and form into a ball, cover with plastic wrap and allow to rest in the refrigerator for two hours.

To make the ratatouille heat the oil in a medium sized sauté pan, add the onion and garlic and sauté until soft. Add the eggplant, capsicum and zucchini and continue cooking until soft. Remove from the heat and stir in the tomato, add salt and pepper to taste. Set aside until required.

Roll the dough through a pasta machine set at the widest setting, fold into thirds and roll again. Set the rollers at the next narrowest setting and roll the dough through again. Repeat the process reducing the opening after each rolling and dusting the dough lightly with flour if necessary until the required thickness is reached.

Using a 7 cm round cutter cut the required amount of rounds. Brush the edges of half the rounds with egg wash and spoon some of the ratatouille into the centre of each round. Cover with the remaining rounds and press the edges firmly, expelling any trapped air and sealing. Using a fluted 6 cm cutter trim the ravioli.

In a large saucepan heat some vegetable oil 7 cm deep and heat to about 190°C. Place the ravioli into the oil and fry until golden brown, remove and place onto a paper towel to drain. Keep warm.

## TOMATO AND CAPSICUM COULIS

*40 ml olive oil*
*2 small cloves garlic, finely chopped*
*3 shallots, finely chopped*
*1 cup reduced fish stock*
*2 small tomatoes, peeled, seeded and chopped*
*2 red capsicums, roasted, peeled, seeded and chopped*
*balsamic vinegar*
*salt and pepper*

In a medium sauté pan heat the oil and add the garlic and shallots, cook until soft. Add the remaining ingredients, reduce the heat and simmer for 20 minutes. Remove from the heat and place into a food processor, process until smooth and strain.

## LOIN OF TATIANA LAMB WITH MACADAMIA NUT CRUST, ROASTED FENNEL AND A ROSEMARY JUS

### CHARDONNAY LODGE

*100 grams macadamia nuts*
*100 grams unsalted butter*
*100 grams fine bread crumbs*
*salt and pepper*
*oil*
*220 grams tatiana lamb loin per portion*
*Rosemary Jus*
*Roasted Fennel*

PLACE THE nuts into a food processor and process until still coarse (it does not matter if there are some larger pieces). In a large saucepan melt the butter over a medium heat, add the nuts and bread crumbs and stir until the ingredients are incorporated, remove from the heat and add salt and pepper to taste.

Heat the oil in a medium pan over a high heat, season the lamb with salt and pepper and place in the pan. Seal the lamb on both sides. Spread some of the macadamia crust on top of the lamb and place in a medium hot oven for approximately 7 minutes or until the lamb is cooked, remove from the oven and allow to rest for 10 minutes.

To serve, place the Roasted Fennel in the centre of the plate. Slice the lamb into three and arrange around the fennel, and pour the Rosemary Jus between the lamb.

## ROSEMARY JUS

*2 sprigs rosemary*  
*50 grams castor sugar*  
*500 ml red wine*  
*1 litre lamb stock*

Place the rosemary, sugar and red wine in a large saucepan. Heat over a medium heat and reduce by two thirds. Add the stock and reduce until a good consistency is reached, strain and keep warm.

## ROASTED FENNEL

*olive oil*  
*1 small fennel bulb, divided into 6 pieces*  
*salt and pepper*

Heat the oil in a large sauté pan over a medium heat, add the fennel, salt and pepper and place the pan into a medium hot oven. Cook until soft, turning occasionally. Remove from the pan and keep warm.

# FRESHLY BAKED LEMON TART WITH BLACK TEA SORBET

### CHARDONNAY LODGE

*8 egg yolks*  
*340 grams icing sugar*  
*140 ml thickened cream*  
*3 drops vanilla essence*  
*1 kg plain flour*  
*2 grams salt*  
*2 grams baking powder*  
*700 grams butter, softened*

*LEMON FILLING:*  
*5 whole eggs*  
*200 grams castor sugar*  
*4 lemons, juice and zest*  
*200 ml double cream*  
*whipped cream, to serve*  
*Black Tea Sorbet*  
*Glass Biscuits (or Tuille Biscuits)*  
*mint*

IN A MIXING machine beat together the egg yolks, icing sugar, cream and vanilla essence. When totally incorporated add the flour, salt and baking powder. Next add the softened butter in two lots, making sure the first lot is fully incorporated before adding the second. Remove the dough from the bowl, cover with plastic wrap and refrigerate for 2 to 3 hours. Working quickly and using plenty of flour to dust, roll out the dough to approximately 3 to 4 mm thick and line a greased tart mould with it. (Approximately 200 grams of the dough will line one 25 cm tart mould.) Rest the pastry for 1 hour and then blind bake (with paper and rice) for 10 minutes at 180°C, then bake for 5 more minutes without the paper and rice. Remove from the oven and allow to cool.

To make the lemon filling, mix together the eggs, sugar, lemon juice and zest. Lightly whip the double cream and add to the lemon mix. Chill the mixture for 1 hour then pour into the pastry case. Bake at 150°C for 1 hour. Remove from the oven and cool.

Place a slice of the lemon tart on a plate, at the tip of the slice place the whipped cream to one side and a quenelle of the Black Tea Sorbet to the other. Top both the sorbet and the cream with a chard of Glass Biscuit and a sprig of mint.

## BLACK TEA SORBET

*1.5 litres spring water*
*600 grams castor sugar*
*200 ml lemon juice*
*15 grams English breakfast tea leaves*
*2 egg whites, lightly whisked*

Brew the tea with ½ a litre of water, dissolve the sugar in the remaining water and add the lemon juice to the sugar water. Strain the tea and add to the sugar solution. Allow to cool then churn through an ice-cream machine. Just before the sorbet is finished, add the egg whites, remove from the machine and place in the freezer.

## GLASS BISCUITS

*200 grams butter*
*180 ml liquid glucose*
*180 grams plain flour*
*360 grams castor sugar*
*30 grams glace ginger, finely diced*

In a bowl over a hot water bath melt the butter and glucose, remove from the heat and mix with the remaining ingredients. Place in a plastic bag and refrigerate for approximately 1 hour. Roll a small amount of the mix in between 2 pieces of silicon paper, remove the top sheet and bake in an oven at 180°C for approximately 6 minutes. Allow to cool slightly until set and remove from the silicon paper.

## TUILLE BISCUITS

*125 grams butter, melted*
*200 grams castor sugar*
*50 grams honey*
*65 grams plain flour*
*125 grams flaked almonds*
*zest of 1 orange, grated*
*100 ml orange juice*

Cream the butter and sugar together. Add the remaining

## FRANKLIN MANOR
### West Coast, Tasmania

*Crayfish medallions and kale salad*

*Emu and mountain pepper sauce*

*Chocolate and walnut dessert cake*

---

ingredients and stir until combined. Chill for 1 hour. Form into rounds on a baking dish and bake at 200°C for 6–8 minutes.

# CRAYFISH MEDALLIONS AND KALE SALAD

### FRANKLIN MANOR

*2 crayfish*
*1 kg salt*
*100 ml vinegar*
*4 litres water*
*200 grams kale lettuce*
*1 medium carrot, julienned*
*⅓ large leek, julienned*
*1 small red capsicum, julienned*
*1 stick celery, julienned*

*STOCK:*
*100 grams butter*
*1 onion, roughly chopped*
*juice of 1 lemon*
*parsley stems*
*3 peppercorns*
*1 bay leaf*
*1 litre water*
*Brandy Hommade Sauce*

DROWN THE crayfish in fresh water.

Place the salt, vinegar and 4 litres of water in a large saucepan and bring to the boil. Place the crayfish in the water and cook for 8 minutes. When cooked, remove the crayfish and cool in cold salted water. Remove the tails from the crayfish bodies, reserving the bodies for the stock.

To make the stock, melt the butter in a saucepan, then add the onion and sauté. Add the lemon juice, parsley stems, peppercorns, bay leaf and reserved crayfish bodies. Crush the bodies, then add 1 litre of water and bring to the boil. Reduce the heat and simmer for 20 minutes. Sieve through a muslin cloth.

Cut the tails into four equal portions. Place on four warmed serving plates, and arrange the kale lettuce, carrot, leek, capsicum and celery around. Spoon over some of the Brandy Hommade Sauce. Serves 4.

# BRANDY HOMMADE SAUCE

*100 ml brandy*
*2 litres crayfish stock*
*300 ml cream*
*oil*

*flour*
*100 grams butter*
*salt and white pepper, to taste*

Place the brandy in a warm saucepan and flame. Add the stock and bring to a simmer. Add the cream, and enough oil and flour to thicken to a sauce consistency. Add the butter and salt and pepper to taste.

---

FRANKLIN MANOR, TASMANIA
*Emu and mountain pepper sauce, page 260*

*S*pring

## EMU AND MOUNTAIN PEPPER SAUCE

### FRANKLIN MANOR

1 medium onion
1 clove garlic
25 ml green ginger wine
25 grams bush tea
10 grams mountain pepper
10 grams blue gum
1 litre demi glaze
600 grams emu, flat fillet, rump flat or flan flat

*Gallette:*
100 grams butter
1 medium onion, roughly chopped
10 spring onions, roughly chopped
1 clove garlic, roughly chopped
4 mushrooms, roughly chopped
70 grams semi sun-dried tomato
salt and pepper, to taste

Sauté the onion, garlic and green ginger wine over high heat until the alcohol is removed. Add the bush tea, mountain pepper, blue gum and demi glaze, reduce the heat and simmer for 25 minutes. Remove from the heat and strain, reserving the flavoured liquid.

Melt the butter over a high heat in a frying pan and sauté the onion, spring onions, garlic, mushrooms, sun-dried tomato and salt and pepper until soft. Set aside and keep warm.

Cut the emu into 100 gram portions (larger if desired) and pan fry until it is medium rare. Slice.

To serve, ladle the sauce on a serving plate, arrange the gallette mixture in a round cutter and fan the emu slices around the gallette mixture. Serves 6.

## CHOCOLATE AND WALNUT DESSERT CAKE

### FRANKLIN MANOR

375 grams dark chocolate
170 grams butter
1 litre water, boiling
460 grams sugar
10 eggs
2 teaspoons vanilla essence
210 grams plain flour

1 teaspoon salt
1 teaspoons baking powder
6 tablespoons sour cream
455 grams ground walnuts
455 grams walnut pieces
Ganache Chocolate Sauce

Preheat the oven to 180°C. Grease and line a 26 cm springform cake tin. Place the chocolate and butter in a stainless steel bowl and melt over a bain marie containing 1 litre of boiling water. Cool to room temperature.

Whisk the sugar, eggs and vanilla essence with an electric mixer. Fold into the chocolate mixture. Add the flour, salt and baking powder, then add the sour cream, ground walnuts and walnut pieces. Place the mixture in the prepared cake tin and bake for

30–40 minutes. Test with a skewer. Rest for 20 minutes. Remove from the tin and cool in the refrigerator for 1 hour. Serve with the Ganache Chocolate Sauce.

## GANACHE CHOCOLATE SAUCE

*1 litre cream*
*70 grams butter*
*70 grams castor sugar*
*680 grams dark chocolate*

Place all of the ingredients in a stainless steel bowl and melt over simmering water, mixing with a wooden spoon to form a sauce.

## ASPARAGUS ROBED WITH MARINATED SALMON DRIZZLED WITH A TRUFFLE SCENTED VIRGIN OLIVE OIL

### ARTHURS RESTAURANT

*filleted side of salmon, approx. 600 to 700 grams (skin on)*
*32–40 thin asparagus spears*
*⅓ cup dry vermouth (80 ml)*
*⅔ cup lemon juice (160 ml)*
*3 teaspoons sugar*
*100 grams salt*
*12 peppercorns*
*1 small clove garlic, crushed*
*1 bay leaf*
*2 sprigs each thyme and rosemary*
*4 tablespoons white truffle infused virgin olive oil (available in gourmet stores)*
*white bread, toasted*
*Parmesan cheese*

Mix the vermouth, lemon juice, sugar, salt, peppercorns, crushed garlic, bay leaf, thyme and rosemary together and leave for the salt and sugar to dissolve.

Remove all the bones from the salmon and place in a porcelain or earthenware dish. Cover with the marinade and leave for approximately 36 to 48 hours depending on the thickness of the salmon.

Remove the salmon from the marinade, dry it and with a knife gently remove all the white flesh, then wrap it in plastic wrap until it will be used.

Peel and cook the asparagus spears in lots of water for 2 to 3 minutes until they are just cooked. Refresh on ice and then drain and dry.

To serve, place 8 to 10 spears in the middle of the plate, cut the salmon into paper thin slices and place over the asparagus, just leaving the tips of the asparagus, showing. Sprinkle the asparagus and salmon generously with truffle infused virgin olive oil.

Serve with white toast baked in the oven and sprinkled with grated parmesan cheese. Serves 4.

---

**ARTHURS RESTAURANT**
Mornington Peninsula, Victoria

•

*Asparagus robed with marinated salmon drizzled with a truffle scented virgin olive oil*

•

*Rump of spring lamb with Chermoula poached in a reduced stock flavoured with sherry*

•

*Reversed chocolate and fromage blanc soufflé with a compote of lightly brandied cumquats*

# RUMP OF SPRING LAMB WITH CHERMOULA POACHED IN A REDUCED STOCK FLAVOURED WITH SHERRY

### ARTHURS RESTAURANT

4 whole lamb rumps removed from the bone and trimmed of all fat (retain the bones)
4 lamb necks
2 litres water, for lamb stock
bouquet garni, for lamb stock
1 bunch baby turnips
1 bunch baby dutch carrots
12 shallots or tiny salad onions
1 cup baby broad beans, skins removed (or fresh peas)
1 tablespoon of butter fat (ghee)
150 ml medium sherry (preferably Amontillado)
50 grams fresh butter

CHERMOULA MIXTURE:
1 medium onion, finely chopped
1 clove garlic
4 tablespoons continental parsley, chopped
4 tablespoons fresh coriander leaves
¼ teaspoon saffron powder
¼ teaspoon cumin powder
¼ teaspoon paprika/cayenne mixture
6 tablespoons olive oil
2 tablespoons lemon juice

HAVE THE butcher bone out the rump and keep the fillet ends and trimmings for other dishes. Remove all fat from the rump.

Make a stock of the neck bones and remaining rump bones by first blanching them in boiling water. Add approximately 2 litres of cold water and the bouquet garni and gently boil for approximately 2 hours. Keep removing any fat or impurities until you have a clear reduced stock of approximately 1 litre.

Clean the turnips, carrots, shallots and beans carefully, leaving half a centimetre of green on all the vegetable tops.

Mix together the chermoula mixture.

Seal the rumps in a hot frying pan with a little clarified butter. Let the rump cool, then generously paste with the chermoula mixture and wrap individually in plastic wrap. Poach in a mixture of two thirds of the remaining stock and the sherry for 6 to 7 minutes but make sure they remain pink. Remove the rumps and reduce the stock to a syrupy consistency.

Glaze the prepared vegetables without the broad beans or peas in 25 grams of butter, starting with the onion. After a few minutes add the turnips and carrots, wet with the retained meat stock and gently cook to al dente for a few minutes, adding the young broad beans in the final moments.

When serving, remove the plastic wrap and slice the pink rumps on a plate. Garnish with the jardiniere of glazed vegetables. Add the retained juices from the rumps to the reduced lamb stock, adjust the seasoning and generously coat the meat.

FRANKLIN MANOR,
TASMANIA
*Crayfish medallions and kale salad, page 258*

*S*pring

**MIETTA'S QUEENSCLIFF HOTEL**
Bellarine Peninsula,
Victoria

•

*Snapper fillet with sea salt in a saffron bouillon*

•

*Veal cutlets baked in paper with asparagus, broad beans and light truffle jus*

•

*Brandy snaps with mascarpone and spring fruits dressed with cognac*

## REVERSED CHOCOLATE AND FROMAGE BLANC SOUFFLÉ WITH A COMPOTE OF LIGHTLY BRANDIED CUMQUATS

### ARTHURS RESTAURANT

*200 grams cumquats*
*125 grams sugar*
*2 tablespoons grenadine syrup*
*200 ml orange juice*
*2 tablespoons cognac*
*butter and sugar, for soufflé dishes*
*3 whole eggs, separated*
*60 grams sugar*
*120 grams fromage blanc or quark*
*15 grams pure cocoa powder*
*cocoa and icing sugar for dusting*

THOROUGHLY prick the cumquats with a needle. Bring ½ a litre of water to the boil and gently cook the cumquats for a few minutes until just soft, drain immediately.

Make a blond (light coloured) caramel with the 125 grams of sugar. Remove from the heat and add the grenadine syrup and orange juice. Then return to the heat and let the caramel dissolve and reduce to a syrupy consistency. Add the cognac, halve the cumquats and remove any pips, and return to the syrup.

Coat the individual soufflé forms generously with butter and dust with sugar. Separate the eggs and place the egg yolks and 60 grams of sugar into a mixing bowl. Beat the mixture vigorously until it becomes frothy and white, then add the fromage blanc and cocoa. Beat the remaining egg whites until stiff and gently fold into the egg and cheese mixture.

Fill the soufflé dishes and place into a baking dish half filled with water. Cook in a preheated oven at 170°C for 20 minutes.

To serve, reverse the baked soufflés onto pre-warmed plates. (If necessary gently loosen the sides with a fine knife.) Dust with a mixture of icing sugar and cocoa. Place the cumquats with a little syrup around the soufflé and serve immediately. Serves 4.

## SNAPPER FILLET WITH SEA SALT IN A SAFFRON BOUILLON

### MIETTA'S QUEENSCLIFF HOTEL

*1.8 kg snapper*
*40 grams olive paste*
*3 teaspoons olive oil*
*1 tablespoon breadcrumbs*
*pepper, to taste*
*Bouillon*
*5 grams saffron threads*
*sea salt*

PREHEAT THE oven to 230°C. Scale and gut the snapper and cut into fillets. Bone the fillets, retaining the bones for the Bouillon.

Place the olive paste, olive oil and breadcrumbs in a bowl and season with pepper. Spread the paste evenly over the snapper fillets.

Place the Bouillon in a saucepan and bring back to the boil. Add the saffron threads and simmer over low heat for 15 minutes.

Trim the fish fillets evenly and cut into 4 even portions. Place them on a greased tray and cook for 8–10 minutes, or until just cooked. Sprinkle with sea salt and keep warm in the oven.

Ladle the Bouillon into bowls and place the fish fillets in the centre. Serves 4.

## BOUILLON

*500 ml white wine*
*water*
*1 onion, chopped*
*1 leek, chopped*
*1 carrot, chopped*
*1 stick celery, chopped*
*1 head garlic, chopped*
*4 tomatoes, chopped*
*50 ml olive oil*
*2 teaspoon fennel seeds*
*salt and pepper, to taste*
*1 bay leaf*

Rinse the fish bones, place in a pot and cover with the wine and enough water to cover by 3 cm. Add the remaining ingredients, bring to the boil and simmer gently for 20 minutes. Strain and then cook further until reduced to 400 ml. Skim off any scum as it comes to the top.

# VEAL CUTLETS BAKED IN PAPER WITH ASPARAGUS, BROAD BEANS AND LIGHT TRUFFLE JUS

MIETTA'S QUEENSCLIFF HOTEL

*4 x 180 gram veal cutlets*
*salt and pepper, to taste*
*40 grams butter, melted*
*1 carrot, julienned*
*1 leek, julienned*
*½ bunch sage, chopped*
*1 truffle, very finely julienned*
*4 teaspoons walnut oil*
*600 grams veal stock*
*30 ml cognac*
*100 ml white wine*
*400 grams asparagus*
*20 grams butter, extra*
*600 grams broad beans, peeled and blanched*

CUT FOUR 30 x 30 cm squares out of greaseproof paper, fold them in half and cut into semi-circles.

Trim the veal cutlets into even shapes and scrape the bones clean. Season to taste and sear lightly over a moderate heat for 30 seconds on each side.

Brush the greaseproof circles liberally with the melted butter and lay on a baking tray. On one half of the paper, place a mound of the combined carrot and leek and sprinkle with the sage. Place a veal cutlet on top, adding a pinch of truffle, season and pour one teaspoon of walnut oil over each cutlet. Fold the other half of paper over the top and, working from one end to the other, twist tightly to seal.

Place the veal stock, cognac, white wine and remaining truffle in a saucepan and bring to the boil. Cook until reduced by half then remove from the heat.

Clean the asparagus and cut them in half at an angle. Place in a saucepan of boiling salted water and cook for 1 minute. Strain.

Bake the paper envelopes at 200°C for 10–15 minutes (they will puff up like a balloon). Meanwhile, bring the sauce back to the boil and whisk in the extra butter. Reduce the heat to low and put in the broad beans. Simmer for a few minutes.

Divide the asparagus between four pre-heated serving plates. Place the paper envelopes on the plates, slit the top with a sharp knife, pour in the sauce and serve. Serves 4.

# BRANDY SNAPS WITH MASCARPONE AND SPRING FRUITS DRESSED WITH COGNAC

## MIETTA'S QUEENSCLIFF HOTEL

*¾ punnet strawberries*
*¾ punnet raspberries*
*¾ punnet blueberries*
*¾ punnet blackberries*

*300 grams mascarpone*
*60 ml cognac*
*icing sugar*
*Brandy Snaps*

Cut the strawberries into quarters and remove the hull. Discard any berries that are bruised. Beat the mascarpone until smooth and sweeten to taste if desired.

Place the Brandy Snaps onto serving plates and arrange the berries around the sides. Divide the mascarpone among the biscuits and make a cavity in the top to hold the cognac. Pour 15 ml of cognac into each cavity and dust lightly with icing sugar. Serves 4.

## BRANDY SNAPS

*90 grams butter*
*90 grams plain flour*

*60 grams golden syrup*
*210 grams icing sugar*

Preheat the oven to 175°C. Line a baking tray with silicon paper.

Cream the butter and beat in the flour. Stir the golden syrup and icing sugar through. Form the dough into balls half the size of an egg, and gently flatten. Bake in the oven for 6–10 minutes or until lightly browned. Remove from the oven and allow them to cool slightly. Remove from the baking tray and place over the bottom of a coffee cup. You need four bowl-shaped biscuits.

---

MIETTA'S QUEENSCLIFF HOTEL, VICTORIA
*Veal cutlets baked in paper with asparagus, broad beans and light truffle jus, page 265*

*S*pring

267

## TAYLOR'S COUNTRY HOUSE
### Byron Bay, New South Wales

*Honey-basted roast quail on roast potato cake with crisp pancetta, preserved eggplant and lemon-infused olive oil*

•

*Char-grilled tuna steak with tapenade and a warm Nicoise style vegetable casserole*

•

*Frozen strawberry dacquari with berries and poppy seed wafers*

# HONEY BASTED ROAST QUAIL ON ROAST POTATO CAKE WITH CRISP PANCETTA, PRESERVED EGG PLANT AND LEMON INFUSED OLIVE OIL

### TAYLOR'S COUNTRY HOUSE

8 medium desiree potatoes, peeled and cut into 1 cm cubes
2 onions, finely sliced
8 medium quails
2 tablespoons Kejap Manis (thick sweet soy)
2 tablespoons Thai sweet chilli sauce
half bunch coriander, finely shredded (including stalks)
1 lime, juice and grated zest
3 cloves garlic, peeled and finely sliced
1 piece ginger, peeled and finely sliced
8 eggplant slices
½ cup honey
½ cup vinegar
fresh mixed herbs
8 pancetta slices
olive oil
watercress

Boil the potatoes until tender but not collapsing, and drain. Sweat the onions in a little oil but do not allow them to colour. Add to the potato and mash lightly to break up the potato, then season.

Oil 8 metal rings, fill the rings with the potato and smooth over the top. Chill until required.

Truss the quails with string.

Mix together the Kejap Manis, chilli sauce, coriander, lime, garlic and ginger. Place the quails in a glass, ceramic or stainless steel container and pour over the marinade. Ensure that all the quails are coated in the marinade, cover and refrigerate.

Brown the eggplant in a little oil on both sides, season and remove to a suitable container. Boil the honey, vinegar and fresh herbs, pour over the eggplant and cover.

Place the pancetta slices on an oven slide, set the oven to 180°C and bake for about 3 minutes until crisp, remove and set aside.

Remove the quail from the marinade and roast in an oven at 200°C. Baste continuously with the marinade and juices until the quail is a deep mahogany colour and cooked through (approximately 8 minutes). When cool enough to handle, remove the legs and breast, and keep warm.

Heat a little oil in a non-stick fry pan. Cook the potato cakes over a medium heat until golden, and repeat on the other side. Sear the preserved eggplant in a hot pan.

To serve, place a potato cake in the centre of each plate and remove the metal ring, then place a slice of eggplant on top of the potato. Arrange the quail on top and finish with a few watercress leaves and a slice of pancetta. Add a little virgin olive oil to the quail juice and spoon this over and around the quail. Serves 8.

# CHAR-GRILLED TUNA STEAK WITH TAPENADE AND A WARM NIÇOISE STYLE VEGETABLE CASSEROLE

### TAYLOR'S COUNTRY HOUSE

*8 x 180 gram mid-cut tuna fillet steaks*
*extra virgin olive oil*
*3 Spanish onions, sliced*
*4 cloves garlic, finely chopped*
*3 pontiac potatoes, cut into 1.5 cm dice and cooked*
*2 red capsicums, roasted, peeled and cut into strips*
*1¼ cups Kalamata olives*
*half bunch basil leaves*
*half bunch continental parsley, leaves shredded*
*balsamic vinegar*
*seasoning*
*3 tablespoons Tapenade (see recipe page 68)*

Heat a char-grill to very hot. Brush the tuna with oil, mark the steaks with a criss-cross pattern, turn and repeat. Cook the tuna until medium rare, taking care not to over-cook as it cooks quickly.

Heat about half a cup of virgin olive oil over a gentle heat and add the onions and garlic. Cook for several minutes then add the potatoes, capsicum and olives, and lastly the fresh herbs.

Swirl in a tablespoon of balsamic vinegar and season. Spoon the vegetables with their liquid so they cover the plate and place the tuna steak on top. Place a small teaspoon of Tapenade on the tuna.

# FROZEN STRAWBERRY DACQUIRI WITH BERRIES AND POPPYSEED WAFERS

### TAYLOR'S COUNTRY HOUSE

*1½ cups crushed ice*
*Strawberry Sorbet*
*¾ cup Bacardi rum*
*1 punnet strawberries*
*1 punnet blueberries*
*1 punnet raspberries*
*Poppyseed Wafers*

Place the ice in a food processor with metal blades, pulse until relatively smooth, add the Strawberry Sorbet and rum, and process until combined. Divide the berries between large cocktail glasses. Pile the frozen Dacquiri on top of the berries. Finish with a thin Poppyseed Wafer placed on an angle.

# STRAWBERRY SORBET

*170 grams castor sugar*
*170 ml water*
*550 ml fresh strawberry purée*

Boil the sugar and water together, pour onto the strawberry purée, cool and churn in an ice-cream maker. Store in the freezer.

## THE PARLOUR AND PANTRY
Northeastern Victoria

•

*Salad of rabbit fillets*

•

*Oven-baked spatchcock with sage butter*

•

*Lemon curd tart*

## POPPYSEED WAFERS

*60 ml egg whites*
*100 grams castor sugar*
*75 grams plain flour*
*50 grams melted butter*
*vanilla extract*
*poppyseeds*

Lightly whisk the egg whites with the sugar until frothy. Stir in the flour, when smooth stir in the butter and the vanilla. Rest the mixture in the refrigerator for 30 minutes. Spread the mixture on a greased baking sheet. Sprinkle with poppyseeds. Bake at 180°C for approximately 5 minutes until golden, remove from the oven. Using a large plain cookie cutter, make perfect circles of biscuit discs.

## SALAD OF RABBIT FILLETS
### THE PARLOUR AND PANTRY

*1 rabbit fillet*
*oil*
*3 slices prosciutto*
*salad leaves to serve 1*
*6 olives*
*3 semi-sundried tomatoes, chopped*
*6 whole seedless red grapes or half a pear, sliced*
*20 grams Parmesan cheese, shaved*
*10 baby capers*
LEMON AND BASIL VINAIGRETTE:
*50 ml lemon juice*
*1 bunch basil leaves*
*150 ml virgin olive oil*
*salt and pepper, to taste*
*25 ml white wine vinegar*

PLACE THE rabbit fillet and a little oil in a pan and sear on all sides until the meat is sealed. Place in a baking dish and cook in a 150°C oven for 5 minutes or until cooked. Remove from the oven and rest for 10 minutes. Cut into diagonal slices.

Combine all of the Vinaigrette ingredients in a food processor and blend until combined.

Place the prosciutto slices on a baking tray and bake in the oven for 2 minutes or until crisp. Assemble the salad leaves on a serving plate. Scatter over the olives, sundried tomatoes, grapes, Parmesan cheese and capers, and dress with the Vinaigrette. Place the rabbit slices on top of the salad, and the prosciutto on top of the rabbit. Serve with fresh bread. Serves 1.

THE PARLOUR AND PANTRY, VICTORIA
*Salad of rabbit fillets*

*S*pring

271

## OVEN-BAKED SPATCHCOCK WITH SAGE BUTTER

### THE PARLOUR AND PANTRY

*1 x No. 12–16 spatchcock*
*50 grams butter, softened*
*1 tablespoon fresh sage leaves, cut into fine strips*
*salt and pepper, to taste*
*juice of 1 lemon*
*50 ml brown chicken stock*

TRIM THE wing tips of the spatchcock to the first joint from the breast. Rinse the bird under running water and pat dry with a paper towel. Combine the butter and sage leaves, and rub into the skin. Season with salt and pepper.

Place the spatchcock in a baking dish and roast at 180°C for 10–12 minutes, or until just cooked and the juices run clear when pierced with a metal skewer. Remove from the oven and rest in a warm place for 10 minutes. Squeeze over some lemon juice. Place the chicken stock in a saucepan and cook over medium heat until heated through.

Place the spatchcock on a serving plate and drizzle around some of the chicken stock. Serve accompanied with baby vegetables such as baby carrots, baby corn, baby turnips, zucchini balls or cherry tomatoes and sugar snap peas. Serve with a dipping bowl for cleaning fingers. Serves 1.

## LEMON CURD TART

### THE PARLOUR AND PANTRY

*5 medium lemons, rind and juice*
*11 x 60 gram eggs*
*480 grams castor sugar*
*380 ml rich cream*
*1 deep, sweet pastry shell*

PLACE ALL of the ingredients except the pastry shell in a food processor and blend until well combined. Pour into the pastry shell. Bake at 170°C for 30–40 minutes, or until just 'wobbly'. Serves 10.

# Spring

## CALVES' SWEETBREADS WITH LEMON
### THE VALLEY COUNTRY HOME

400 grams calves' sweetbreads  
1 bay leaf  
1 onion, quartered  
few black peppercorns  
75 grams plain flour  
pinch salt  
pinch pepper  
pinch ground paprika  
pinch ground cumin  
pinch ground coriander  
75 grams clarified butter  
fresh bush lemons  

SIT THE sweetbreads in enough cold water to cover, leave for 1 hour.

Remove the sweetbreads from the water and place in a saucepan with the bay leaf, onion and peppercorns. Cover with cold water, bring to the boil then reduce the heat and simmer for 10 minutes. Remove the sweetbreads from the liquid and gently peel the membrane and small tubes away. Place under a weight and set aside to cool.

Combine the flour, salt, pepper, paprika, cumin and coriander. Cut the sweetbread into 5 mm thick slices, dust with the spiced flour and sauté in the butter over high heat until golden. Serve with fresh bush lemons.

## TILBA SUPREME CHEESE SOUFFLÉ WITH RED PEPPER PURÉE
### THE VALLEY COUNTRY HOME

500 ml milk  
1 onion coloute  
50 grams butter  
50 grams flour  
1 tablespoon cream  
nutmeg  
50 grams cheese, grated  
3 egg yolks  
6 egg whites  
breadcrumbs  
Red Pepper Purée  

PLACE THE milk and onion coloute in a saucepan and steep. In a separate pan, melt the butter then add the flour and stir, but do not brown. Add the flour mixture to the milk and stir until it forms a thick sauce. Add the cream and nutmeg and remove from the heat. Add the grated cheese and mix thoroughly. Add the egg yolks and stir.

Whisk the egg whites until stiff peaks form and fold carefully through the egg yolk mixture. Ladle into buttered soufflé dishes lined with breadcrumbs and bake in a 180°C oven for 20 minutes. Remove from the moulds and serve in a pool of Red Pepper Purée.

---

**THE VALLEY COUNTRY HOME**  
Tilba Tilba, Southern Coast, New South Wales

•

Calves' sweetbreads with lemon

•

Tilba Supreme cheese soufflé with red pepper purée

•

Fillets of John Dory poached with Eden mussels

•

Strawberry sponge

## RED PEPPER PURÉE

2 red capsicums, roasted and peeled
1 medium onion
1 bay leaf
500 ml chicken stock
salt, to taste
ground white pepper, to taste

Place all of the ingredients in a saucepan, bring to the boil and cook for 30 minutes. Remove the bay leaf. Blend in a food processor and season with the salt and pepper.

## FILLETS OF JOHN DORY POACHED WITH EDEN MUSSELS

### THE VALLEY COUNTRY HOME

300 ml fish stock
300 ml dry white wine
Eden mussels (6 per serve), cleaned and scrubbed
150 ml cream
John Dory (1 medium fish per serve), filleted
4 tablespoons chives, finely chopped

Put the fish stock and wine into a saucepan and bring to the boil. Add the mussels, removing them as soon as they begin to open. Set aside until cool enough to handle, then remove the meat.

Strain the stock into a fresh saucepan and return to the heat. Add the cream and cook over medium heat until reduced a little. Turn off the heat, add the fish fillets and mussels and leave to cook in the sauce for 1–2 minutes.

Remove the fish and mussels from the sauce and place on a serving plate. Bring the sauce back to the boil, add the chives and cook for 30 seconds. Pour over the fish and serve with an asparagus and seaweed salad.

## STRAWBERRY SPONGE

### THE VALLEY COUNTRY HOME

1 cup sugar
4 eggs
1 cup plain flour
1 teaspoon baking powder
1 tablespoon boiling water
1 punnet strawberries
2 tablespoons sugar
2 tablespoons water or juice of 1 orange
Muscat
whipped cream

Beat the sugar and eggs together for at least 10 minutes. In a separate bowl, sift together the flour and baking powder. Add to the egg mixture and beat gently; do not overwork. Pour in the boiling water, stirring in thoroughly.

*The Parlour and Pantry, Victoria*
*Lemon curd tart, page 272*

*S*PRING

**WARRENMANG VINEYARD RESORT**
Pyrenees, Central Victoria

•

*Mousseline of rabbit*

•

*Oven-roasted loin of spring lamb with olive pastry, potato purée and white wine sauce*

•

*Iced nougat with praline, glace fruits and Cointreau*

Pour into a greased and floured cake tin and bake at 190°C for 45 minutes or until the top of the cake springs back. Turn out and cool.

Cut the strawberries in half. Place in a saucepan with the sugar and water and bring to the boil. Remove from the heat and cool.

Split the cake in half and sprinkle with lashings of the Muscat. Spread with whipped cream and spoon over half the strawberry mixture. Replace the top half of the cake and spread that with another layer of cream and strawberries.

## MOUSSELINE OF RABBIT
### WARRENMANG VINEYARD RESORT

*50 gram rabbit fillet, cleaned*
*½ beaten egg*
*150 ml cream*
*⅓ bunch lovage, finely chopped*
*20 grams sun-dried tomatoes, finely chopped*
*salt and pepper, to taste*

Place the rabbit fillet and egg in a food processor and purée until smooth. Place in a large stainless steel bowl and slowly add the cream, beating continuously with a wooden spoon.

Add the lovage and sundried tomatoes and season to taste. Place into dariole moulds and cover with foil.

Place the moulds in a bain marie and cook at 220°C for approximately 30 minutes or until firm. Serves 2.

## OVEN-ROASTED LOIN OF SPRING LAMB WITH OLIVE PASTRY, POTATO PURÉE AND WHITE WINE SAUCE
### WARRENMANG VINEYARD RESORT

*1 lamb fillet or lean mince*
*1 egg*
*lemon zest, chopped*
*parsley*
*Parmesan cheese*
*salt and pepper, to taste*
*150 gram lamb loin*
*10–20 gram crepinette*
*½ zucchini, sliced lengthwise*
*50 grams cooked potato*
*milk*
*butter*
*salt and pepper, to taste*
*Olive Pastries*
*White Wine Sauce*

Place the lamb fillet and egg in a food processor and blend until smooth. Combine with the lemon zest, parsley, Parmesan cheese and salt and pepper.

Season the lamb loin. Encase it with the lamb farce and wrap with crepinette. Roast in a 200°C oven until cooked, remove from the oven and allow to rest. Slice thinly.

Mash the potatoes with enough milk and butter to form a creamy texture. Season to taste.

Place the potato purée on a serving plate and top with slices of the lamb. Garnish with olive pastries and sliced zucchini. Finish with the white wine sauce. Serves 1.

## OLIVE PASTRIES

*1 kg Kalamata olives, seeded*
*1 kg puff pastry*
*eggwash*

Place the olives in a food processor and blend to a fine paste. Spread the olives over the puff pastry sheets, roll up and slice thinly. Coat with an eggwash and bake at 225°C for 10 to 12 minutes. This quantity is enough for 10 servings.

## WHITE WINE SAUCE

*3 carrots, chopped*
*3 onions, chopped*
*2 litres white wine*
*5 litres beef or veal stock*
*1 small bunch thyme*
*200 grams butter*

Sweat the carrots and onions in a saucepan. Add the wine and cook over a medium heat until almost all of the liquid has disappeared. Add the stock and herbs and cook further until reduced by one-third. Strain, then reduce again until thick. Stir in the butter. These quantities are enough for 30 to 40 portions.

# ICED NOUGAT WITH PRALINE, GLACE FRUITS AND COINTREAU

### WARRENMANG VINEYARD RESORT

*6 egg whites*
*80 ml water*
*360 grams sugar*
*600 ml double cream*
*chopped glace fruits: mixture of*
  *pear, orange, peach and pineapple*
*Cointreau, to taste*
*Praline*
*fresh raspberries*
*raspberry coulis*

Beat the egg whites until stiff peaks form. Place the water and sugar in a heavy-based saucepan and heat to 120°C. Pour the sugar syrup in a long, thin stream into the egg whites, whisking continuously until cool.

Fold into the cream and add the glace fruits, Cointreau and praline. Freeze overnight. Serve sprinkled with Praline and surrounded with raspberry coulis and fresh raspberries.

# Fine Food from Country Australia

**WILLOWVALE MILL**
Southern Highlands, New South Wales

•

*Spring potato and leek soup*

•

*Country leg of spring lamb baked on top of potatoes*

•

*Fruit tart*

## PRALINE

¼ cup roasted almonds
2 tablespoons water

⅓ cup sugar

Chop the almonds finely. Place the water and sugar in a saucepan and stir over low heat until the sugar has dissolved. Bring to the boil and boil rapidly until it is pale golden in colour. Add the almonds and stir until dark golden. Remove from the heat.

Pour onto a lightly oiled oven tray and leave to harden. When set, chop roughly.

## SPRING POTATO AND LEEK SOUP

### WILLOWVALE MILL

500 grams potatoes (preferably Desiree, King Edward or Red Craig Royal)
salt and pepper
water
2 leeks

milk
butter
salt
1 litre chicken stock
1 cup white wine
cream

DICE THE potatoes and put in a pan with the salt and pepper and just enough water to cover. Cook until soft, topping up with water if necessary. Don't allow the pan to go dry.

Slice the two leeks and simmer in some milk with a dash of butter and salt. Set aside.

When the potatoes are cooked, skim any scum from the top then mash. Add the chicken stock, the wine and the leek mixture. Gently simmer for 15 minutes and serve with a swirl of cream on top.

## COUNTRY LEG OF SPRING LAMB BAKED ON TOP OF POTATOES

### WILLOWVALE MILL

1 leg of lamb
olive oil
salt and pepper, to taste
1.5 kg potatoes (Bintje or Nicola), washed and cut into 1.5 cm slices

2 onions, sliced (optional)
salt and pepper, extra, to taste
fresh rosemary
500 ml stock

RUB THE lamb leg with olive oil and sprinkle with salt and pepper. Place in a large baking dish and cook at 190°C. When half-cooked (depending on the size of the leg and how you like it cooked—the instructions are for medium), remove from the baking dish and set aside on a large plate.

**WILLOWVALE MILL, NEW SOUTH WALES**
*Spring potato and leek soup*

*S*pring

Add the potatoes, onions, extra salt and pepper, a handful of rosemary and the stock to the baking pan. Place the lamb on top, including any juice from the plate, and continue to roast for another 30 minutes or until the potatoes are cooked. This dish is delicious served with a mixture of seasonal fresh garden vegetables. Serves 4.

# FRUIT TART
### WILLOWVALE MILL

*250 grams butter, cubed*
*500 grams plain flour*
*135 grams icing sugar*
*1 egg, or milk, or water*

*Blackberry Jam, freshly made*
*1 cooking apple, peeled and cored*
*cream*
*icing sugar*

PLACE BUTTER, flour and sugar into a food processor. Pulse until the mixture resembles fine breadcrumbs. Add 1 egg for a strong pastry or a little milk or water. Process lightly and tip out onto a bench. Knead the mixture until it comes together.

Press into a tart dish and trim the edges. Bake until nearly cooked in a moderate oven.

Fill the pastry case with the freshly made Blackberry Jam, then slice a good cooking apple thinly and fan it out over the top of the jam. Return to the oven and bake through. Serve the tart hot or cold with cream. If you are serving it cold sprinkle with icing sugar.

# BLACKBERRY JAM

*1.5 kg blackberries*
*3 teaspoons lemon juice*

*1.5 kg sugar*

Put the blackberries in a pan with the lemon juice and simmer until the berries are well softened. Add the sugar and stir over a low heat until the sugar has dissolved. Bring to the boil and boil rapidly until setting point is reached.

# SOUTHWEST MARRON, GRILLED OVER A JULIENNE OF CARROT, SNOW PEAS AND LEEK TOSSED IN GARLIC, GINGER, SAKE AND A HINT OF HARVEY ORANGE

### LEEUWIN ESTATE

*4 x 250 grams marron*
*2 carrots*
*100 grams snowpeas, topped and tailed*
*1 leek*
*250 grams butter, melted*
*salt and white pepper*
*1 clove garlic, crushed*
*12 mm ginger, finely chopped or grated*
*1 good splash sake (Japanese rice wine)*
*1 splash freshly squeezed Harvey orange juice*
*salt and pepper*
*1 tablespoon chives, chopped*

PLUNGE THE marron into boiling water for 2 to 3 minutes until the shells are just beginning to turn red, remove from the boiling water and refresh in iced water. Split each marron in half lengthwise, wash the 'coral' out and discard, also removing the sand track in the same process.

Slice the carrots into long thin lengths and then slice into julienne strips of about matchstick size in length. Slice the snowpeas finely lengthwise. Wash the leek and slice into julienne strips, matchstick length.

Brush the marron halves with melted butter and season with salt and finely ground white pepper. Place under a grill until the marron are just cooked and hot.

While the marron are grilling, heat 2 tablespoons of butter in a pan, add the garlic, ginger and vegetables and sauté very quickly, leaving the crispness in the vegetables. Add the sake and orange juice, reduce a little (about 2 minutes) and season with salt and pepper.

Arrange the julienne of vegetables on 8 plates, place the marron on top and garnish with chopped chives. Serves 8.

---

## LEEUWIN ESTATE
### Margaret River, Western Australia

•

*Southwest marron, grilled over a julienne of carrot, snow peas and leek tossed in garlic, ginger, sake and a hint of Harvey orange*

•

*Lamb medallions with eggplant, sweet peppers, assorted mushrooms*

•

*Karridale ewe's milk, pecorino and Metricup vintage havarti cheeses with raddichio, witlof, red globe grapes and lignon bread*

•

*Pecan and nougat terrine with caramelised pears and cinnamon essence syrup*

# LAMB MEDALLIONS WITH EGGPLANT, SWEET PEPPERS AND ASSORTED MUSHROOMS

### LEEUWIN ESTATE

*1 eggplant, sliced to about 1 cm thick, salted and washed, patted dry*
*1 red capsicum*
*1 yellow capsicum*
*100 grams button mushrooms, washed*
*olive oil*
*black pepper, cracked*
*salt*
*8 abalone mushrooms*
*8 enoki mushrooms (straw mushrooms)*
*24 lamb rack cutlets (3 each)*
*16 button onions, peeled*
*100 ml Rosemary Pinot Noir Jus*
*parsley, chopped finely*
*8 rosemary sprigs*

Char-grill the sliced eggplant, slice into 1 cm strips and season with cracked pepper.

Roast the capsicums until the skins have turned black, skin and seed them, then slice into 2.5 cm strips. Gently sauté the button mushrooms in 30 to 40 ml of olive oil, season with cracked pepper and salt. Gently char-grill the abalone and enoki mushrooms then season with cracked pepper and salt. Set the vegetables aside and keep warm.

Char-grill the lamb cutlets to make grill markings on each side. Place on a roasting tray and add the button onions brushed with olive oil to the tray. Brush the lamb with olive oil and season the onions and lamb with cracked pepper and salt. Roast at 190°C until the lamb medallions are still pink and juicy.

Arrange the vegetables in a rustic pile in the centre of each plate using abalone and enoki mushrooms as a garnish. Place 3 lamb cutlets around the vegetables and drizzle with 50 ml of the Rosemary and Pinot Noir Jus per plate. Garnish with finely chopped parsley and a rosemary sprig. Serves 8.

## ROSEMARY AND PINOT NOIR JUS

*1.5 litres lamb stock*
*250 ml Pinot Noir*
*sprigs of rosemary to flavour*
*1 carrot, cut in half*
*1 onion, unpeeled, cut in half*
*2 tablespoons sugar to sweeten if necessary*

Bring the lamb stock to the boil, reduce the heat and simmer until the stock has reduced by half. Bring the Pinot Noir to the boil, reduce the heat and simmer until the wine is reduced to approximately 2 tablespoons. Add the reduced stock to the wine reduction, add the rosemary, carrot and onion, and reduce by simmering until half is left.

WILLOWVALE MILL, NEW SOUTH WALES
*Country leg of spring lamb baked on top of potatoes, page 278*

*S*PRING

Check the consistency of the jus, it should be a little sticky when a few drops are rolled between the thumb and forefinger—if not reduce a little more. Strain through a fine sieve and thicken very lightly with a little arrowroot mixed in cold water. Strain again and bring to the boil, just as you are ready to serve.

## KARRIDALE EWES MILK PECORNIO AND METRICUP VINTAGE HAVARTI CHEESES WITH RADDICHIO, WITLOF, RED GLOBE GRAPES AND LIGNON BREAD

LEEUWIN ESTATE

*500 grams rye meal*
*200 grams rye meal flour*
*100 grams mixed peel*
*1 teaspoon salt*
*1 teaspoon bicarbonate of soda*
*100 grams sultanas*
*6 tablespoons walnuts, crushed*
*1 teaspoon fennel powder*
*800 ml milk*
*150 grams golden syrup*
*8 small wedges Karridale ewes milk pecorino (careful as it can be very crumbly)*
*8 small wedges Metricup vintage havarti (made by Fonti Farms in Metricup, Western Australia and available from most good gourmet shops)*
*8 leaves witlof, washed*
*8 leaves raddichio, washed (use only the tender heart leaves)*
*8 small bunches red globe grapes, washed*

To make the lignon bread, combine the rye meal, rye meal flour, mixed peel, salt, bicarbonate of soda, sultanas, crushed walnuts and fennel powder in a bowl.

Combine the milk and golden syrup in a heavy saucepan and bring to the boil. Combine this with the dry ingredients and mix into a sticky dough (this should not resemble a bread dough, it should be moist).

Place the mixture in a lined and oiled loaf tin and bake at 200°C for approximately 75 minutes or until a skewer inserted in the middle comes out clean. Slice the bread, cutting 8 slices then cutting each one diagonally in half.

Arrange the cheeses and lignon bread slices on 8 plates with witlof, raddichio leaves and red globe grapes. Serves 8.

# PECAN AND NOUGAT TERRINE WITH CARAMELISED PEARS AND CINNAMON ESSENCE SYRUP

### LEEUWIN ESTATE

*100 grams pecans*
*480 grams sugar*
*4 egg whites, whipped to soft peaks*
*6 egg yolks*
*65 grams sugar, extra*
*10 grams gelatine leaves*
*30 ml Galliano, warmed*
*400 ml cream, semi whipped*
*75 grams glace cherries, red and green, chopped*
*30 grams glace ginger, chopped*
*Caramelised Pears and Cinnamon Essence Syrup*

ROAST THE pecans in a moderate oven for 10 minutes, cool and chop coarsely. Place 280 grams of sugar in a heavy based pan and cover with enough water to wet the sugar. Cook over a medium heat and boil until the sugar turns golden brown.

Lay the chopped pecans on a lightly oiled tray and pour the caramel over the pecans. Cool and crush the praline.

Place 200 grams of sugar in a heavy based pan and cover with water, bring to the boil and simmer until it forms a thick syrup. Pour the sugar syrup into the beaten egg whites whilst whisking. Whisk until cool.

Whisk together the egg yolks and 65 grams of sugar to ribbon stage (pale and frothy). Soften the gelatine in a little cool water and dissolve in warm Galliano, then mix into the egg yolk and sugar. Fold in ⅓ of the meringue. Fold in the cream. Fold in the chopped fruit. Fold in ANOTHER ⅓ of the meringue. Fold in the praline. Lightly mix in the remaining meringue, leaving little clumps through the mixture. Pour into a lined terrine mould and chill overnight.

Arrange the Caramelised Pears on plates with a slice of terrine and the Cinnamon Syrup (reduced poaching liquid). Serves 8.

## CARAMELISED PEARS AND CINNAMON ESSENCE SYRUP

*4 pears slightly green (hard)*
*500 grams soft light brown sugar*
*2 cinnamon sticks*
*1 pod star anise (1 star only)*
*water to just cover pears*
*100 grams castor sugar*

Peel the pears and remove the seeds by hollowing in from the bottom of the pear. Place in the light brown sugar. Place the cinnamon, star anise and pear peelings into a stainless steel saucepan with the pears and brown sugar then add enough water to just cover the pears. Bring to the boil and simmer until the pears are just cooked, remove and chill the pears.

**SKILLOGALEE**
Clare Valley,
South Australia

•

*Goat's cheese soufflé with marinated capsicum and a hazelnut and balsamic dressing*

•

*Rack of Burra lamb with oven roasted vegetables and quince jelly*

•

*Quandong pie with Kangaroo Island cream*

Continue simmering the poaching liquid until it forms a slightly thickened syrup. Strain and cool, it will thicken a little more as it cools.

Slice the pears in half lengthwise and fan out by slicing through, but only to where the stem is attached. Press down on the pear with the palm of your hand to make the fan shape.

Sprinkle the pears liberally with castor sugar and caramelise with a blow torch or by placing under a grill. (Don't let the caramelised sugar become too dark as the sugar gets very bitter — a light golden colour is best.)

# GOAT'S CHEESE SOUFFLÉ WITH MARINATED CAPSICUM AND A HAZELNUT AND BALSAMIC DRESSING

SKILLOGALEE

*30 grams hazelnuts*
*30 grams fresh white breadcrumbs*
*30 grams butter*
*30 grams flour*
*200 ml milk*
*2 egg yolks*
*250 grams goat's cheese, mashed*
*salt and freshly ground pepper*
*8 egg whites*
*1 teaspoon lemon juice*
*boiling water*
*4 parts olive oil*
*1 part hazelnut oil*
*1 part balsamic vinegar*
*rocket leaves*
*Marinated Capsicum*
*hazelnuts, chopped*

TOAST THE hazelnuts in the oven until golden. Rub off the skins and place in the food processor until they resemble breadcrumbs. Mix with the breadcrumbs.

Butter 8 cm soufflé dishes. Put some of the nut mixture into each and shake to coat the base and sides. Tip out and reserve the remaining nut mixture.

Melt the butter in a pan over a low heat, add the flour and cook for 2 minutes, stirring constantly. Using a metal whisk gradually add the milk, whisking all the time. Bring to the boil and simmer for 1 minute. Remove from the heat and beat in the egg yolks. Add 170 grams of mashed goat's cheese and mix it in. Season with salt and pepper.

In a clean stainless steel bowl whisk the egg whites with the lemon juice until they form stiff peaks. Using a metal spoon fold one third of the egg whites into the cheese mixture. Fold in the rest of the egg whites in two lots. Half fill the soufflé dishes with this mixture. Divide the remaining goat's cheese between the soufflé dishes then top them up with the remaining soufflé mixture. Scatter the tops with the hazelnut mix.

Place the soufflés in a roasting tin and pour in enough boiling

SKILLOGALEE,
SOUTH AUSTRALIA
*Goat's cheese soufflé with marinated capsicum and a hazelnut and balsamic dressing,*
*Rack of Burra lamb with oven roasted vegetables and quince jelly*
*Quandong pie with Kangaroo Island cream*

*S*PRING

water to come half way up their sides. Bake in a 180°C oven for 15 minutes. Remove and cool. At this point they can be left for several hours.

When preparing to serve, turn the soufflés out and place on a greased oven tray. Cook in the oven for 10 more minutes.

To make a hazelnut vinaigrette, put the olive oil, hazelnut oil and balsamic vinegar in a screwtop jar and shake well.

Serve on a small bed of rocket leaves and drizzle with vinaigrette. Place several strips of Marinated Capsicum on one side and sprinkle with a few chopped hazelnuts.

## MARINATED CAPSICUM

*1 kg red capsicums*
*2 cloves garlic, peeled*
*3 sprigs thyme*
*2 red chillies, split lengthwise*
*2 tablespoons sugar*
*½ cup olive oil*
*½ cup Riesling*

Roast the capsicums in a 180°C oven until the skins blacken. Put them in a plastic bag and leave for a few minutes to cool slightly. Peel the skin from the capsicums and cut into strips.

Put all the other ingredients in a saucepan and bring slowly to the boil. Pack the capsicum strips into jars and pour over the liquid. Seal and store in the refrigerator.

## RACK OF BURRA LAMB WITH OVEN ROASTED VEGETABLES AND QUINCE JELLY

### SKILLOGALEE

*6 racks of lamb with 4 chops each*
*2 tablespoons grainy mustard*
*2 tablespoons parsley, chopped*
*2 tablespoons olive oil*
*1 clove garlic, minced*
*black pepper, freshly ground*
*2 potatoes, unpeeled*
*1 onion, peeled and cut in wedges*
*2 zucchini*
*½ a small butternut pumpkin, peeled*
*1 sweet potato, peeled*
*1 red capsicum, cut into wedges*
*olive oil*
*black pepper, freshly ground*
*Quince Jelly*

TRIM THE lamb of all fat and sinew. Mix together the mustard, parsley, olive oil, garlic and pepper. Spread this mixture over the meat.

Cut all the vegetables into chunks roughly the same size. Put into a roasting tin and drizzle over some olive oil and sprinkle with black pepper. Toss. Roast in a 180°C oven for 45 minutes or until tender.

Roast the lamb in a 180°C fan-forced oven for 18 minutes and rest covered in a warm place for 4 minutes. Carve the chops and arrange, overlapping against a mound of oven-roasted vegetables. Garnish with a sprig of rosemary and a spoonful of Quince Jelly.

## QUINCE JELLY

*8 large quinces or 12 medium quinces*
*480 ml water*
*2 kg castor sugar*

Rub the fluff from the quinces, put them uncut into a preserving pan, add the water and the sugar. Bring to the boil and simmer for 4 hours. After 4 hours the jelly should be pink, clear and slightly thickened. Strain the liquid into sterilised jars and seal.

## QUANDONG PIE WITH KANGAROO ISLAND CREAM

### SKILLOGALEE

*500 grams quandongs, halved and stones removed*
*250 grams sugar*
*125 ml water*
*250 grams cold butter*
*500 grams plain flour*
*3 to 4 tablespoons iced water*
*1 egg yolk, beaten with a little milk*
*castor sugar*
*double cream*

PUT THE quandongs, sugar and 125 ml of water in a pan and gently stew until tender. Quandongs should be soft but not completely broken down. If the mixture becomes too dry, add a little more water.

In a food processor mix the butter and the flour until they resemble breadcrumbs. With the motor running add just enough iced water to form the dough into a ball. Remove and roll out to line a 22.5 cm pie plate. Fill the pie with the quandong mixture. Roll the remaining pastry out for a lid and decorate with pastry leaves. Brush with the egg yolk glaze and rest in the refrigerator for 30 minutes. Bake at 180°C for 30 to 35 minutes. Dust with castor sugar and serve with rich cream.

**RED OCHRE GRILL**
Cairns, Queensland

•

*Hot pecan, oyster and orange salad with lemon aspen mayonnaise*

•

*Steamed fish and yabbies in banana leaf with coconut, lemon myrtle and green mango, lime salsa*

•

*Wattle seed pavlova with passionfruit glaze and sugar bark*

# HOT PECAN, OYSTER AND ORANGE SALAD WITH LEMON ASPEN MAYONNAISE

### RED OCHRE GRILL

*16 freshly shucked oysters*
*3 oranges*
*200 grams salad mix (mesculan) with rocket for extra zing*
*480 ml macadamia oil*
*24 pecan nuts (40 grams)*
*120 ml Lemon Aspen Mayonnaise*

DO NOT wash the oysters! Freshly opened oysters should be lying in their own salt water. Segment the oranges into 24 segments, retaining any juice to add to the salad. Check the salad mix for dirt or sand and if necessary wash and drain. Chill in a mixing bowl.

Arrange the salad on four plates. Divide the orange segments evenly between the plates. Remove the oysters from their shells, discarding any shell fragments. Place the oysters on the salad (perhaps retaining one oyster in a shell to use as a garnish).

Heat the macadamia oil in a pan and toss the pecans until they are warm. Sprinkle the pecans over the salad. Drizzle each plate of salad with 30 ml of Lemon Aspen Mayonnaise. Finish with the garnishing oyster and serve. Serves 4.

## LEMON ASPEN MAYONNAISE

*100 grams lemon aspen*
*300 ml white vinegar*
*30 grams castor sugar*
*200 ml lemon juice*
*50 ml dijon mustard*
*10 egg yolks*
*500 ml vegetable oil*
*480 ml macadamia oil*

Purée the lemon aspen and boil with the vinegar, sugar and lemon juice. Reduce by approximately one third. Cool and strain.

Beat the lemon aspen vinegar with the mustard and egg yolks. Slowly add the oil mix to form a light mayonnaise consistency. Refrigerated, this will keep for up to one month.

**FRANKLIN MANOR, TASMANIA**
*Chocolate and walnut dessert cake, page 260*

$\mathcal{S}$PRING

# STEAMED FISH AND YABBIES IN BANANA LEAF WITH COCONUT, LEMON MYRTLE AND GREEN MANGO, LIME SALSA

### RED OCHRE GRILL

½ bird's eye chilli, finely chopped
5 grams ginger, finely chopped
5 grams coriander, finely chopped
8 lemon myrtle leaves, finely chop 4 leaves
juice of ½ a lime
100 ml coconut cream
splash of fish sauce
8 large red claw yabbies
800 grams fresh red emperor fillet, coral trout or similar
4 pieces banana leaf 20 cm square (if not available locally enquire at a quality fruit wholesaler or Asian food store)
Lime Salsa

Mix the chilli, ginger, coriander, finely chopped myrtle leaves, lime juice, coconut cream and fish sauce together to make a marinade.

Boil the yabbies for 3 minutes in salty water. Peel and de-vein. Retain and wash out 4 heads. Slice the fish fillet into 8 x 100 gram, 1 cm thick pieces. Lay the fish and yabby tails on a tray and drizzle with marinade. Chill so the coconut cream sets.

Blanch the banana leaf pieces in boiling water then refresh in cold water. Place the leaves shiny side down and stack 2 fish fillet pieces and 2 yabby tails in the centre of each leaf piece. Apply more marinade, then place 1 whole myrtle leaf on top. Wrap by folding the sides over, then the front, then roll into the back edge. Trim any excess from the back edge. Hold the parcel firmly and put it straight into the steamer tray. Repeat for each parcel. Store the parcels on the steamer tray in the refrigerator until you are ready to cook them. They can be prepared the day before.

Steam at a rapid boil for 12–15 minutes, checking if the fish is cooked by either opening one or seeing if the juices seeping out are white and coagulated — then the fish is cooked.

Garnish by slicing open the banana leaf and peeling it back to expose the steaming white fish, spoon some Lime Salsa down the edge of the parcel and onto the plate. For an extra touch put a yabby head on a bed of curled julienne of vegetables and sprinkle with black sesame seeds. Serves 4.

## LIME SALSA

1 large greenish mango (ie. very firm, cuts like a raw potato)
1 lime
½ bird's eye chilli
5 grams coriander, 5 to 6 sprigs
50 ml rice wine vinegar
100 ml peanut oil
salt and pepper

Dice the mango into 5 mm pieces. Zest, segment and juice the lime. Finely chop the chilli and coriander. Gently mix all the remaining ingredients and season to taste.

# WATTLE SEED PAVLOVA WITH PASSIONFRUIT GLAZE AND SUGAR BARK

### RED OCHRE GRILL

*5 egg whites*
*225 grams castor sugar*
*5 ml lemon juice*
*2.5 grams cornflour (a pinch)*
*50 grams castor sugar, extra*
*25 grams macadamia nuts, ground*
*2 grams cinnamon, ground*
*300 grams wattle seed*
*100 ml water*
*40 grams castor sugar*
*400 ml whipping cream*
*icing sugar, optional*

WHIP TOGETHER the egg whites, sugar, lemon juice and cornflour in an electric mixer until the whites are shiny and stiff. Spread the mixture 1 cm thick on oiled greaseproof paper or a sheet of silicon paper.

Mix together the extra castor sugar, macadamia nuts and cinnamon. Sprinkle this macadamia crust over the egg white mixture evenly. Slide onto a flat baking tray and bake at 160°C for 20 to 25 minutes. Allow to cool but do not place in a refrigerator.

Make some wattle seed essence by placing the wattle seed, water and castor sugar together in a pot and simmering for 5 minutes. Set aside to cool.

Turn the pavlova over onto a clean tea towel. Whip the cream with 30 ml of the wattle seed essence until stiff. Spread the cream over the pavlova base. Roll up using a tea towel as a support. Allow it to set in the refrigerator for 1 hour. Open the tea towel and cut it at a 45° angle into 6 pieces. Stand the pavlova pieces upright on cool plates. Pour on approximately 50 ml of Passionfruit Glaze and garnish with a Sugarbark shard poked carefully into the top of the pavlova. Dust with icing sugar if desired. Serves 6.

## PASSIONFRUIT GLAZE

*50 ml fresh passionfruit pulp*
*150 ml water*
*150 grams castor sugar*
*10 ml white rum*

Simmer all the ingredients together for 20 minutes in a stainless steel pot. Strain out the pips, adding approximately one quarter of the pips back into the sauce, then chill.

## SUGARBARK

*100 grams coffee sugar*
*100 grams castor sugar*
*100 grams raw sugar*

Combine the sugars and sprinkle about 2 mm thick on a flat baking tray. Melt to a dark golden colour in a hot oven, cool slightly. Cut into 10 cm squares and twist to form bizarre shapes. Hold for a few moments until cool, store in a dry airtight container.

**LAMONT'S WINERY AND RESTAURANT**
Swan Valley,
Western Australia

•

*Prawn salad with guacamole and crispy bacon*

•

*Venison salad with fresh asparagus and eggplant croutons*

•

*Chocolate nougat ice-cream with roast coconut anglaise*

# PRAWN SALAD WITH GUACAMOLE AND CRISPY BACON

LAMONT'S WINERY AND RESTAURANT

*3 ripe avocadoes, peeled*
*2 tablespoons sour cream*
*salt and pepper, to taste*
*½ red onion, finely diced*
*juice of 2 lemons*
*salad leaves, for 6 serves*
*24 –30 tiger prawns (depending on size), peeled with tails left on*
*3 rashers bacon, roughly chopped and pan fried until crisp*
*pepper, to taste*
*chopped chives, to garnish*
*Balsamic Vinaigrette*

MASH THE avocadoes roughly with a fork. Add the sour cream, salt and pepper and onion. Add lemon juice to taste.

Season and dress the salad leaves with Balsamic Vinaigrette in a large mixing bowl. Divide the salad leaves between 6 plates and pile 4 or 5 prawns on top of each other. Place a large dessertspoon of guacamole on top of the prawns.

Finish with a sprinkling of the bacon. Season with the pepper and garnish with the chives. Serves 6.

## BALSAMIC VINAIGRETTE

*100 ml balsamic vinegar*
*300 ml olive oil*
*1 teaspoon salt*
*1 teaspoon pepper*

Combine all of the ingredients in a jar or bottle and shake vigorously until combined.

# VENISON SALAD WITH FRESH ASPARAGUS AND EGGPLANT CROUTONS

LAMONT'S WINERY AND RESTAURANT

*24 spears asparagus*
*18 slices 1 cm thick venison*
*olive oil*
*salt and pepper*
*1 sourdough stick*
*100 ml raspberry vinegar*
*300 ml olive oil*
*1 teaspoon salt*
*1 teaspoon pepper*
*salad leaves, for 6 serves*
*salt and pepper, extra, to taste*
*fresh Parmesan cheese, grated*
*Eggplant Jam*

CUT THE ends off the asparagus (about 2 cm) and discard. Immerse the tops in boiling salted water for 1 minute. Refresh immediately in a bowl of iced water and stand until cool. Remove and pat dry.

Marinate the venison in olive oil and salt and pepper until tender. Remove from the marinade and seal on a high heat under a char-grill or on a flat top for 2 minutes on either side. Rest for 15 minutes in a warm place.

Slice the sourdough stick diagonally across into 5 mm thick toasts. When you have 12, fry in hot oil or a deep fryer until crisp and golden brown. Drain on kitchen paper.

Pour the raspberry vinegar, olive oil and seasoning into a jar or bottle and shake vigorously until the oil and vinegar are combined.

Season and dress the salad leaves with the raspberry vinaigrette in a large mixing bowl. Add the asparagus spears and venison slices, pouring in any residual juices from the venison.

Distribute evenly between 6 plates and season with salt and pepper. Garnish with a sprinkling of fresh Parmesan cheese. Spread some Eggplant Jam on the croutons and arrange two around each plate. Serves 6.

## EGGPLANT JAM

*1.5 kg eggplant*
*salt*
*7 tablespoons olive oil*
*3 cloves garlic, minced*
*2 teaspoons sweet paprika powder*

*2 teaspoons cumin*
*¾ teaspoon harissa*
*5 tablespoons lemon juice*
*salt and pepper, to taste*

Preheat the oven to 190°C. Cut the stems off the eggplant and peel the skin every 2 cm so you get a striped eggplant. Discard the unwanted peel. Slice the eggplant horizontally into 2 cm slices. Place in a colander, sprinkle with salt and stand for 30 minutes. Rinse well and pat dry.

Using 3 tablespoons of the olive oil, brush the eggplant on both sides and brown on a grill or flat top. Place on a baking tray and bake in the oven for 20 minutes or until quite soft.

Process with the garlic, paprika, cumin, harissa and remaining oil. Stir in the lemon juice. Season with the salt and pepper. This quantity makes much more than you need, since you only need 1 cup for the salad.

# CHOCOLATE NOUGAT ICE-CREAM WITH ROAST COCONUT ANGLAISE

### LAMONT'S WINERY AND RESTAURANT

*Chocolate Cream:*
200 ml cream
300 grams dark chocolate buttons
*Gelato Base:*
12 egg yolks
100 grams castor sugar
1.5 litres cream
200 grams honey
*Roast Coconut Mix:*
½ cup whole raw peanuts, blanched
½ cup whole raw almonds
4 cups coconut threads
750 grams Italian nougat, cut into small, rough dice
*Coconut Anglaise:*
1 cup roasted coconut threads
1.2 litres cream
8 egg yolks
200 grams sugar

Place the cream in a saucepan and bring to the boil. Remove from the heat and whisk in the dark chocolate. Set aside to cool.

To make the gelato base, whisk the egg yolks and sugar together in a large bowl. Place the cream and honey in a saucepan and gently heat over the stove. Combine with the egg yolk mixture, return to the stove and cook on low heat, stirring constantly, until the mixture coats the back of a wooden spoon. Cool.

To make the roast coconut mix, chop the peanuts and almonds roughly in a food processor. Roast the coconut threads and nuts in a slow, 100–120°C oven until they have browned slightly. Set aside to cool. Combine with the nougat.

Add 3 cups of the roast coconut mix to the chocolate cream and mix thoroughly. Mix together with the gelato base.

Pour the mixture into an ice-cream machine and churn until firm. Spoon into a log mould and freeze overnight.

To make the coconut anglaise, place the coconut and cream in a saucepan and bring to the boil. Remove from the heat and set aside for 30 minutes. Strain through a fine sieve and add to the egg yolks and sugar as for the gelato base. Set aside to cool.

To serve, turn out the ice-cream and cut into 2–3 cm thick slices. Divide between six serving plates. Pour the coconut anglaise over the top. Serves 6. This dish has been adapted from a recipe by Stephano Manfredi.

## CHAR-GRILLED QUAIL ON A BED OF SPINACH
### TYNWALD

*4 slices bread, diced*
*4 rashers bacon, diced*
*100 ml good olive oil*
*30 ml balsamic vinegar*
*1 clove garlic, crushed*
*salt and pepper*
*24 spinach leaves*
*4 quails*

PLACE THE diced bread on a baking sheet and bake in a medium to hot oven until golden, keep warm. Cook the bacon in a little oil. Blend together the oil, balsamic vinegar, garlic, salt and pepper to make a balsamic dressing. Wash and remove the stalks from the spinach. Grill the quail until cooked. Arrange 6 spinach leaves on each plate. Cut each quail into 8 pieces and arrange on the spinach. Sprinkle with the bacon and toasted bread, then dress with the balsamic dressing. Serves 4.

## CARPACCIO OF MILK-FED LAMB AND WARM PINK EYE POTATO SALAD
### TYNWALD

*300 grams lamb loin, sliced thinly*
*2 tablespoons oil*
*5 stems mint*
*12 pink eye potatoes (4 per person)*
*125 ml olive oil*
*50 grams white wine vinegar*
*1 teaspoon French mustard*
*salt and pepper*
*parsley, chopped*
*1 red capsicum, char-grilled*
*8 black olives, sliced (2 per person)*
*1 onion, diced*
*4 butter lettuce leaves*

PAT THE sliced lamb loin with the 2 tablespoons of oil and place the mint leaves on top. Cover with plastic wrap and set aside to marinate.

Leaving the skins on, boil the potatoes in water until cooked. Drain and cut each potato into four. Blend together the olive oil, white wine vinegar, mustard and salt and pepper to make a vinaigrette. Sprinkle the parsley over the potatoes and add the vinaigrette. Peel the skin from the grilled capsicum and slice into a julienne.

Arrange the lamb on four plates with some mint leaves. Put the sliced olives to one side of the lamb and some of the onion to the other side. Place a lettuce leaf on each plate and fill it with some potato salad. Top the salad with slices of red capsicum. Serves 4.

---

**TYNWALD**
New Norfolk, Southern Tasmania

•

*Char-grilled quail on a bed of spinach*

•

*Carpaccio of milk-fed lamb and warm pink eye potato salad*

•

*Berry Tiers*

## BERRY TIERS

### TYNWALD

*2 kg mixed berries*
*250 ml water*
*3 tablespoons corn flour*
*Tiers Biscuits*

*Crème Patissier*
*1 kg strawberries, washed and hulled*
*icing sugar*

Place 1 kg of berries together with the water into a saucepan and bring to the boil. Remove to a food processor and process until well blended. Strain back into the saucepan and bring to the boil again. Mix the cornflour with a little extra water and whisk into the berry coulis. Set aside to cool.

Pour enough berry coulis to cover the bottom of each plate. Place a Tiers Biscuit in the middle. Spread the biscuit with some of the creme patissier and scatter some of the remaining berries over the creme patissier. Repeat this, building up the tiers. Top with a biscuit dusted with icing sugar. Serves 8 to 10.

## TIERS BISCUITS

*240 grams egg whites*
*400 grams castor sugar*
*½ teaspoon vanilla essence*

*200 grams butter, melted at room temperature*
*240 grams plain flour*
*60 grams cocoa*

Whisk the egg whites and sugar together until the mixture forms soft peaks. Fold in the vanilla and melted butter. Sift the flour and cocoa together and mix these in.

Spoon onto a buttered baking tray and spread in thin circles. Bake in a preheated 160°C oven until the biscuits have darkened slightly. Remove from the tray and allow the biscuits to cool completely. Store in an airtight container.

## CRÈME PATISSIER

*2 vanilla beans, split and scraped*
*1 litre milk*
*200 grams castor sugar*

*3 tablespoons cornflour*
*10 egg yolks*

Place the vanilla beans and milk in a saucepan and bring to the boil. Whisk the sugar, cornflour and egg yolks together. Pour the boiling milk onto the egg mixture and mix well. Transfer to a saucepan and stir over a low heat (80°C) until it has thickened.

---

Willowvale Mill,
New South Wales
*Fruit tart, page 280*

*S*PRING

**DEAR FRIENDS GARDEN RESTAURANT**
Swan Valley, Western Australia

•

*Tian of smoked crocodile and corn-fed chicken*

•

*Fresh Darling Range trout*

•

*Fruit sushi*

•

*The Gippsland Blues*

# TIAN OF SMOKED CROCODILE AND CORN-FED CHICKEN

## DEAR FRIENDS GARDEN RESTAURANT

*20 tomatoes, blanched*
*10 bush tomatoes*
*assorted lettuce leaves*
*5 ml sherry vinegar*
*5 ml red wine*
*salt and pepper, to taste*
*20 ml peanut oil*
*5 ml olive oil*
*½ apple, peeled and cored*
*¼ avocado*
*juice from ¼ lemon*
*120 grams shredded smoked crocodile*
*120 grams shredded smoked corn-fed chicken*
*lemon myrtle chilli sauce*
*1 teaspoon mayonnaise*
*chervil leaves*
*green mayonnaise*
*2 chervil leaves, extra, to garnish*
*Tomato Coulis*

CHOP BOTH lots of tomatoes into rectangles. Cut the lettuce leaves into chiffonnade. Combine the sherry vinegar, red wine, salt and pepper and stir to dissolve. Add the peanut and olive oils and whisk to an emulsion, taste and adjust the seasoning if necessary. Pour over the lettuce leaves. Cut the apple and avocado into 3 mm dice, combine and sprinkle with the lemon juice. Mix the meats with the lemon myrtle chilli sauce, mayonnaise and dressed lettuce leaves.

Layer the tomatoes, lettuce leaf mixture, apple mixture and chervil leaves on a plate, finishing with tomato. Cut to form a diamond shape, top with Tomato Coulis and garnish with the green mayonnaise and extra chervil leaves. Serves 4.

## TOMATO COULIS

*200 grams tomatoes or bush tomatoes, chopped*
*50 ml red wine vinegar*
*40 grams tomato purée*
*dash tabasco sauce*
*dash ketchup (tomato sauce)*
*50 ml virgin olive oil*

Place all of the ingredients except the olive oil in a food processor and blend to a purée. Add the oil, blend for 30 seconds, and repeat three times. Measure out 30 ml (use the remainder for other dishes).

## FRESH DARLING RANGE TROUT
### DEAR FRIENDS GARDEN RESTAURANT

*4 x 150–180 gram trout darne*
*salt and pepper, to taste*
*60 grams butter*
*25 ml fresh lime juice*
*45 ml lime cordial*
*30 ml white wine*
*90 ml cream*
*30 grams lilly pilly*
*butter, extra*
*few sprigs lemon thyme*
*5 ml squid ink*
*10 ml yoghurt*

LIGHTLY SEASON the trout and brush with the butter. Grill or pan fry over very low heat until the centre bone comes away easily.

Heat a saucepan and add the lime juice, lime cordial and white wine. Cook over medium heat until reduced by half. Add the cream, reduce again, then add the lilly pilly. Thicken the sauce with the extra butter.

Place the trout on serving plates, and run the sauce around. Garnish with the lemon thyme and the combined squid ink and yoghurt. Serves 4.

## FRUIT SUSHI
### DEAR FRIENDS GARDEN RESTAURANT

*1 mango, pulp only, puréed with 30 grams sugar*
*1 pawpaw, pulp only, puréed with 30 grams sugar*
*135 grams strawberries, pulp only, puréed with 30 grams sugar*
*375 grams white rice*
*395 ml cold water*
*45 ml coconut milk*
*30 grams sugar*
*pinch salt*
*15 ml coconut liqueur*
*175 grams assorted fruit, chopped*
*lemon slices, kiwifruit, orange julienne and mint leaves, to garnish*

STRAIN THE mango, pawpaw and strawberries separately.

Rinse the rice and cook in the water until soft. Drain and stand for 10 minutes. Transfer to a large bowl, add the coconut milk, sugar, salt and coconut liqueur and mix gently until cooled.

Form the rice into oval shapes with moistened hands. Place on serving plates and arrange the assorted fruit on top. Serve with the fruit purées and garnish with the lemon slices, kiwifruit, orange julienne and mint leaves. Serves 4.

## THE GIPPSLAND BLUES
### DEAR FRIENDS GARDEN RESTAURANT

*Sauce:*
250 grams plums
35 grams sugar
120 grams redcurrant jelly, melted
½ teaspoon English mustard
75 ml port
120 grams sweet Davidson plum purée
75 ml orange juice
juice from ½ lemon
15 grams shallots, finely chopped
zest from ½ orange, julienne
60 grams butter
120 grams flour
3 eggs, beaten
300 ml water
35 grams Gippsland Blue cheese, grated
olive oil
*Straws*
rambutan slices, mint leaves, redcurrants and caramelised orange, lemon, grapefruit and lime zest, to garnish

To make the sauce, stew the plums with the sugar and strain three times. Place in a bowl with the redcurrant jelly and mustard. Whisk in the port, plum purée and orange and lemon juices. Blanch the shallots, add to the plum mixture and stir in the orange zest. Set aside

Melt the butter in a saucepan and stir in the flour. Gradually add the beaten eggs and water, stirring constantly, until smooth. Stir in the cheese. Pipe out onto greased paper, then deep fry in the oil until golden. Drain well.

Serve with the straws and sauce and garnished with the rambutan, mint, redcurrants and caramelised zests. Serves 5 or 6.

## STRAWS

120 grams flour
salt and cayenne pepper, to taste
60 grams butter
60 grams Gippsland Blue cheese, grated
1 egg yolk
water
salt

Sift the flour, salt and cayenne pepper. Rub in the butter, then blend in the cheese. Add the egg yolk and enough water to make a firm dough. Roll out to 4 mm thick. Cut into straws 7.5 cm long and 7 mm wide and twist. Bake at 180° C for 7 minutes, remove from the oven and sprinkle with the salt. If preferred, ready made puff pastry can be used.

---

MOUNT LOFTY HOUSE,
MERCURE GRAND HOTEL,
SOUTH AUSTRALIA
*Scallop ravioli with wholegrain mustard and crustacean oil, page 304*

*S*PRING

## MOUNT LOFTY HOUSE, MERCURE GRAND HOTEL
### Adelaide Hills, South Australia

*Scallop ravioli with wholegrain mustard and crustacean oil*

•

*Double breast of baby chicken with potato and sage galettes, chicken liver parfait, sweet corn in red wine vinegar sauce and rocket salad*

•

*Strawberries flamed with white curacao, vanilla bean mascapone and orange lace biscuits*

# SCALLOP RAVIOLI WITH WHOLEGRAIN MUSTARD AND CRUSTACEAN OIL

MOUNT LOFTY HOUSE, MERCURE GRAND HOTEL

*wonton wrappers*
*1 egg white*
*Scallop Mousse*
*Crustacean Oil*
*deep-fried leek julienne*

Lay the wonton wrappers out on a bench and brush with a very light amount of egg white. Pipe the Scallop Mousse on top of the wonton wrappers, then carefully cover with another wrapper. Cut with a cutter and press the edges well.

Cook the ravioli in boiling salted water for 2–3 minutes. Drain, and toss in a bowl with the Crustacean Oil. Arrange on a serving plate and garnish with the leek julienne. Serve immediately.

## SCALLOP MOUSSE

*400 grams fresh scallops, cleaned*
*1 egg white*
*pinch cayenne*
*pinch salt*
*pepper, to taste*
*300 grams cream*

Ensure all of the ingredients are chilled. Place the scallops in a food processor and blend until smooth. Add the egg white and seasonings and blend again as quickly as possible.

Remove the mixture and place in a bowl over ice. Fold the cream through with a spoon, then pan the scallop mousse through a drum sieve. Keep chilled at all times over ice.

## CRUSTACEAN OIL

*bones from 1 crayfish*
*200 ml vegetable oil*
*50 ml olive oil*
*50 ml whole grain mustard*
*pinch of salt*

Chop the crayfish bones until small, then spread out on a tray and roast at 170°C until totally dry. Place the dried bones in a saucepan and pour the vegetable and olive oils over. Bring to a simmer over a low heat to get the last of the moisture out of the bones. Pour the bones and oil into a container, cover and store in a cool room or refrigerator for 48 hours. Drain the oil through a very fine muslin cloth and mix with the mustard and salt.

# Spring

## DOUBLE BREAST OF BABY CHICKEN WITH POTATO AND SAGE GALETTES, CHICKEN LIVER PARFAIT, SWEET CORN IN RED WINE VINEGAR SAUCE AND ROCKET SALAD

### MOUNT LOFTY HOUSE, MERCURE GRAND HOTEL

*8 double chicken breasts, skin on*
*balsamic vinegar*
*garlic, chopped*
*olive oil*
*rocket leaves, picked and washed*
*150 ml bordelaise (red wine) sauce*
*20 ml red wine vinegar, or to taste*
*pinch chopped parsley*
*pinch chopped sage*
*fresh sweet corn, cooked and removed from the cob*
*1 teaspoon butter*
*salt and pepper, to taste*
*Potato and Sage Galettes*
*fresh sage leaves*
*Chicken Liver Parfait*

BOIL, STEAM, microwave or fry the chicken breasts until tender.

Combine the balsamic vinegar, garlic and olive oil to make a vinaigrette. Toss the vinaigrette through the rocket leaves.

Place the bordelaise sauce, red wine vinegar, parsley, sage, corn and butter in a saucepan and bring to a simmer over a medium heat just until the butter melts. Add salt and pepper to taste. Serve immediately.

Serve the chicken on top of the Potato and Sage Galettes (two per serve), garnished with the fresh sage and red wine sauce, and with the rocket salad and chicken liver parfaits alongside. Spoon the corn over the parfaits. Serves 4.

### POTATO AND SAGE GALETTES

*500 grams potato*
*150 grams plain flour*
*salt and pepper, to taste*
*50 ml cream*
*2 eggs*
*sage, chopped*
*3 egg whites*

Peel the potato and cook in boiling salted water until tender, then pan through a drum sieve while still very hot. Place in a bowl with the flour, salt and pepper, cream, eggs and sage, and mix. Whisk the egg whites and fold through the potato mixture. Drop tablespoonfuls into a frying pan with a little oil and fry until golden.

## CHICKEN LIVER PARFAIT

*200 grams chicken liver, cleaned*
*4 shallots, chopped*
*good pinch chopped parsley*
*salt and pepper, to taste*
*50 ml bordelaise (red wine) sauce*
*2 eggs*
*50 grams softened butter*

Place the liver, shallots, parsley, salt and pepper, bordelaise sauce and eggs in a food processor and process until smooth. Add the butter and mix well. Pour into four buttered dariole moulds, cover with foil and cook in a water bath at 150°C for 20–25 minutes.

## STRAWBERRIES FLAMED WITH WHITE CURACAO, VANILLA BEAN MASCARPONE AND ORANGE LACE BISCUITS

### MOUNT LOFTY HOUSE, MERCURE GRAND HOTEL

*125 grams sugar*
*water*
*1 lemon, juice and zest*
*1 orange, juice and zest*
*500 ml orange juice*
*20 ml brandy*
*50 ml Cointreau*
*50 ml white Curacao*
*100 ml cream*
*seeds from ½ vanilla bean*
*100 grams mascarpone*
*icing sugar, to taste*
*3 punnets strawberries, hulled*
*butter*
*white Curacao*
*butter, extra*
*Orange Lace Biscuits*
*sprig woodruff, to garnish*

Place the sugar and a little water in a saucepan and cook over a medium heat until the sugar has dissolved. Carefully add the lemon juice and zest and orange juice and zest and simmer gently for 5–10 minutes, or until no hard caramel lumps are left. Add the brandy, Cointreau and white Curacao and remove from the heat.

Semi-whip the cream, then gently fold the vanilla seeds, mascarpone and icing sugar through.

Heat the strawberries in some butter in a frying pan, then flame with Curacao. Add some sauce and a knob of butter and simmer. Quickly spoon into warm bowls with the remaining sauce. Top with mascarpone and serve with lace biscuits. Garnish. Serves 4.

## ORANGE LACE BISCUITS

*60 grams butter*
*100 grams sugar*
*30 grams plain flour*
*50 ml orange juice*
*zest of 1 orange*

Mix the butter and sugar, then stir in the flour, juice and zest. Spread onto baking paper on a baking tray and bake at 180°C until golden. Remove from the tray with a spatula and cool over a rolling pin.

---

CARRINGTON HOUSE,
NEW SOUTH WALES
*Lemon-chocolate charlotte with a blueberry compote, page 313*

$\mathcal{S}$PRING

**PICNICS AT FAIRHILL**
Sunshine Coast,
Queensland

•

*Crocodile shoi mai in clear soup with native herbs*

•

*Barramundi fillet with mud crab and shallot crust*

•

*Black sapote and macadamia tartlet*

# CROCODILE SHOI MAI IN CLEAR SOUP WITH NATIVE HERBS

### PICNICS AT FAIRHILL

*150 grams crocodile tail meat*
*2 egg whites*
*½ teaspoon fish sauce*
*½ teaspoon sweet chilli sauce*
*2 teaspoons chopped coriander*
*50 ml cream*
*1 packet of wonton wrappers*
*rice flour (or cornflour)*
Soup:
*1.5 litres water*
*2–3 teaspoons dashi powder*
*2 teaspoons fish sauce, extra*
*12 lemon myrtle leaves*
*1 finger lime, sliced*
*6 mountain pepper leaves*
*2 barbed wire grass stems*
*2 sprigs sago bush*
*6 scrambling lily shoots*
*24 warrigal greens leaves*

BLEND THE crocodile meat, egg whites, fish sauce, chilli sauce, coriander and cream together in a food processor to form a coarse mousseline.

Spread the wonton wrappers and brush their edges lightly with water. Drop a teaspoon of filling onto each wrapper. Gather the corners together and pinch tightly to seal. Place on a tray dusted with rice flour and store in the refrigerator.

To make the soup, place the water, dashi powder and extra fish sauce in a saucepan and bring to a simmer. Add the wontons and poach for 8 to 10 minutes.

Add the remaining ingredients. Return to a simmer, then remove from the heat and infuse for 35 minutes. Serve in hot bowls. Serves 6.

# BARRAMUNDI FILLET WITH MUD CRAB AND SHALLOT CRUST

### PICNICS AT FAIRHILL

*200 grams mud crab meat*
*3 egg whites*
*6 golden shallots, peeled, finely sliced and lightly sautéed*
*2 tablespoons Parmesan cheese, grated*
*60 ml cream*
*½ teaspoon fish sauce*
*barramundi fillets (140–150 grams per serve)*

COMBINE THE crab meat, egg whites, shallots, Parmesan cheese, cream and fish sauce well by hand. Spread the mixture over the barramundi.

Bake at 180°C for 15 minutes, then place under a griller for a few minutes to brown. Serve with salad. Serves 6 to 8.

# BLACK SAPOTE AND MACADAMIA TARTLET

## PICNICS AT FAIRHILL

1 cup very ripe black sapote flesh
2 small eggs (or 1 egg and 1 egg yolk)
⅓ cup sugar
½ teaspoon vanilla essence
1½ tablespoons cognac or brandy
⅛ teaspoon nutmeg
¼ cup milk
¼ cup cream
prebaked shortcrust pastry shells (5–6 cm diameter)
¾ cup light brown sugar
1 tablespoon unsalted butter
1 cup macadamia nuts, chopped
1 tablespoon cream, extra

COMBINE THE black sapote flesh, eggs, sugar, vanilla, cognac, nutmeg, milk and cream. Mix until smooth. Pour into the prebaked pastry shells and bake at 200°C for 15 minutes, then reduce the heat to 180°C and bake for a further 35 minutes. Remove from the oven and allow to cool.

For the crust, combine the brown sugar, unsalted butter, macadamias and cream, then spread over the tarts. Place under a hot griller and grill until brown. Serve either hot or cold with Caramel Sauce. Serves 6.

## CARAMEL SAUCE

125 grams butter, melted
1 cup brown sugar, sieved
225 gram can reduced cream

Combine the butter and brown sugar in a saucepan and stir over a medium heat until the sugar has dissolved. Increase the heat and boil rapidly for 3 minutes without stirring. When golden, add the cream. Makes 1½ cups.

# MUD CRAB AND PAWPAW SALAD

## SEVEN SPIRIT BAY

3 capsicums, yellow, green and red
3 cloves garlic, crushed
8 bird's eye chillies, finely diced
6 limes, zest and juice
3 tablespoons brown sugar
¼ cup chives, sliced
400 ml can coconut cream
1 tablespoon ground sea salt
2 tablespoon fresh coriander, chopped
4 cooked mud crabs, flesh taken out
2 small pawpaws, melon balls
½ lettuce chiffonnade (finely sliced)

CUT THE four sides out of the capsicums, thinly cut these horizontally then slice thinly lengthwise. Place in ice water and leave to curl.

Mix together the garlic, chillies, lime juice, sugar, chives coconut

---

**SEVEN SPIRIT BAY**
Cobourg Peninsula,
Northern Territory

•

*Mud crab and pawpaw salad*

•

*Barramundi fillet with a tempura of Arafura sea bugs and tamarind sauce*

•

*Iced Pineapple and mango mousse*

cream, salt and coriander. Put aside the lime zest to be used later.

Place the crab meat in a large bowl with the dressing. Add half the pawpaw balls. Clean the crab shells and place the chiffonnade of lettuce in the shells. Then place the crab salad on top of the lettuce. Garnish with the capsicum curls, lime zest and the remaining pawpaw.

This dish can be served as an entreé or main meal. For an entreé, simply halve the quantities and place the mixture in pawpaw shells rather than crab shells. Serves 4 as a main course.

## BARRAMUNDI FILLET WITH A TEMPURA OF ARAFURA SEA BUGS AND TAMARIND SAUCE

### SEVEN SPIRIT BAY

*8 large tomatoes, finely diced*
*1 tablespoon turmeric*
*1 tablespoon ginger*
*1½ tablespoon tamarind pulp*
*¼ cup palm sugar*
*1 tablespoon shrimp paste*
*1½ litres water*
*1 cup jasmine rice*
*6 egg whites*
*pinch salt*

*1 cup rice flour*
*12 Arafura sea bug tails*
*½ cup rice flour, for dredging bugs*
*2 limes*
*10 peppercorns*
*10 lemon balm leaves*
*1 tablespoon sea salt*
*1 litre water*
*4 x 150 grams barramundi fillets*
*lime wedges and coriander sprigs, to garnish*

To make a sauce, sauté the tomatoes, turmeric, ginger, tamarind pulp, palm sugar and shrimp paste together. Then add the water and reduce for ½ an hour on a slow simmer. Add the rice to the simmering sauce and cook for a further 20 minutes, stirring continually.

Whisk the egg whites and salt until soft peaks form, fold in the rice flour.

Dredge the bugs in the flour and dip in the batter. Deep fry to a golden brown.

Place the limes, peppercorns, lemon balm, sea salt and water in a steamer base. Bring to a simmer. Place the barramundi in the steamer and steam for approximately 5 minutes or until the fish is just cooked when touched.

Place the sauce on the base of the serving plates and serve the fish on top with the tempura bugs. Garnish with lime wedges and a coriander sprig. Serves 4.

CARRINGTON HOUSE, NEW SOUTH WALES
*Moussaka of John Dory, haloumi mousse, eggplant and tomato, page 313*

*S*pring

**CARRINGTON HOUSE**
Newcastle,
New South Wales

•

*Blackened red pepper stuffed with fetta cheese and olives*

•

*Moussaka of John Dory, haloumi mousse, eggplant and tomato*

•

*Lemon-chocolate charlotte with a blueberry compote*

# ICED PINEAPPLE AND MANGO MOUSSE

### SEVEN SPIRIT BAY

*125 ml water*
*250 grams sugar*
*1 lime, zest*
*1 pineapple, skin removed*
*2 mangoes, peeled*
*½ cup whipped cream*
*1 sheet gelatine*
*4 eggs, separated*
*½ cup castor sugar*
*½ cup mango purée*
*½ cup pineapple purée*
*mango, garnish*
*native mints*

PLACE THE sugar, lime zest and the water in a saucepan. Simmer for 15 minutes. Remove from the heat and allow to cool.

Slice the pineapple and mango wafer thin and remove the skin. Place in the sugar syrup for 30 seconds then drain on a rack.

Dissolve the gelatine with ¼ cup of the sugar syrup. Place the sliced fruit around the base of dariole moulds. Brush with the gelatine syrup and freeze.

Whisk the cream until stiff. Whisk the egg whites until stiff. Whisk the egg yolks and sugar until smooth. Fold together the cream, egg whites and egg yolk mixture. Place equal amounts of the mixture in two bowls. In one bowl mix in the pineapple purée and in the other mix in the mango purée.

Remove the dariole moulds from the freezer and layer them with the two mousses. Freeze for two hours. Remove the mousse from the mould and serve with fresh mango segments and native mints. Serves 4.

# BLACKENED RED PEPPER STUFFED WITH FETTA CHEESE AND OLIVES

### CARRINGTON HOUSE

*4 medium sized red peppers*
*1 handful small beans, trimmed and blanched*
*200 grams fetta cheese, crumbled*
*1 tablespoon black dried olives, sliced*
*¼ small red onion, finely sliced*
*½ teaspoon garlic, finely chopped*
*½ teaspoon chilli*
*½ teaspoon ginger*
*2 pinches salt*
*2 ripe tomatoes, peeled, seeded and cubed*
*1 Lebanese cucumber, diced and salted*
*tuna or chicken, optional*
*black olives, garnish*
*chopped parsley, garnish*
*diced tomato, garnish*
*olive oil, garnish*
*balsamic vinegar, garnish*

ROAST THE red peppers over a naked flame until they are well blackened all over. Remove this blackened skin by washing the pepper immediately under running water. Carefully remove the seeds through a vertical slit in the side.

Toss together the beans, fetta cheese, sliced olives, red onion, garlic, chilli, ginger, salt, tomatoes, cucumber and optional tuna or chicken. Stuff the peppers with the tossed ingredients. Decorate with the garnish ingredients scattered around on the plate.

## MOUSSAKA OF JOHN DORY, HALOUMI MOUSSE, EGGPLANT AND TOMATO
### CARRINGTON HOUSE

*2 large onions, peeled and sliced*
*4 garlic cloves, peeled and chopped*
*2 small hot chillies*
*½ teaspoon fennel seeds*
*1 teaspoon salt*
*2 cans whole tomatoes*
*1 haloumi twist*
*2 whole eggs*
*1 clove garlic, peeled*
*12 slices eggplant*
*olive oil*
*12 John Dory fillets*
*grated cheese*
*fresh herbs*

Lightly sauté the onions, garlic, chilli and fennel seeds. Add the salt and tomatoes and simmer slowly for 1½ hours.

To make the haloumi mousse, combine the haloumi, eggs and whole garlic clove in a food processor and blend well.

Place 3 slices of eggplant per person onto a roasting tray that has been well oiled with olive oil. Spread a spoonful of the haloumi mousse on top of the eggplant, then place the John Dory fillets over the haloumi mousse. Roast the eggplant layers in a very hot oven until the fish is cooked through.

To serve, stack three eggplant layers, with the largest slice on the bottom, on each plate. Put a spoonful of the tomato sauce between each layer. Garnish with grated cheese and fresh herbs.

## LEMON-CHOCOLATE CHARLOTTE WITH A BLUEBERRY COMPOTE
### CARRINGTON HOUSE

*5 gelatine leaves, softened in chilled water*
*200 ml cream, boiled*
*160 grams egg yolks (about 8)*
*2 x 75 grams castor sugar*
*150 grams calibaut lemon-flavoured white chocolate*
*200 grams egg whites (about 8)*
*Nut Sponge*
*Blueberry Compote*
*icing sugar*

Strain the gelatine leaves and discard the water. Melt the gelatine in the hot cream. Whisk the egg yolks with 75 grams of castor sugar. Pour the cream onto the beaten yolks and mix well, then add the chocolate.

In a steel or glass bowl placed over simmering water, beat the mixture until it reaches 80°C or 'coats the back of a spoon'.

Place the bowl into cold water to allow the mixture to cool to room temperature.

Whisk the egg whites with the remaining lot of sugar until firm. Fold the egg whites into the custard mixture to make a mousse.

Line two loaf tins with plastic wrap and then with a layer of Nut Sponge. Fill with the mousse mixture and allow to set overnight.

Remove from the tins. Discard the plastic wrap and cut into slices with a warm knife. Serve with Blueberry Compote and dust with icing sugar.

## NUT SPONGE

*130 grams nuts, eg. almonds*
*130 grams pure icing sugar*
*70 grams egg whites*
*6 egg yolks*

*250 grams egg whites*
*80 grams castor sugar*
*110 grams plain flour*

In a food processor purée the nuts with the icing sugar until fine and then add the 70 grams of egg whites along with the egg yolks.

Whisk the 250 grams of egg whites with the castor sugar until they have formed stiff peaks. Fold these whites into the nut mixture. Finally fold the flour into this mixture.

Spread out onto a non-stick tray and cook for about 10 minutes at 180°C. Freeze any sponge that is not used.

## BLUEBERRY COMPOTE

*2 cups white sugar*
*2 cups water*

*juice of 1 lemon*
*1 punnet blueberries*

Stir together the sugar, water and lemon juice. Bring to the boil and reduce until only a light gold in colour, then add the blueberries. Cook for a further 1 minute. Cool and chill.

# Restaurants and Guest Houses

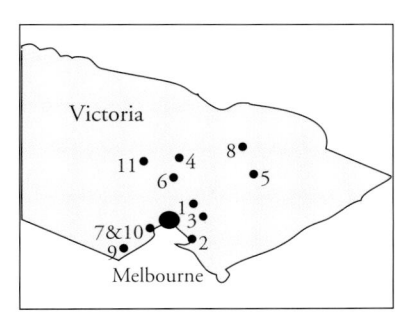

## VICTORIA

**1 ADAMS OF NORTH RIDING RESTAURANT**
1726 Heidelberg-Kinglake Road
St Andrews, Victoria 3761
Tel. (03) 9710 1461  Fax. (03) 9710 1541

**2 ARTHURS RESTAURANT**
Arthurs Seat Scenic Road
Arthurs Seat, Victoria 3937
Tel. (03) 5981 4444
Fax. (03) 5981 0651

**3 COTSWOLD HOUSE RESTAURANT**
Blackhill Road,
Menzies Creek, Victoria 3159
Tel. (03) 9754 7884

**4 ELLIMATTA**
233 Barker Street
Castlemaine, Victoria 3450
Tel. (03) 5472 4454
Fax. (03) 5470 5093

**5 HOWQUA DALE GOURMET RETREAT**
Howqua River Road,
Via Mansfield, Victoria 3722
Tel. (03) 5777 3503
Fax. (03) 5777 3896

**6 LAKE HOUSE**
King Street
Daylesford, Victoria 3460
Tel. (03) 5348 3329
Fax. (03) 5348 3995

**7 MIETTA'S QUEENSCLIFF HOTEL**
16 Gellibrand St
Queenscliff, Victoria 3225
Tel. (03) 5258 1066
Fax. (03) 5258 1899

**8 THE PARLOUR AND PANTRY**
69 Ford Street
Beechworth, Victoria 3747
Tel. (03) 5728 2575
Fax. (03) 5728 2575

**9 SUNNYBRAE COUNTRY RESTAURANT**
Corner Cape Otway
& Lorne Roads
Birregurra, Victoria 3242
Tel. (03) 5236 2276

**10 VUE GRAND HOTEL**
46 Hesse Street
Queenscliff, Victoria 3225
Tel. (03) 5258 1544
Fax. (03) 5258 3471

**11 WARRENMANG VINEYARD RESORT**
Mountain Creek Road
Moonambel, Victoria 3478
Tel. (03) 5467 2233
Fax. (03) 5467 2309

## NEW SOUTH WALES

**1 BAWLEY POINT GUEST HOUSE**
17-23 Johnston Street
Bawley Point, New South Wales 2539
Tel. (044) 57 1011  Fax. (044) 57 1436

**2 CARRINGTON HOUSE**
130 Young Street
Newcastle, New South Wales 2294
Tel. (049) 61 3564  Tel. (049) 69 6564

**3 THE COTTAGE RESTAURANT**
109 Woollombi Road
Cessnock, New South Wales 2325
Tel. (049) 90 3062  Fax. (049) 90 7039

**4 DARLEYS RESTAURANT**
Lilianfels
Lilianfels Avenue
Katoomba, New South Wales 2780
Tel. (047) 80 1200  Fax. (047) 801 300

**5 THE MOUNT INN**
Bells Line of Road
Bilpin, New South Wales 2758
Tel. (045) 67 1354

**6 ROBERTS AT PEPPERTREE**
Halls Road
Pokolbin, New South Wales 2320
Tel. (049) 987 330  Fax. (049) 987 329

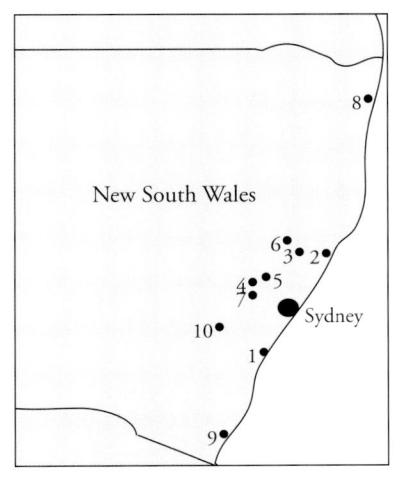

**7 SILK'S BRASSERIE**
128 Leura Mall
Leura, New South Wales 2780
Tel. (047) 84 2534  Fax. (047) 84 2706

**8 TAYLOR'S COUNTRY HOUSE**
McGettingan's Lane
Byron Bay, New South Wales 2481
Tel. (066) 847 436  Fax. (066) 847 526

**9 THE VALLEY COUNTRY HOME**
Post Office Box 10
Central Tilba, New South Wales 2546
Tel. (044) 737 405  Fax. (044) 737 300

**10 WILLOWVALE MILL**
Laggan via Crookwell,
New South Wales 2583
Tel. (048) 37 3319

## SOUTH AUSTRALIA

**1 CHARDONNAY LODGE**
Main Highway,
Coonawarra, South Australia 5263
Tel. (08) 8736 3309
Fax. 08 8736 3383

**2 MOUNT LOFTY HOUSE, MERCURE GRAND HOTEL**
74 Summit Road
Crafers, South Australia 5152
Tel. (08) 8339 6777
Fax. (08) 8339 5656

**3 PADTHAWAY ESTATE**
Padthaway, South Australia 5271
Tel. (08) 8765 5039
Fax. (08) 8765 5097

# Fine Food from Country Australia

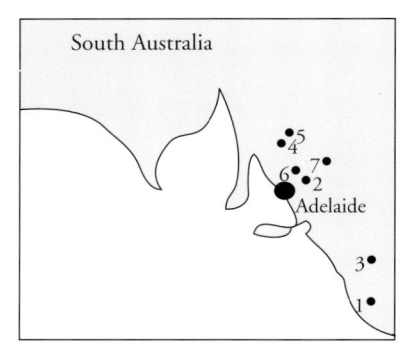

**4 SKILLOGALEE**
Hughes Park Road
Sevenhill, South Australia 5453
Tel. (08) 8843 4311
Fax. (08) 8843 4343

**5 THORN PARK COUNTRY HOUSE**
College Road,
Sevenhill, South Australia 5453
Tel. (08) 8843 4304
Fax. (08) 8843 4296

**6 THE URAIDLA ARISTOLOGIST**
Corner Greenhill and Basket Range Road
Uraidla, South Australia 5142
Tel. (08) 8390 1995

**7 THE WILD OLIVE**
Pheasant Farm Road
(Off Samuel Road)
Nuriootpa, South Australia 5355
Tel. (08) 8562 1286
Fax. (08) 8562 1032

## WESTERN AUSTRALIA

**1 DEAR FRIENDS GARDEN RESTAURANT**
100 Benara Road
Caversham, Western Australia 6055
Tel. (09) 279 2815  Fax. (09) 377 4018

**2 FLUTES OF BROOKLAND VALLEY**
Brookland Valley Vineyards
Caves Road
Willyabrup, Western Australia 6284
Tel. (097) 55 6250  Fax. (097) 55 6214

**3 LAMONT'S WINERY AND RESTAURANT**
Bisdee Road
Millendon, Western Australia 6056
Tel. (09) 296 4485  Fax. (09) 2961663

**4 LEEUWIN ESTATE**
Margaret River, Western Australia 6285
Tel. (097) 57 6253  Fax. (097) 57 6364

**5 LOUISA'S RESTAURANT**
15 Clifton Street
Bunbury, Western Australia 6230
Tel. (097) 219959  Fax. (097) 912726

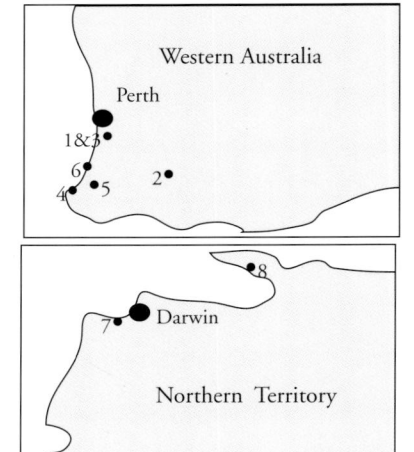

**6 NEWTOWN HOUSE**
Bussell Highway
Vasse, Western Australia 6280
Tel./Fax. (09) 7554485

## NORTHERN TERRITORY

**7 SAN SOLARO BAY**
Cox Peninsula
Northern Territory
Tel./Fax. (08) 8978 5010

**8 SEVEN SPIRIT BAY**
Cobourg Peninsula
GPO Box 4721
Darwin, Northern Territory 0801
Tel. (08) 8979 0277
Fax. (08) 8979 0284

## TASMANIA

**1 ANABELS OF SCOTTSDALE**
46 King Street
Scottsdale, Tasmania 7260
Tel. (03) 6352 3277
Fax. (03) 6352 2144

**2 ARCOONA**
East Barrack Street
Deloraine, Tasmania 7304
Tel. (03) 6362 3443
Fax. (03) 6362 3228

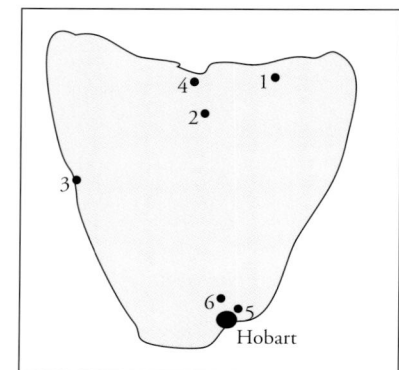

**3 FRANKLIN MANOR**
The Esplanade
Strahan, Tasmania 7468
Tel. (03) 6471 7311
Fax. (03) 64 71 7267

**4 LUCINDA**
17 Forth Street
Latrobe, Tasmania 7307
Tel. (03) 6426 2285
Fax. (03) 6426 2290

**5 PROSPECT HOUSE**
Richmond
Tasmania 7025
Tel. (03) 6260 2207
Fax. (03) 6260 2551

**6 TYNWALD**
Willow Bend Estate
New Norfolk, Tasmania 7140
Tel. (03) 6261 2667
Fax. (03) 6261 2040

## QUEENSLAND

**1 PEREGIAN PARK HOMESTEAD RESTAURANT**
Monak Road
Peregian Beach, Queensland 4573
Tel. (07) 5448 1628
Email: pph@peg.apc.org

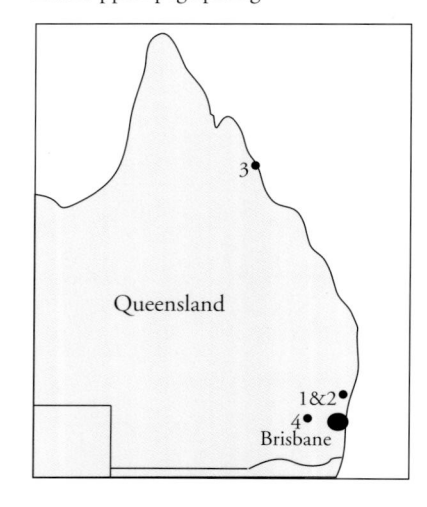

**2 PICNICS AT FAIRHILL**
Fairhill Road
Yandina, Queensland 4561
Tel. (07) 5446 8191
Fax. (07) 5441 7399

**3 RED OCHRE GRILL**
43 Sheilds Street
Cairns, Queensland 4870
Tel. (070) 510 100  Fax. (070) 510 025

**4 TALGAI HOMESTEAD**
Dalrymple Creek Road
Allora, Queensland 4362
Tel. (076) 663444  Fax. (076) 663780

# INDEX

almond
    meringue, 96
    and orange baskets, 18, *19*
    praline, 125
amaretto ice-cream, 96
anchovy and parmesan
    dressing, 49
anglaise
    chocolate, 174
    coconut, 296
    vanilla, 214
aniseed myrtle parfait, 206
apple
    baked, 124
    and brandy cake, 133
    crepe gateau, 178
    crumble, 161
    feuilletée, 132
    fruit crumble, 150, *155*
    glazed Harcourt, 141, *143*
    pear, banana and date tart, 116
    and polenta pie, 137
apricot
    bread and butter pudding, 237
    sorbet, 30
    soufflé, 30
Arcoona's lavender ice-cream, 65
artichokes Barigoule, 252
Asian marinade, 66
asparagus, 30, 49, 261
Atlantic salmon, 65, *67*

banana
    bread pudding, 174
    coulis, 233
    pudding, *99*, 100
    spring rolls, 88
barramundi, fillet, 92, 308, 310
basil
    linguini, *51*, 53
    pesto, 134, 170
    scented jus, 16
bavarois, rhubarb, *115*, 121
beef
    cheek, crepinette of boned oxtail and, *243*, 244
    fillet, 26, 68, 222
        grain-fed, 190
        sesame, 162
        tournedos, 144
    salad of marinated, 52
    tenderloin, 154
    vegetable and, samosas, 97
beetroot
    baby, glazed, 94, *95*
    confit, 45, *55*
    and creme fraiche salad, 177
    ravioli, 248
berry
    mille feuille, 33

sauce, *87*, 89
savarin, 14
tiers, 298
biscuit
    almond and orange baskets, 18
    brandy snaps, 266
    garlic tuille, 21
    glass, 157, 257
    honey wafers, 38
    lace, 112
    orange lace, 306
    poppyseed wafers, 270
    shortcrust shards, 68, 189
    straws, 302
    sugared shortbread, 41
    tiers, 298
    tuilles, 257
black beans, 86
blackberry jam, 280, *299*
blackeyed peas, 64
blueberry
    compote, *307*, 314
    coulis, 88
    tart, *87*, 89
borsodo, 246, *247*
bouillon, 265
brandy snaps, 266
bread
    lignon, 284
    olive and parmesan, 24
    pumpkin, 162
brioche, 214
    with wild mushrooms, 198, *199*
broccoli timbale, 233
brulée
    peach, 57
buckwheat noodles, 66
bunya nut pizza dough, 134
bush tomato
    and bunya nut pizza, 134
    relish, 206
buttermilk polenta, 229
butternut pumpkin soup, 69
butterscotch sauce, 178, 194

cabbage, braised caraway, 13
cake
    apple and brandy, 133
    chocolate and hazelnut torte, 210
    chocolate and walnut dessert, 260, *291*
    Hungarian chocolate walnut cake, 245, *247*
    nut sponge, *307*, 314
    orange and almond, 70
    strawberry sponge, 274
caramel sauce, 157, 176, 226, *227*, 309
carrot
    cumin, 18

and oatmeal soup, 176
capsicum
    coulis, 60
    marinated, *287*, 288
    purée, red, 236, 274
    roasted, 53, 70, 84, 113
    stuffed, red, 312
chantilly cream, 18
charlotte, lemon-chocolate, *307*, 313
cheese
    Ashgrove pepperberry, 64
    blue cheesecake, 213
    custards, 236
    Gippsland blue, 93, 302
    goat's cheese, 82, *83*, 138, *139*
        soufflé, 286, *287*
        terrine, 212
    Karridale ewes milk pecorino, 284
    Kervella goat's with pasta, 221
    King Island double brie, 88
    Metricup vintage harvarti, 284
    mozzarella, 102
    ricotta fritters, 50
    soufflé, 273
Chermoula, 262
chervil mousseline, 28
chiboust, 160, *163*
chicken
    baby, breast, 305
    char-grilled, *51*, 53
    corn-fed, 72
    tian, 300
    farce, *171*, 172
    liver, hazelnut and mushroom paté, 45, *55*
    parfait, 306
    nonya, 56
    salad, 40
    sausages, 205
    slow cooked coated in Moroccan spices, salad, *107*, 109
    in smoked salmon, with Thai noodles, 25
    stock, 72
    wontons, 182
chocolate
    anglaise, 174
    baked, pudding, 181, *183*
    and black cherry roulade, 144
    chiboust, 160, *163*
    cream, 246, *247*
    and hazelnut torte, 210
    lover's fantasy, 233
    marquise, 192, *195*
    nougat ice-cream, 296

reversed, and fromage blanc soufflé, 264
sauce, 176
    bitter, 181, *183*
soufflé, 230, 242
walnut cake
    Hungarian, 245, *247*
    dessert, 260, *291*
chutney, fresh mint, 56
coconut milk, laksa, 40
coffee sauce, 192, *195*
coral trout with ginger and black beans, 86
corn
    and prawn fritters, 220
    soufflé, 1178
coulis
    banana, 233
    blueberry, 88
    capsicum, 60
    pistachio, 160
    raspberry, 26
    strawberry, 81
    tomato, 300
    tomato and capsicum, 255
couscous, *235*, 236
crab, 16
    gratin of sandcrab, 106
    mud, 308, 309
    pots, 117
    and pumpkin mulligatawny soup, 92
    stock, 117
crayfish
    medallions, 29, 30, *31*, 258, *263*
    redclaw, and scallops, 77
crème patissier, 298
crepes
    apple, gateau, 178
    strawberry, Rasputin, 64
crepezes, 190, *191*
crocodile
    shoi mai, 308
    smoked, tian, 300
    tempura, 42
crustacean
    oil, 304
    salad, 194
cucumber soup, 56
cumquats, brandied, 264
custard
    cheese, 236
    old fashioned, 210
    vanilla bean, 218

daiquiri, strawberry, 269
date
    ginger pudding, 226, *227*
    pudding, 249
doughnuts, Turkish, 208
dressing
    anchovy and parmesan, 49

dressing *continued*
  balsamic, 29, 294
  hazelnut and balsamic, 286, *287*
  herbed wine vinegar, 52
  Kakadu plum and wasabi, 42
  Thai herbs, 36
  wattle seed, 65
  vindaloo, 40
duck
  confit, 188, 200, *211*, 238
  honey-glazed, 17, *19,*
  livers with pancetta, 132
  ravioli, 232
  roast, 13
  roast quail and, livers, 138, *139*
  sausage, 200, *211*
  trio of birds poached, 209
  warm salad, 46
dumpling, spinach, 130, *131*

eggplant
  char-grilled, 52
  jam, 295
  preserved, 268
  roast, 68
  smoked, 204
eggs, quail, 49
emu fillet, 62, *259*, 260

fennel
  braised, 140
  creamed, and leeks, 241
  fondue, 101
  roasted, 256
figs
  brandied, 13
  cream flavoured, with kirsch, 108
  and ginger cognac sauce, 188
  poached, *39* , 41
  roast black Genoa, 93
  and rocket salad, 152
fish
  Atlantic salmon, 65
  barramundi, 92, 308, 310
  bluefin tuna, 84, *78*
  Clover Cottage trout, 186
  coral trout, 86
  John Dory, 274
    moussaka, *311,* 313
  leather jackets, 98
  prawns, 36
  rock, soup, 133
  salmon
    marinated, 261
    parcel, 184, *187*
    smoked salmon, 25, 149, *223,* 224
    Tasmanian, baked, 74
  sauce, 141
  scallops, 32, 69
  seafood, 140
  snapper, 264
    pink, 61
  squid, 36
  smoked trout, 57
  steamed, and yabbies, 292
  stock, 76
  tuna
    char-grilled, 269
    grilled, *78*, 84

  tartare, 20, *23*
  whiting
    fillets, steamed, *27*, 28
    King George, 101
Flinders mussels, 106
fritters
  corn and prawn, 220
  ricotta fritters, 50
fruit
  fresh, *18,* 18
  spring, 266
  stone fruit, poached, 30, 149
  sushi, 301
  tart, 280, *299*
  Tasmanian berry fruit, 33
  tropical, ice-cream, 26
  winter, tart, 170
galettes, potato and sage, 305
game pudding, steamed, *175,* 177
ganache, 174
  chocolate, 261, *291*
garlic
  roasted, and baby Spanish onions, 136
  roasted, and wild mushroom risotto, 104
  tuilles, 22
gaucamole, 294
gelato, mascarpone, 242
ginger ice-cream and strawberry sorbet layered terrine, 81
glass biscuits, 157, 257
goat
  cheese, 16
  terrine, 212
  with pasta, 221
  kid, 173
  tagine, 234, *235*
golden nugget scallops, 142
gooseberry tart, 253
granita, 202, *203*
grapefruit and coriander salsa, 48
green pea butter, 140
Guinness
  oyster and, soup, 246

hare
  saddle, 212
  stock, 213
harissa sauce, *235*, 236
honey
  ice-cream, 93, 157
  wafers, 38
horseradish cream, 216, *223*, 224
Hungarian chocolate walnut cake, 245, *247*

ice-cream
  almond praline, 124
  amaretto, 96
  Arcoona's lavender, 44
  blood orange and grand marnier, 230
  chocolate nougat, 296
  cinnamon, 142, *143*
  ginger, 81
  honey, 93, 133
  lavender and honey, 112
  Leeuwin Estate 'brut', 138

  mascarpone, 105
    gelato, 242
  prune and cognac, 68, 189
  rosella flower, 45
  tropical fruit, 26
  vanilla bean, 46, *47,* 145
Illawarra plum and chilli sauce, 196

jelly
  port, 213
  quince, *287*, 289
  vin santo, 202, *203*
jerusalem artichoke
  soup, 122
  and trout ravioli, 240
John Dory, 274
  moussaka, *311*, 313

Kakadu plum and wasabi dressing, 42
kale salad, 258, *263*
kangaroo
  fillet, 161
  roasted, 196
  roast sirloin, 106
  and Skillogalee shiraz pie, 193
  and venison pie, 248
kidneys, lamb, 114
kumera mash, 205

lace biscuits, 112
la dolce vita, 201, *203*
laksa, 40
lamb
  brains, 204
  carpaccio, 297
  char-grilled rump, *58*, 58
  chops, 252
  Greek, and lettuce stew, 220
  kidneys, 114
  leg, 278, *283*
  loin, 255
  medallions, 282
  oven-roasted, 276
  rack, *287*, 288
  rump, 262
  shanks, braised, 169
lasagne, scallop, 113
lavender
  ice-cream, 65
  and honey ice-cream, 112
leather jackets with ginger and lime, 98
leeks, garden, 72
lemon
  Aspen and rosella flower ice-cream, 44
  Aspen mayonnaise, 204, 290
  butter, 158
  chocolate charlotte, *307*, 313
  curd tart, 272, *275*
  myrtle beurre blanc, 164
  preserved, 60
    Moroccan-style, *235*, 236
  tart, 272
  thyme butter sauce, 70
lentils, green, 110, *111*
lime
  salsa, 292
  scented jus, 78
  syrup, 88, 208

terrine, semi-freddo, 165
liver, duck, 132, 138, *139*
loukma, 208
macadamia nut
  black sapote and, tartlet, 309
  crust, 255
  lamb's brains, 204
  soufflé, 93
  tart, 61, *63*
mango, 50
  and macadamia tart, 85
  and passionfruit mousse, 85
  sorbet, 46, *47,* 85
marron
  grilled, 281
  sweet potato fritters, 48
mascarpone
  cream, 24, 38
  gelato, 242
  ice-cream, 105
  vanilla bean, 306
mayonnaise
  lemon Aspen, 205, 290
  strawberry, 30
meringue, almond, 96
mille feuille, Tasmanian berry fruit, 33
mint chutney, 56
moussaka of John Dory, *311*, 313
mousse
  haloumi, *311*, 313
  mango and passionfruit, 85
  pheasant, 225
  pineapple and mango, 312
  scallop, 304
  sour cream, 181, *183*
mud crab and pawpaw salad, 309
mulberry pudding, 73
mulloway brandade, *78*, 84
mushroom
  field, 136
  menage, 193
  pine forest, *123*, 124
  wild
    brioche with, 198, *199*
    blue mountains, ragout, 146
    fumet, 232
    risotto, *119*, 120
    roasted garlic and, risotto, 104
    soup, *215*, 216
    sweetbreads and, 100
mussels
  Eden, 274
  Flinders, 106
  Portarlington, *243*, 244

nectarines, 96
nougat
  iced, 277
  pecan and, terrine, 285

ocean trout, 70
olive
  and parmesan bread, 24
  pastries, 277
onion
  gravy, 190
  marmalade, 26
  soup, *179*, 180

# INDEX

orange
  and almond cake, 70
  blood, and grand marnier ice-cream, 230
  butter sauce, 100, 172
  lace biscuits, 306
osso bucco, 185
oxtail
  braised, 148
  char-grilled, 177
  crepinette, and beef cheek, *243*, 244
  stew, 126, *127*
ox tongue, braised, 114
oysters, 28
  and Guinness soup, 246
  poached, 34
  soupiere of fruit of the sea, *231*, 232

pancakes
  lacy, 56
  saffron noodle, 94, *95*
  strawberry crepe Rasputin, 64
parfait, aniseed myrtle, 206
parsnip chips, 150, *151*
passionfruit
  curd tart, 76
  glaze, 293
  mango and, mousse, 85
pasta
  basil linguini, *51*, 53
  beetroot ravioli, 248
  fried ravioli, 254
  Jerusalem artichoke and trout ravioli, 240
  Kervella goat's cheese and winter greens, 221
  scallop ravioli, *303*, 304
  tomato and fresh basil, 53
pastry
  lard short, 181
  sweet, 170
paté
  chicken liver, hazelnut and mushroom, 45, *55*
pavlova, wattle seed, 293
pea
  green, butter, 140
peach
  brulée, 57
  poached yellow, 108
  roast, 38
  sorbet, 73
pear
  caramelised, 285
  date and ginger upside down pudding, 197
  fruit crumble, 150, *155*
  glazed, 156
  poached, 121, 210
  spiced poached, 102
pecan
  and nougat terrine, 285
  oyster and orange salad, 290
persimmon and raisin pudding, steamed, 221
pesto, basil, 134, 170
pheasant
  breast, 225
  mousse, 225
pickled lotus root, 81

pigeon
  pork and, rillettes, 125
pig's
  ear salad, *171*, 172
  trotter, stuffed, 114
pineapple and mango mousse, 312
pistachio coulis, 160
pizza
  bush tomato and bunya nut, 134
plum sorbet, 52
poaching
  stock, 78
  stone fruit, 149
polenta
  apple and, pie, 137
  buttermilk, 229
  soft, 241
  wild mint, diamonds, 196
poppyseed wafers, 270
pork
  cheeks, 216, *219*
  and pigeon rillettes, 125
port jelly, 213
potato
  cake, 268
  and leek soup, 278, *279*
  mashed, 148
  and parsnip, mashed, 49
  purée, 22
  rosti, 163
  and sage galettes, 305
  salad, 297
  sweet, 21, 48
praline, 278
prawn
  corn and, fritters, 220
  crustacean salad, 194
  laksa, 40
  salad, 294
  soupiere of fruit of the sea, *231*, 232
  and squid, 36
  and sweet potato flat cakes, 86
  tempura, 152
preserved lemon, 60
  Moroccan-style, 236
prune
  brandied, 129, *131*
  and cognac ice-cream, 68
pudding
  apricot bread and butter, 237
  banana bread, 237
  chocolate, 181
  date, 249
  date and ginger, 226, *227*
  game, steamed, *175*, 177
  mulberry, 73
  rhubarb and orange roly poly, 222
  steamed, 217
    persimmon and raisin, 221
  toffee, 194
pumpkin
  bread, 162
  crab and, mulligatawny soup, 92
  ginger tart brulée, 105
  soup, *43*, 69
    Asian, 160

quail
  barbecued boneless, 21
  char-grilled, 297
  deboned, 128, *135*
  eggs, 49
  honey basted, 268
  jus, 21
  roast, 138, *139*
  salad, 74
  smoked, 80
  trio of birds, 209
quandong
  chilli glaze, 44
  pie, 289
quince
  in syrup, 68, 189
  jelly, *297*, 289
  poached, 121, 214
  sorbet, 129
  tart, raised, 126
  wine sabayon, 102

rabbit
  braised, 110, *111*
  in shiraz, 129, *131*
  fillets, 270, *271*
  mousseline, 276
  stuffed saddle, 104
raspberries, *15*, 18, *19*, 65
  coulis, 26
  in Cointreau, 65
ravioli
  beetroot, 248
  duck, 232
  fried, 254
  scallop, *303*, 304
  sweet potato, 110, *111*
red cabbage and apple, 229
relish, bush tomato, 206
rhubarb
  bavarois, *115*, 121
  and orange roly poly, 222
ricotta fritters, 50
rillettes, pork and pigeon, 125
risotto
  cakes, 168
  roasted garlic and wild mushroom, 104
roly poly, rhubarb and orange, 222
rosemary
  jus, 256
  and pinot noir, 282
roulade, chocolate and black cherry, 144
rum and coconut sabayon, 44

sabayon
  champagné, 16
  quince wine, 102
  rum and coconut, 45
saffron
  bouillon, 265
  noodles, 96
sage butter, 272
salads
  beetroot and creme fraiche, 177
  chicken, slow cooked, *107*, 109
  dhal, 12
  duck breast, artichoke and sun-dried capsicum, 46
  fig and rocket, 152
  hot, summer greens, 65
  kale, 258, *263*
  marinated beef, 52
  mud crab and pawpaw, 309
  pecan, oyster and orange, 290
  pig's ear, *171*, 172
  potato, 297
  prawn, 294
  quail, 74
  rabbit fillets, 270, *271*
  roast quail and duck livers, 138, *139*
  rocket, 168
  snow pea and chinois, 42
  soba noodle, 36
  venison, 294
  witlof and orange, 128, *135*
  yabbie, 161
salmon
  baked Tasmanian, 74, *75*
  grilled with scallops, 32
  marinated, 261
  parcel, 184, *187*
  smoked, 25, 149
    gateau, *223*, 224
salsa
  grapefruit and coriander, 48
  lime, 292
  tomato and coriander, 12
samosa, 97
  pastry, 98
sapote, black, 309
sauce
  beurre blanc, 137
  bitter chocolate, 181, *183*
  and red wine, 62
  black peppercorn, 161
  brandy hommade, 258, *263*
  butterscotch, 178, 194
  caramel, 157, 176, 226, *227*, 309
  champagne, 28
  and chive, 234
  chilli beurre blanc, 25
  chocolate, 176
    anglaise, 174
  cinnamon essence syrup, 285
  coffee, 192, *195*
  coral, 32
  essence of tomato and saffron, 184
  fig and ginger cognac, 188
  fish, 141
  ganache, 174
    chocolate, 261, *291*
  green pea, 113
  Illawarra plum and chilli, 196
  jasmine, 17
  lemon myrtle beurre blanc, 164
  lemon thyme butter, 70
  madiera, 37
  marmalade treacle, 218
  mixed berry, *87*, 89
  mountain pepper, *259*, 260
  orange butter, 100, 172
  port wine and balsamic, 180, *239*

sauces *continued*
  red currant stock, 150, *151*
  red wine shallot, 156
  rosemary jus, 256
  rosemary and pinot noir jus, 282
  Scotchmans Hill pinot noir, 158, *159*
  sorrel, 252
  tamarind, 310
  thyme flavoured cream, 186
  toffee, *99*, 100
  tomato essence, 184
  truffle jus, 265, *267*
  veal jus, 173
  walnut and butterscotch, 197
  white wine, 277
  wild honey demi-jus, 162
scallops
  golden nugget, 142
  lasagne, 113
  mousse, 304
  and Penola trout, 254
  ravioli, *303*, 304
  redclaw crayfish, and, 77
  seared, 134
  soupiere of fruit of the sea, *231*, 232
  spicy seared, 69
seafood chowder, 228
shortbread, sugared, *38*, 41
shortcrust shards, 68, 189
smoking mix, 80
snails, 158, *159*
snapper, 264
  pink, 61
soba noodles, 36
somen noodles, 20
sorbet, 54
  apricot, 30
  black tea, 257
  mango, 46, *47*, 85
  peach, 73
  plum, 52
  quince, 129
  stone fruits, 54
  strawberry, 81, 269
soufflé
  apricot, 30
  bone marrow, *179*, 180
  cheese, 273
  chocolate, 230, 242
  cinnamon and macadamia nut, 93
  corn, double-baked, 117
  goat's cheese, 286, *287*
  reversed chocolate and fromage blanc, 264
soup
  carrot and oatmeal, 176
  clear with native herbs, 308
  crab and golden nugget pumpkin mulligatawny, 92
  cucumber, 56
  jerusalem artichoke, 122
  laksa, 40
  onion, *179*, 180

oyster and Guinness, 246
  potato and leek, 278, *279*
  pumpkin, 69, *43*
  rock fish, 133
  saffron bouillon, 264
  seafood chowder, 228
  tomato consommé, 34, *35*
  vegetable, 182, *207*, 208
  watermelon, 77
  wild mushroom, *215*, 216
soupiere of fruit of the sea, *231*, 232
sour cream mousse, 182, *183*
spatchcock, 164
  oven-baked, 272
  trio of birds, 209
spatzellie, 62
spinach
  blackeyed peas and, 64
  dumplings, 130, *131*
  wilted, 70
spring rolls, banana, 88
squab
  breast, 228
  pot-roasted, 180, *238*
  roast, 118, *119*
squid with prawns, 36
steamed
  persimmon and raisin pudding, 221
  pudding, 217
stew
  Greek lamb and lettuce, 220
  oxtail with celery, 126, *127*
stock
  chicken, 72
  crab, 117
  fish, 76
  hare, 213
  veal, 173
strawberry
  coulis, 81
  crepes, Rasputin, 64
  daiquiri, 269
  flamed, 306
  marinated, 165, 185
  mascarpone, and, 22
  mayonnaise, 30
  sorbet, 269
  sponge, 274
straws, 302
sugarbark, 293
sushi, fruit, 301
sweetbreads
  calves, 273
  feuilletée, and wild mushrooms, 100
  poached veal rolled with, 37
sweet potato
  chips, 74
  mash, 205
  and marron fritters, 48
  prawn and, flat cakes, 86
  purée, 22
  ravioli, 110, *111*
syllabub, 149

tagine of kid, 234
tapenade, 68, 70

tarts and pies
  apple and polenta, 137
  apple, pear, banana and date, 116
  black sapote and macadamia, 309
  blueberry, *87*, 89
  fruit, 280, *299*
  gooseberry, 253
  kangaroo and Skillogalee shiraz pie, 193
  kangaroo and venison pie, 248
  lemon, 256
  lemon curd, 272, *275*
  macadamia nut, 61, *63*
  mango and macadamia nut, 85
  passionfruit curd, 76
  pumpkin ginger, brulée, 105
  quandong pie, 289
  quince, raised, 126
  tomato with goat's cheese, 82, *83*
  truffle, 180, *239*
  winter fruit, 170
tempura
  batter, 153, 310
  sea bugs, 310
tiers biscuits, 298
timbale
  broccoli, 233
  smoked salmon, 149
  Thai noodle, chicken, smoked salmon, 25
toffee
  pudding, 194
  sauce, *99*, 100
tomato, 16, *19*
  consommé, 34, *35*
  coulis, 300
  and capsicum, 255
  essence, 184, *187*
  fresh basil linguini, 53
  pressed terrine, 102
  soft-dried with basil and beans, 71
  tart with goat's cheese, 82, *83*
trifle, 22
  moulded, *115*, 121
trout
  Clover Cottage, 186
  Darling Range, 301
  jerusalem artichoke and, ravioli, 240
  ocean, 70
  Pemberton emperor, 137
  rainbow, *123*, 124
  scallop and Penola, 254
  smoked, 57
tuille
  biscuits, 257
  garlic, 22
tuna
  char-grilled, 269
  grilled, *78*, 84
  tartare, 20, *23*

Turkish doughnuts, 208
turnips, buttered, 130, *131*

vanilla
  anglaise, 214
  bean ice-cream, 46, *47*, 125
  ice-cream, 145
veal
  cutlets, 265, *267*
  jus, 173
  medallions, 158
  osso bucco, 185
  rolled and poached, 37
  stock, 173
  sweetbreads, 37
  with parsley and bone marrow, 49
vegetables
  Asian style, 200, *211*
  and beef samosas, 97
  char-grilled, 29, *31*, *58*, 58
  niçoise style casserole, 269
  pistou, 238
  roast, 222, 288
    root, 169
  soup, 182, *207*, 208
  stock pot, 216, *219*
venison
  kangaroo and, pie, 248
  pepper-crusted, 94, *95*
  salad, 294
  shanks, 241
  Tasmanian, 150, *151*
vinaigrette 71
  balsamic, 29, 294
  orange and mustard, 81
vin santo jelly, 202, *203*

wallaby
  char-grilled, 44
  medallions, 89
watermelon
  pickle, 57
  soup, 77
wattle seed
  dressing, 65
  pavlova, 293
wild cherry farce, 21
wild mint polenta diamonds, 196
witlof and orange salad, 128, *135*
whiting
  King George, 101
  steamed 26, *27*
wontons
  braised leg meat, 17
  chicken, 182
  fried, 40

yabbies, 12
  crustacean salad, 194
  salad, 71, 161
  steamed fish and, 292
  tails in Asian marinade, 66
Yorkshire pudding, 190

zabaglione
  borsodo, 246, *247*
  Cointreau, 185